EXPLORATIONS
in
SPIRITUALITY

History, Theology, and Social Practice

PHILIP F. SHELDRAKE

Paulist Press
New York/Mahwah, NJ

Cover design by Joy Taylor
Book design by Lynn Else

Library of Congress Cataloging-in-Publication Data

Sheldrake, Philip.
    Explorations in spirituality : history, theology, and social practice/ Philip F. Sheldrake.
      p. cm.
    Includes bibliographical references and index.
    ISBN 978-0-8091-4647-5 (alk. paper)
    1. Spirituality—Catholic Church. I. Title.
    BX2350.65.S45 2010
    248.09—dc22

                                                                    2009046244

Published by Paulist Press
997 Macarthur Boulevard
Mahwah, New Jersey 07430

www.paulistpress.com

Printed and bound in the
United States of America

CONTENTS

iii

PREFACE

This book is a series of "explorations" in the field of Christian spirituality that express some of my particular interests and concerns by gathering together a number of unpublished lectures delivered in a variety of contexts, as well as material from journal articles and book essays. All of these have been significantly revised, added to, and sometimes amalgamated together. Although it is not a definitive exposition of the subject, nevertheless, I hope that this volume will offer readers an interesting perspective on contemporary Christian spirituality as an area of study and reflection.

The chosen subtitle, "History, Theology, and Social Practice," expresses three of the clear convictions that frame my thinking and teaching. The first conviction is that, while spirituality has established itself as an interdisciplinary subject that allows for a range of perspectives, the particularity of Christian spirituality means that we cannot separate it from how we articulate Christian belief—that is, from theology. I also believe, however, that while spirituality is shaped by Christian beliefs, its relationship to theology is not simply derivative. Within the wider field of theology, spirituality acts as a balance, even a corrective, that persistently recalls theology to its self-implicating and transformative purpose. In other words, spirituality questions any attempt by theology to retreat into abstraction by detaching itself from Christian practice and from wider social engagement.

My second conviction is that because the doctrine of the incarnation places God at the heart of human history, Christian spirituality affirms the world of time and place as the essential context for human transformation. Despite a certain contemporary suspicion of "tradition" and "history" in Western cultures, a historical consciousness is vital to human flourishing. It will therefore be central to a critical study of Christian spirituality.

My final conviction is that, despite a sometimes unbalanced rhetoric of interiority in some versions of theology and spirituality, the overall logic of Christian spirituality is to be deeply concerned with the practice of everyday life in the outer, social world. From the second half of the twentieth century onward, Christian spirituality has also embraced an explicit concern with social transformation. One corollary of this social concern has directed spirituality toward reflection on the nature of "place" in relation to human identity, and this trajectory is explored in different ways in the final two chapters of the book.

Certain acknowledgments are in order. Chapter 1 is based partly on an essay "The Wisdom of History" published in *Spirituality and Time, The Way Supplement* 96 (Autumn 1999): 17–26, supplemented by additional material. Chapter 2 is a revision and expansion of the essay "Interpretation" in *The Blackwell Companion to Christian Spirituality*, ed. Arthur Holder (Oxford/Malden, MA: Blackwell Publishing, 2005): 459–77. Chapter 3 draws on a published essay, "Spirituality and Theology," in *Halvårsskrift för Praktisk Teologi* (2003/2): 27–37, and some material from my book *Spirituality and Theology* (Orbis Books, 1998), which is no longer in print. Chapter 4 was given as the keynote lecture at the conference "The Trinity in Contemporary Perspective" at The Milltown Institute of Theology, Dublin, 2008. Chapter 5 was originally a presentation at the 2004 Lilly Endowment colloquium "Religion and Social Engagement: Practices, Visions and Complexities" at the Evangelical Academy in Berlin. Chapter 6 is a revision of "Unending Desire: Michel de Certeau's 'Mystics,'" published in *Christianity and the Mystical, The Way Supplement* 102 (Autumn 2001): 38–48, combined with material from a public lecture on Christian mysticism at Ampleforth Abbey, England, 2006. Chapter 7 is a revision of a public lecture given at The Merton Center, Bellarmine University, Louisville, Kentucky, 2004. Chapter 8 draws upon material from two presentations given to the House of Bishops of The Episcopal Church (USA), 2005. Chapter 9 is adapted from material from several public lectures given in the UK, USA, and Canada, 2001–2008. Finally, Chapter 10 combines material from an essay "Church Buildings as Classical Spiritual Texts," in ed. Kees Doevendans and Gertjan van der Horst, *Het kerkgebouw in Postindustriële Landschap* (Zoetermeer: Uitgeverij Boekencentrum,

2004), 29–40, and from "Reading Cathedrals as Spiritual Texts" in *Studies in Spirituality* 11 (2001), 187–204.

I am particularly grateful to Nancy de Flon at Paulist Press for suggesting that I gather together material for this volume and for her constructive and thoughtful reactions to the text. The Joseph Visiting Professorship in the Theology Department of Boston College (2008–2009) gave me the time and space to create this book. I am very grateful for the warm hospitality of the Department and the School of Theology and Ministry as well as for many stimulating conversations with faculty and students. Finally, but by no means least, I dedicate the book to Susie, whose love and thoughtful responses are a continual encouragement and support in everything I write.

Philip Sheldrake
Joseph Visiting Professor,
Boston College, 2008–2009

INTRODUCTION
What Is Spirituality?

While, for reasons that will become clear, I believe that the contemporary field of spirituality is necessarily interdisciplinary, explicitly Christian spirituality is also inherently related to theology. Indeed, to my way of thinking, the field of spirituality may be thought of as a kind of reform movement within Christian theology that reminds it of its fundamental purpose and therefore method. Second, while the value of tradition and the role of history are questioned by many people in Western cultures, I am convinced that to forget history is profoundly dangerous. Many contemporary approaches to "spirituality" seek to detach it from "religion." This bypasses both specific belief systems and any organic connection with the classic spiritual traditions of the past. Yet, the Christian spiritual tradition in its plurality has depths of wisdom to offer. The question, of course, is how traditions and classic texts are to be interpreted and continually reappropriated in ever-changing social, cultural, and religious contexts. To value "tradition" is not the same as "traditionalism"—the defense of a fixed, antiquarian artifact. On the contrary, tradition is a living, dynamic force. Finally, spirituality has sometimes been confused with some kind of detached and individualized interiority, disengaged from everyday existence, from public and political worlds and from the quest for social as well as personal transformation. I hope that this book will go some way to righting the balance.

Contemporary Meanings

In her classic work, *Mysticism: The Nature and Development of Spiritual Consciousness*, Evelyn Underhill suggests that human beings are vision-creating beings rather than merely tool-making animals.[1] In other

1

words, humans are driven by goals that are more than a mere desire for physical satisfaction or mental supremacy. Humans seek what might be thought of as spiritual fulfillment.

Spirituality is a word with an increasing contemporary currency. However, the contemporary usage of the word *spirituality* is often vague and difficult to define precisely because it is increasingly detached from religious beliefs and specifically from its Christian origins. Yet, the sharp distinction often made between "spirituality" and "religion" is unhelpful. Such a polarized view is too uncritical. On this reading of contemporary culture, spirituality is in process of *replacing* religion in a kind of evolutionary development that implies that "spirituality" rather than "religion" is a better fit with contemporary needs. The trouble with this way of describing things is that it depends on an old-fashioned post-Enlightenment understanding of human existence as an inevitable crescendo of progress. If the study of history teaches us anything at all, it is that making such assumptions about some kind of complete break with the past is an illegitimate move. Even what we understand about the present moment is ambiguous. While, in terms of Western societies, it is true that increasing numbers of people in both traditional religious as well as nontraditional contexts are exploring a diversity of spiritual theories, experiences, and practices, it is also true that other people, often young and intelligent people, are turning to highly conservative forms of "religion" as their chosen answer to the quest for ultimate meaning. If we move beyond Western cultures, assessments of the definitive demise of conventional religion are highly questionable.

There are two other significant problems about distinguishing "spirituality" from "religion." In both cases, the problem is involved with how we define "spirituality" and "religion." In the case of "spirituality," this is assumed to be a set of practices, sometimes specifically "spiritual," sometimes generally life-framing, that are distinct from systems of belief. Spirituality may be associated with *values* (for example, the pursuit of human "well-being" in discussions of spirituality and health care), but these are treated as somehow free-standing or self-evident rather than based on prior assumptions or judgments about the meaning and purpose of human existence. In reality, everyone has some kind of worldview—whether explicit or implicit—and this gives rise to a hierarchy of values. Such worldviews are clearly not self-evident (or all humans would have the same view) but are in fact based on some kind of belief system, however loosely defined. Such belief systems are usually derived from a mixture of factors such as personal life experience, family "formation" during childhood, and also a range of social and cultural values and viewpoints (often originally derived from the historic religious foundations of a given society) that have been absorbed, often unconsciously, into the bloodstream. Conversely, the distinction between "spirituality" and "religion" depends on a reductionist view of religion—even a caricature of it. Thus one recent American commentator on the contemporary spirituality phenomenon notes that, whatever the deeper reality, "religion" in the popular mind is increasingly associated with complex and unhelpful dogmatic systems, heavy and judgmental moralism, authoritarian clerical hierarchies, the constraints of social expectations, and an excessive concern with buildings and money.[2]

What is undoubtedly true is that Christianity has not always done itself any favors in terms of making its rich and varied spiritual traditions accessible to its own adherents let alone to unaligned spiritual seekers. In that sense, it is not only the uncommitted spiritual seekers but equally many members of the Christian Church themselves who are dissatisfied with Christianity's apparent overconcentration on hierarchy, institutional structures, buildings, rationalist styles of religious teaching, and a preoccupation with moralistic approaches to religion.

Although I do not wish to denigrate or criticize all elements of the contemporary hunger for spirituality, let alone the dedication of many people to spiritual practice, there are also some dangers in the modern taste for optional spiritualities detached from traditions and beliefs. Such rather ill-defined spiritualities tend to bypass issues of commitment—which, for some people, is part of their attraction but is also one of their weaknesses. Equally, such approaches to spirituality do not as effectively help us to address fundamental questions of human meaning in the way that the wisdom of spiritual traditions associated with the historic religions such as Christianity does. Nor do they offer a framework to help us distinguish between different, even between constructive or unbalanced, versions of "the sacred," or "the divine," and their implications for good or ill. Another serious issue is the degree to which this free-floating approach to spirituality is capable of challenging an uncritical desire for fulfillment, happiness, satisfaction, and self-enhancement. Not that any of these things are bad in themselves but, without criteria of judgment, they can so easily become unbalanced or self-regarding.

One task of spirituality is surely to teach judgment and discernment in some form. Many of the greatest spiritual teachers and traditions in Christianity, for example Augustine, Julian of Norwich, or Ignatius Loyola, focus on the language of "desire" as the fundamental key to spiritual growth. What such teachers also note, however, is that, while desire is a God-given dissatisfaction that leads us onward in the spiritual quest, not all immediate "wants" or "yearnings" necessarily point us toward our deepest desires. An adequate spirituality also needs a language to identify some object of desire worthy of our human possibilities and that draws us beyond the superficial, the immediate, and the self-absorbed. The danger is that "optional" spiritualities offer personal practices to assuage spiritual hunger, yet can all too easily turn into another form of individualistic consumerism. Such spiritualities do not necessarily offer a language of solidarity or communion with other people. Equally, many of them are not particularly well equipped to offer a vision of public values, let alone of social transformation in the face of injustice. Yet, despite the fuzziness of the contemporary use of the word *spirituality*, it is possible to suggest that the word refers to the deepest values and meanings by which people seek to live. In other words, "spirituality" implies some kind of vision of the human spirit and of what will assist it to achieve full potential.

Commentators sometimes suggest that the current interest in spirituality reflects a subjective turn in contemporary Western culture. Spirituality therefore tends to focus either on individual self-realization or on a kind of inwardness. There is considerable justification for this assertion in consumerist "lifestyle spirituality" that promotes fitness, healthy living, and holistic well-being.[3] Since the beginning of the new millennium, however, there are also signs that the understanding of "spirituality" has expanded beyond an individualistic quest for fulfillment. Spirituality increasingly appears in discussions about public values or the transformation of social structures—for example, in reference to the ultimate focus of health care, the purpose of education, more reflective approaches to economic systems and to business practice, and, as chapter 9 of this book illustrates, the re-enchantment of urban life.

The term *spirituality* has a more defined content when it is associated with a historic religious tradition such as Christianity. In fact, the original source of the word *spirituality* lies in Christianity, although it has now been adopted by other faith traditions, not least Eastern religions such as Buddhism and Hinduism.[4] In specifically Christian terms, the notion of "spirituality" refers to the way our fundamental values, lifestyles, and spiritual practices reflect understandings of God, human identity, and the material world as the context for human transformation. All Christian spiritual traditions are ultimately rooted in, and are interpretations of, the Hebrew and Christian scriptures and particularly in the four Gospels. The connection to these foundational texts is not simple, however. Spiritual traditions and texts, in all times and places, are also attempts to reinterpret these foundational scriptural texts, and the values they portray, within specific historical and cultural circumstances. There is, therefore, a tension between a thread of continuities in Christian spirituality and the fact that spirituality is always also a response to particular contexts. This tension is expressed in an interesting way by Michel de Certeau, the French Jesuit historian of spirituality.

> Christianity implies a *relationship to the event* which inaugurated it: Jesus Christ. It has had a series of intellectual and historical social forms which have had two apparently contradictory characteristics: the will to be *faithful* to the inaugural event: the necessity of being *different* from these beginnings.[5]

In de Certeau's terms, the particularity of the event of Jesus Christ is the measure of all authentic forms of Christian discipleship in the sense that they presuppose that event but are not identical repetitions of it. In de Certeau's language, the particularity of the event of Jesus Christ "permits" the placed nature, the particularities of all subsequent discipleship. There, too, God may eternally say Yes to us without condition.

Origins of the Word *Spirituality*

The origins of the English word *spirituality* lie in the Latin noun *spiritualitas* associated with the adjective *spiritualis* (spiritual). These derive from the Greek *pneuma*, spirit, and the adjective *pneumatikos* as they appear in Paul's letters in the New Testament. It is important to note that "spirit" and "spiritual" are not the opposite of "physical" or "material" (Greek *soma*, Latin *corpus*) but of "flesh" (Greek *sarx*, Latin *caro*) in the sense of everything contrary to the Spirit of God. The intended contrast is not therefore between body and soul but between two attitudes to life. A "spiritual person" (see 1 Cor 2:14–15) was simply someone within whom the Spirit of God dwelt or who lived under the influence of the Spirit of God.

The Pauline moral sense of "spiritual," meaning "life in the Spirit," remained in constant use in the West until the twelfth century. Under the influence of the "new theology" of Scholasticism, influenced by the retrieval of Greek philosophy, "spiritual" began to be used to distinguish intelligent humanity from non-rational creation. Yet the Pauline and the supra-material senses of "spiritual" continued side by side in the thirteenth-century writings of a theologian like Thomas Aquinas. Interestingly, the noun *spirituality* (*spiritualitas*) during the Middle Ages most frequently referred not to an area of study or practice but to "the clergy." The noun only began to be established in reference to "the spiritual life" in seventeenth-century France—and not always in a positive sense. It then disappeared from theological circles until the end of the nineteenth and beginning of the twentieth centuries when it again appeared in French in reference to the "spiritual life." From there it passed into English in translations of French writings.

The use of the word *spirituality* as an area of study gradually reemerged during the twentieth century, but it was only by the Second Vatican Council in the early 1960s that it began to dominate and replace older terms such as ascetical theology or mystical theology. The emergence of "spirituality" as the preferred term to describe historical or theological studies of the Christian life increased after the Council until it was the dominant term from the 1970s onward. First, it countered older distinctions between a supernatural, spiritual life and a purely natural everyday one. Second, it recovered a sense that "the spiritual life" was collective in nature rather than exclusively individual. Third, spirituality was not limited to interiority but integrated all aspects of human experience and life in the light of a relationship with God. The British theologian Rowan Williams firmly rejects an understanding of spirituality as the science of spiritualized and private experience. "It must now

6

touch every area of human experience, the public and social, the painful, negative, even pathological byways of the mind, the moral and relational world."⁶ Contemporary spirituality as an area of reflection attempts to integrate religious and human values rather than to concentrate exclusively on such narrowly conceived matters as abstract notions of perfection or on mathematical analyses of the stages of prayer. Fourth, it reengaged with mainstream theology, not least biblical studies. Finally, it became an area of reflection that crossed the boundaries between different Christian traditions and was often a medium for ecumenical growth. By the end of the twentieth century this had extended further into the wider ecumenism of interfaith dialogue.

The Assumptions behind Definitions

Within the context explicitly of the Christian tradition, I want to suggest that how "spirituality" is defined and employed depends on prior and sometimes unexamined assumptions, especially theological ones. Interestingly, graduate courses in Christian spirituality on both sides of the Atlantic still tend to prioritize relatively sophisticated literary texts (notably mystical, monastic, and contemplative ones) over other more "popular" or broadly based forms of spirituality. Clearly the classic texts are a central part of the Christian spiritual tradition. Yet, to give these virtually exclusive attention suggests an intellectual preference for the classic academic disciplines and more generally for abstract or theoretical thinking over applied or engaged approaches.

I also sense that these priorities and preferences mask *theological* assumptions that are frequently unexamined. These can be represented by reference to a number of polarities (expressing a hierarchy of value) such as inwardness versus outer existence, personal experience versus social action (which tends to underpin a separation of spirituality and ethics), an elevated spiritual realm versus the mundane, an idealized future versus the present. At the root of these polarities lies a more fundamental contrast—between "the sacred" and "the secular." If we say, for example, that spirituality is concerned with the "lived experience" of God or the sacred, as well as with a vision of the human spirit and what assists it to achieve its fullest potential, two questions arise.

Where do we locate the sacred? And where is the human spirit most truly itself?

The Sacred as Wholly Other

Without doubt many conventional interpretations of the sacred, at least implicitly, reflect the approach of the great historian of religion Mircea Eliade.[7] Here, "the sacred" is "wholly other" than the mundane and separated from everyday life and experience. For Eliade, the manifestations of the sacred (hierophanies) take place in discontinuity with the ordinary. What is manifested is "something of a wholly different order, a reality that does not belong to our world."[8] Thus, "the sacred" is associated with special places and with special activities. "The sacred" is set over against "the profane," and so an important question is what Eliade means by "profane." For Eliade, this is everything that lies outside what is *explicitly* dedicated to the sacred. In pre-Christian antiquity, "the profane" implied what lay "outside the temple precinct" (in Latin, *pro fano*), outside the domain of religious cult. In other words, "the profane" simply implied the mundane or everyday. Under the impact of Christianity's high doctrine of the everyday and ordinary, "the profane" ceased to imply the realm of everyday life and took on a narrower, more negative connotation of what is actively *opposed* to the "sacred." By contrast, the notion of "the secular" (Christian in origin, not least in Augustine) was distinguished from "the profane" and took over part of its original sense of "the everyday world." The secular is thus the neutral sphere of the *saeculum*, the Latin for "this age," space and time, the here and now.[9] The difficulty with Mircea Eliade's influential approach to "the sacred" is that he once again collapses together the two terms *profane* and *secular* in ways that underwrite a radical contrast between a spiritual realm and the everyday or mundane.

It is worth bearing in mind that Eliade's ideas were strongly influenced by Rudolph Otto's classic work *Das Heilige* (in English *The Idea of the Holy*). Otto, for all his interest in world religions, was fundamentally a traditional Protestant theologian influenced by a particular understanding of Martin Luther's distinction between two realms or Two Kingdoms and by a theology of God imaged as awesome mystery and sovereign power *(mysterium tremendum et fascinans)*.

Private or Social?

On this reading of "the sacred," the practice and study of spirituality are set apart from mundane concerns and from everyday activities. This has an impact both on the kind of primary sources given prominence in the study of spirituality and on the kind of knowledge or wisdom that is taken seriously. In a world described in terms of the polarities of sacred and secular-profane, the human spirit is most truly itself and most effectively enhanced when in special locations such as church and monastery or in the protected privacy of "home" or in an interiorized self—the soul, the heart, or the mind. In either case the human quest for "the spiritual" all too frequently tends to be neither fully embodied nor wholeheartedly social.

If the contexts for the pursuit of the sacred or the enhancement of the human spirit tend to be special locations withdrawn from the everyday world, an interesting variant eventually became the idealization of "the home." The paradox is that while "home" was associated with everyday life, it was at the same time a *private* space protected from the evils of the outside, public world. The widespread Western mystique of "home" begins in the late seventeenth and eighteenth centuries with changes in house design that introduced a wider range of separate rooms and increasingly distinguished family rooms from spaces readily accessible to outsiders. However, the idealization of home became particularly prominent in the early Victorian era in Britain and North America and is, to some extent, prolonged into the present era with an emphasis on the need to defend "family values." There are many reasons for this, but the mystique is particularly associated with the sanctification of domesticity as the shaping symbol of a satisfactory life. To some extent, this reflects a sense of loss and distaste in the face of industrialization and the growing squalor, crowding, noise, and danger of the outside streets in ever-expanding cityscapes. It also reflects a growing shift toward a sense that private spaces, reflecting a new form of interiority, are where human beings are most truly themselves. In traditional Roman Catholicism this mystique of the home as a particularly spiritual place, protected from the profanity of the "outside," the streets, was often enhanced by ceremonies of house blessing, collective family devotions, statues or shrines in many rooms, stoups of holy water at the entrance of bedrooms. In effect this created

9

a kind of domestic monastic cloister. In Protestant England there were particular links to the nineteenth-century Evangelical revival and the sense that the way people organized their most intimate spaces reflected their moral character and spiritual temperament. Interior design expressed who people thought they were or what they valued and at the same time was itself creative of vision and value. Clergy were even involved as design consultants—as one commentator recently noted, it was a time when the priests chose the drapes![10]

My fundamental point is that neither life in public nor, generally speaking, the practices of everyday life have conventionally been considered the stuff of spirituality. Yet, at the heart of Christian theology lies the doctrine of incarnation—that God becomes human and that the sacred is now to be encountered within time and space, "heaven in ordinary" in the memorable phrase of the seventeenth-century Anglican priest-poet George Herbert. The orthodox Christian way of viewing the world understands it to be the gift of God's creation and a revelation of divine presence. Consequently, Christian theology radically reconfigures human conceptions of "the sacred." No part of the material world or of human activity is inherently profane, although it may be profaned by sinful human action. The everyday world is an authentic theological *locus*.

In this regard, the thought of Michel de Certeau is once again particularly interesting. He appears at several points in this book. What is interesting and important for our purposes is that de Certeau began as a historian of Christian spirituality even though he moved more in the direction of the social sciences and cultural studies in later life. The motivations behind his preoccupation in later years with everyday human practices are complex. His two-volume project on *The Practice of Everyday Life* is an exercise in social history and cultural studies rather than in spirituality. At a time when de Certeau is being recovered as a religious thinker, however, and given the evidence for his lifelong concern with the nature of Christian practice, it is not too far-fetched to see his concern with everyday practices as influenced by spiritual-theological as well as social and political values. De Certeau wrote reflections on the city, travel, food, cooking, and shopping.[11] A similar sense that spirituality should be concerned with the mundane and "the vernacular" also informed the editorial decision in the new English-language dictionary of Christian spirituality to include contributions on such topics as clothing, food, architecture, sexuality, public life, work, business, leisure, and sport.[12] This decision embodied a quite specific theological viewpoint—one that sought to counter an unbalanced polarization of sacred and profane. Unsurprisingly, this expansion of the themes that might be considered under the heading of spirituality did not meet with universal approval.

The Characteristics of Christian Spirituality

If we accept that all spiritualities are particular and cannot be separated from belief systems, there are clearly distinctive features to Christian spirituality. There has been some debate about whether Christian spirituality should be treated as essentially a single reality or as a plurality of different traditions.[13] In fact the question of unity or plurality is a matter of viewpoint. Clearly, all Christian spiritualities take the life and teachings of Jesus Christ as their fundamental and privileged starting point. Yet, different historic and contemporary traditions of spirituality emerge precisely when people seek to respond to the gospel of Jesus Christ in the context of their own time and place.

In all its forms, Christian spirituality is, first of all, intimately related to a specific understanding of God and of God's relationship to the world and to humanity. God is understood to be Trinity, a dynamic interrelationship of "persons in communion." This complex understanding of God, beyond any rational equation, clearly underlines that God's existence is totally "other," beyond the capacity of human language to define and beyond human powers to control. Second, however, this understanding of God also embraces a belief that the divine life overflows into an eternal dynamism of creativity. Christian spirituality is creation-centered in the sense that it understands all material reality as the gift and reflection of a loving God. Third, and closely related to this, is a belief in God's incarnation—that God's engagement specifically with humanity is expressed particularly by taking on embodied, historic existence in the person of Jesus Christ. This makes all Christian spiritual traditions Christ-centered in different ways. A fundamental framework for understanding the Christian life is "discipleship," which implies both *metanoia*, conversion, and also following a way of life in the pattern of Jesus Christ and as a prolongation of his mission. Fourth, as a conse-

11

quence, Christian spirituality, when it is true to its foundations, has a positive view of the material world and of the human body. Such an approach to spirituality may be said to be "sacramental" in the sense that material reality (including our embodied selves and everyday experience and action) is seen as the medium for God's self-revelation and for human encounters with the sacred. This sacramentality is expressed particularly in the rituals of Christian sacraments, notably the Eucharist. Fifth, despite this positive view of the material world as a revelation of the sacred, a Christian understanding of God's creativity and relationship to humanity is not naively optimistic. It recognizes disorder and sin in the world. Consequently, God's relationship to humanity is also seen as redemptive. That is, in Jesus Christ, God is said to confront human disorder with a call to repentance and at the same time promises ultimate restoration. Sixth, Christian discipleship is not individualistic but is essentially communal, within the community of believers, sustained by a common life and shared rituals, and expressed ideally in mutual love and acceptance. In fact, the heart of Christian spirituality is precisely a way of life rather than an abstract code of beliefs. Seventh, at the center of the Christian understanding of spiritual transformation is both the notion of God's abiding presence in the Christian community and also God's indwelling in every person as Spirit, empowering, guiding, and inspiring the journey of the community and of each person toward an ultimate union with the divine in eternal life. Finally, while Christian spirituality affirms the value of creation and of history, the trajectory of spiritual transformation is beyond history into an eschatological future. In that sense, authentic spirituality responds to everyday life yet, at the same time, subverts our tendency to settle on what we can see, grasp, and control as the measure of existence.

The Study of Spirituality

The study of Christian spirituality has established itself as an interdisciplinary field rather than merely a subset of doctrinal theology or of church history. Indeed, the role of interdisciplinary study has become a central methodological principle of spirituality.[14]

The criticism used to be leveled at spirituality that it sought to use as many methods and tools as possible only because there was no adequate sense of disciplinary identity. There is certainly a "cheap" interdisciplinarity that merely plunders the language of different disciplines without a real literacy in those disciplines. At its best, however, interdisciplinarity is not a matter of expediency but is a principled position, as critical theory underlines. Critical theory has a growing impact on theology overall and is derived from postwar French philosophers influenced by social analysis, including Christian thinkers such as Paul Ricoeur, Jean-Luc Marion, and Michel de Certeau. The breakdown of closed systems of analysis, based on a post-Enlightenment mechanization of knowledge that demanded the purity and isolation of disciplines, has also underlined that the ways we think are bound up with power issues. Thus, interdisciplinarity is not merely a potential enrichment of the ways we approach what we study, spiritual classics for example, but is also a discipline (*askesis*) of learning to live with what is multifaceted rather than simple and easily controllable.[15]

Because Christian spirituality engages with the traditions of a faith community, certain disciplines are necessarily involved in its study. Sandra Schneiders has written of these disciplines as "constitutive," inherently associated with the Christian nature of what is being studied. She identifies these as the history of Christianity and scripture. In addition there are what she calls "problematic disciplines." These are disciplines that allow access to the particular problematic of whatever is being studied. Schneiders identifies the leading "problematic disciplines" in the study of spirituality as psychology, the social sciences, literature, and the sciences. For Schneiders, theology lies somewhere in between. My own view is that while it is important to move away from thinking of theological doctrine as in some way a priori, and everything else, including spirituality, as merely deducible from these first principles and derivative, it nevertheless seems impossible to detach a wider sense of theology from the study of Christian spirituality at any point.[16]

Spirituality and Ethics

One specific area where there is a fruitful dialogue between theology and spirituality is the interrelationship between spirituality and Christian ethics (or moral theology). This is paradoxical given that in

Roman Catholic theology in the past, the predecessors of spirituality, ascetical and mystical theology, used to be considered merely as a subdivision of moral theology. Indeed, it could be argued that traditional approaches to ethics or moral theology helped to reinforce the split between theology and spirituality. Both moral theology and ascetical theology were preoccupied with sinfulness and the enfeebled nature of the human condition. This overpowered any wider theological consideration of Christian understandings of human existence or of the quest for holiness and gave the impression that ascetical theology had very little if anything to say theologically in its own right. It appeared to deal merely with some subsidiary (even optional) aspects of the moral life which was itself derived from dogmatic theology.

Nowadays, however, Christian ethics is no longer focused primarily on the rightness or wrongness of particular actions. There has been a shift from abstract actions to the human agent. Here, spirituality and ethics find a common language in a renewed theology of the human person (anthropology) and of grace. There is an increasing awareness of the basic unity between the ethical and the spiritual life. Among the themes that focus the joint task of contemporary spirituality and Christian ethics is how we understand "virtue" (that is, what enables a person to become truly human within a commitment to Jesus Christ and aided by the action of grace) and "identity" (what moral theology classically referred to as "character"), or what we should *be*, rather than do, if we are to become fully human persons. Ethicists increasingly emphasize that our ultimate guide to goodness is not abstract codes of behavior or moral rule books but the presence within us of the Holy Spirit. The indwelling of God grounds the recovery of a fruitful relationship between ethics and spirituality. Yet these are not wholly synonymous. Spirituality in its fullest sense includes the whole of a person's or group's spiritual experience or orientation. In that sense, spirituality overlaps with ethics but cannot be reduced to it.[17]

Conclusion

This book is divided into three broad parts. The first, "History, Theology, and Interpretation," explores questions of definition and method in the study of spirituality. Its four chapters in turn address

"Spirituality and History," the problem of "Interpreting Texts and Traditions," the contentious relationship of "Spirituality and Theology," and finally "Trinity and Anthropology," which relates theologies of God and of human existence in an exploration of what we mean by spiritual transformation. The second part of the book concerns "Spirituality and Social Transformation" and underlines that our understanding of Christian spirituality must expand beyond traditional preoccupations with subjective experience, interiority, and narrowly spiritual practices. Its four chapters in turn explore "Prayer and Social Engagement," "Mysticism and Social Practice" in the work of Michel de Certeau, the tension between monastic solitude and social action in "Thomas Merton and Twentieth-Century Spirituality," and, finally, "Spirituality and Reconciliation"—human reconciliation being, in the words of the South African theologian John de Gruchy, "the inspiration and focus of all doctrines of the Christian faith." The third part of the book, "Space and the Sacred," develops comments made earlier in the book that "spiritual texts" involve more than literary sources. The section also explores and expands the notion that spirituality is intimately concerned with our sense of place as constitutive of human identity. The first chapter, "Spirituality and the City," develops the theme that the future of cities is one of the most challenging and critical *spiritual* as well as social and economic issues of our age. Among other things, the chapter explores some of the ways in which Christianity has reflected upon and even designed cities as "spiritual texts." Finally, the last chapter, "Materializing the Sacred: Churches as Spiritual Texts," directly addresses the notion of sacred space and how religious buildings both express a spiritual vision and are intended to be catalysts of spiritual transformation.

Part One

HISTORY, THEOLOGY, AND INTERPRETATION

1
SPIRITUALITY AND HISTORY
Contexts and Memories

On the face of it, Christianity is a world faith critically preoccupied with "history" and deeply embedded in "time." The doctrines of Trinity and incarnation place God firmly at the heart of human history and of the stories of individuals. "By affirming that all 'meaning,' every assertion about the significance of life and reality, must be judged by reference to a brief succession of contingent events in Palestine, Christianity—almost without realising it—closed off the path to 'timeless truth.'"[1]

At its heart, Christianity demands an affirmation of "history" not only as meaningful but also as the context for the process of spiritual transformation. On a more ordinary level, Christianity is a religion that marks special times and seasons, celebrates feasts and fasts. Memory and re-membering are among the most critical hallmarks of Christian liturgy and sacraments. The Church is built around the dynamism of a story. Tradition, *traditio*, is to hand on this story, but also to *hand it over*, so that it may be freely retold by each generation.

Philosophers, historians, and anthropologists are also concerned with the importance of a historical consciousness. "History" and, more broadly, "time" are important categories in our understanding of human cultures. Here I am using the term *culture* in the sense understood by anthropologists. That is, culture signifies the prevailing worldview of any given society. "Few factors in a culture express the essential nature of its world picture so clearly as its way of reckoning time: for this has a determining influence on the way people behave, the way they think, the rhythm of their lives and the relationships between them and things."[2]

The Concept of Time

Interestingly, time is not a prominent theme in books on Christian spirituality even though time and the sanctification of time are central to a religion whose foundational doctrine is God's "incarnation" at a particular historical moment. Christian spirituality exists *in time*—in other words, it is always historical and contextual.[3]

We apprehend our world in terms of space and time, and these provide the framework of our experience. In that sense, "time," like "place," is a critical cultural category through which human beings organize their understanding of human existence and the world around them. How we perceive time determines our rhythms of life, how we behave, and how we value the different elements of our lives.

The human concept of time has changed, and consequently the way history is written has also changed. The concept of time has gone through three historical phases: cyclical, linear, and "chaotic."[4] Although cyclical and linear conceptions of time have coexisted throughout much of history, linear time gradually asserted its superiority. In this context, the Old Testament writings are very important, especially the Genesis creation story. In contrast to the beauty of a cycle with no beginning and no end, the Book of Genesis posits a unique act of creation that inaugurated change and the flow of time. Judaism retained cyclical themes of recurrence but preferred a predominantly linear model of time. Particular events might be repeated or be echoed (e.g., the annual commemoration of the Passover), but history taken as a whole was unique. This view passed over into both Christianity and Islam. In Christianity, the linear model of time was reinforced by the unique event of the incarnation and the emphasis on the permanent sufficiency of Christ's sacrifice on the cross made "once for all." In turn, this belief pointed forward to the final victory of God in Christ—a teleological-providential view of history led by God ever onward toward a redemptive climax.

Such a view of time is now confronted by the arrival, in Western cultures at least, of a concept of time that is no more than chaotic flux. This is partly a philosophical question of denying the "objective" nature of cultural categories such as "time" and its consequent relegation to a subjective, mental construction that is necessarily plural and contested. This new conception of time was reinforced by the work of Albert

Einstein and subsequent scientific studies on "time." Time is not absolute but depends on the observer's standpoint (literally and metaphorically). Equally, some cosmologists speculate that time might itself be reversible and actually be reversed if, in some unimaginable future, the universe begins to contract.

Since Augustine's *Confessions*, Christianity has engaged with philosophical questions about time. Time is the condition of human existence, and of human becoming, and time is inextricably linked to the contingent-created order (time and the world are created together). Time is, if you like, the measure of the absolute difference between God and human existence. Unlike humankind, God is conceived as having neither memory nor expectation of future possibility but as existing in a complete and joy-filled "present." How, then, can time-bound humanity and the eternal God engage with each other? In a sense, such philosophical issues are not the paramount ones for spirituality. Yet, from another angle they stand forcefully for the sheer otherness of God, the mysterious nature of divine-human encounters, and for the priority of an apophatic-mystical stance not only to religious language but also to the nature of spiritual experience.

Christian life and practice have been dominated by concepts of time. The Church's life is marked by a series of temporal cycles—although one has to admit that their power is considerably diminished in contemporary Western culture where time has become increasingly fluid rather than rhythmic. Each day celebrates liturgically the division between day and night (and symbolically between light and dark) and in some Christian communities, for example monastic ones, the whole day is punctuated by times of prayer. These operate on a number of levels as thresholds between different activities, as a framework for a rhythmic rather than random pattern of life, and as regular moments for recollecting the continuous presence of God. A weekly cycle not only provides a regular Holy Day set aside for worship but a boundary between labor and rest. The cycle of the year is to be lived out in redemptive terms in relation to Christ's life from conception to ascension, marked by alternating fasting and feasting, rather than simply in terms of the natural seasons (although there are clearly many ways in which these two views of the year's passing overlap).

It has been suggested that Christianity lives with at least four concepts of "time."[5] In reality, these are not alternatives but are to be held in creative tension. "Catastrophic time" highlights the inexorable process of time moving toward death and the fact that "destiny is dust," as it were. The contemplation of such contingency and of time's ruin has played a significant part in the development of Christian spiritual discipline or asceticism. "Apocalyptic time" expresses a spirituality of waiting and anticipation—that ultimate meaning will "come to us" rather than be artificially constructed by our limited imaginations. "Kairic time" (from the Greek *kairos*, implying "time-as-opportunity") focuses attention on the vital importance of the present moment and of finding meaning in the ordinary, in what is *given now*. In many respects *kairos* time is in the foreground of the New Testament. God's saving action in the life-death-resurrection of Jesus is said to be "in the fullness of time" (Gal 4:4). This overflows into the sense that for all whom Jesus addresses, "this is the favorable time," now "the time is ful-filled" (Mark 1:15; Matt 4:17). The call to welcome the kingdom of God, to turn to God, is an urgent *now*. Finally, "prophetic time" does not accept things as they are but both envisions and then actively pro-motes an ideal "end" for time (both in the sense of completion and pur-pose). Such a view of time fuels different forms of political or liberation spiritualities.

In the broadest possible terms, Christianity treats time as a tightly bound, threefold pattern of memory, engagement with the pres-ent, and anticipation of the future. On the one hand, past and future are not escape routes from dissatisfaction with the present. On the other, a sense of being involved in a stream of time breeds a sense of responsibility for a time beyond ourselves and relativizes an obsession with the unique importance of our "present moment." For the Christian community, "time" conceived as a whole is portrayed in eschatological terms as emanating from and returning to divine eter-nity. Both the Christ-centered and eschatological dimensions of time are most powerfully realized in the regular celebration of the Eucharist. Here, Christ's redemptive life, death, and resurrection are re-presented as real and effective for each succeeding generation. At the same time, in every contingent eucharistic "moment," past, present, and future are mystically gathered in an intersection of time and eternity.

The Problem of Time

A number of features of contemporary Western culture underline the shifting patterns of "time" and provide a challenging context for Christian approaches to time to be reconceived. In summary, these features involve the crumbling away of the time boundaries that defined people's lives for centuries. For example, the impact of microtechnology, among other factors, means that we live increasingly in a twenty-four-hour world where distinctions between night and day are blurred. Equally the traditional boundaries between a working week and sabbath rest are rapidly being eradicated. The resulting "crisis" of time presents itself as a fragmentation of time and the problem of a lack or loss of time. This heightens our awareness of "running out of time," the imperative of "saving time," the pressure to avoid anything that is "a waste of time," and so on. The cultural pressures are toward immediacy, speed, obvious productivity, and completion *now*. In this context, Christian spiritual values such as attentiveness and waiting, recognizing our unfinished nature, and living in hope and expectation take on a new urgency and prophetic potency. Faithfulness and perseverance become critical challenges for everyone. It is worth recalling that one of the most powerful symbols of time in both the Hebrew Scriptures and the Gospels is the desert. The desert is both a space and a time. Desert "time," whether for the people of Israel in Exodus or for Jesus in the Synoptic gospels, is a period both of waiting and of testing (see, e.g., Deut 8:2). Symbolically, the "time of the desert" stands for an apparent non-time, a between-time, a "useless" time, yet the kind of time that, if allowed for, teaches humanity the crucial lessons of patience and perseverance.

Contemporary Suspicion of History

In approaching the relationship between spirituality and history, another fundamental factor is the way we view the importance or otherwise of "history" itself. We also exist in a time of cultural change when the question is often asked concerning whether history has a point any longer. Are we in the West rapidly becoming a history-less and memory-less culture? If this is the case, then in the long term it will surely have a serious impact on our spiritualities. There seems to be a problem in Western culture at the moment in that it is possible to detect a weariness with history and with the notion of being involved in a tradition or a stream of continuities throughout time. To base one's life on tradition or to hark back to the past appears to be a distraction. It is much more common these days for people to believe that "history" only signifies the past and that the past is what happened rather than something that enables our present to come into being or that invites us to reflect on the future and on what we aspire to.

In Booker Prize–winner Pat Barker's recent novel *Another World*, Geordie, a centenarian veteran of the Somme, is dying. He has particularly close relationships with two people. Helen, the professional historian who has recorded interviews with him and other veterans, is a representative of "modernity" with its strong historical consciousness. She has a fervent commitment to preserving memories for the sake of posterity. Geordie's grandson Nick is, if you like, a postmodern man who not only believes that "history" has no message for us but in fact does not really believe in history at all.

> "Well, you see the first thing is I don't believe in public memory. A memory is a biochemical change in an individual brain, and that's all there is." And secretly, what he wants to say is that raking about in the detritus of other people's memories is a waste of time and energy. The only true or useful thing that can be said about the past is that it's over. It no longer exists.[6]

This weariness with history probably relates to a number of factors. Rapid social changes and the decline of traditional social or working communities have broken many people's sense of a living connection with the past. Our sense of a living past and our sense of "place" are intimately connected. Our disconnection from familiar landscapes, places of family origin, and "home" consequently undermine our awareness of continuities. "History," and its sibling "tradition," is also perceived by some people as a conservative force from which we need to break free if we are to become a more rational society. The power of "history" (or, more accurately, of history-as-myth) to sustain entrenched social, religious, and political divisions in different places around the world tends to reinforce this negative view in the minds of many people.

History is a battleground because it is a matter of identity. I only have to recall my childhood experiences in England of heated exchanges about the *true* ownership of history in the four hundred years since the Reformation. Our identity as a Roman Catholic minority in a predominantly Protestant country demanded that we wrest "history" back from the opposition. Once again, history and places were closely related as our wistful attention was often fixed on local medieval churches that had once been "ours"!

Then there is the desire for immediacy sustained by consumerism (and reinforced, to some extent, by information technology) that tends to encourage a memory-less culture without a sense of historical identity. Perhaps the most powerful factor of all is the death of a notion of "history as destiny" that was dominated by faith in the inevitability of progress after a century of industrial growth and imperialistic expansion. This belief in "history" as a progressive force evaporated during the twentieth century in the face of the multiple hammer blows of the mass slaughter of the 1914–1918 war, the horrors of midcentury totalitarianism, the Holocaust, and Hiroshima.

Narrative and History

So, is history dead? The internationally influential French philosopher Paul Ricoeur (unusual in his intellectual world by being a Christian) has been greatly preoccupied with the importance of reconstructing a viable sense of "time" and "historical consciousness." These, he argues, are vital to our individual and collective identities—and, implicitly, to our spiritual well-being. "[T]ime becomes human time to the extent that it is organized after the manner of a narrative; narrative, in turn, is meaningful to the extent that it portrays the features of temporal existence."[7]

At first glance, Ricoeur appears to be something of a paradox. On the one hand, he shares a postmodern skepticism for metanarratives and is profoundly suspicious of "giving in to the temptation of the completed totality."[8] Ricoeur shares with postmodernist thinkers the belief that we must renounce any attempt by history "to decipher the supreme plot." However, Ricoeur also rejects a tendency to equate this renunciation with the impossibility of seeing history as a form of narrative at all. In fact he argues that the former search for a supreme plot or meta-narrative actually undermined true narrative because it reduced history to "the totalization of time in the eternal present."[9] If we reject the possibility of mediating narratives altogether this is not the liberating experience that it may appear. On the contrary, it is profoundly oppressive. The reason is that without narrative we risk two things. First, we undermine a key element of human solidarity (we bond together by sharing stories), and, second, we reduce or remove a key incentive for changing the status quo as well as an important means of bringing this about. "We tell stories because in the last analysis human lives need and merit being narrated. The whole history of suffering cries out for vengeance and calls for narrative."[10]

Narrative is a critical key to our identity, for we all need a story to live by in order to make sense of the otherwise unrelated events of life and to find a sense of dignity. It is only by enabling alternative stories to be heard that an elitist "history" may be prised open to offer an entry point for the oppressed who have otherwise been excluded from public history. "Without a narrative, a person's life is merely a random sequence of unrelated events: birth and death are inscrutable, temporality is a terror and a burden, and suffering and loss remain mute and unintelligible."[11] Rather than abolish narrative we need to ask: "Whose narrative is told?" "Who belongs within the story?"

Narrative and history are closely related. Ricoeur seeks to overcome the absolute dichotomy between history as "true" and stories as "fiction."[12] Both history and fiction refer to the historicity of human existence. Both share a common narrative structure. Both employ a "plot" to suggest a pattern for otherwise episodic events. Any and every plot chooses a sequence for events and characters that suggests a direction or movement. This is shaped by a particular point of view. Ricoeur rejects the positivist view of history (that is, history is only what is scientifically verifiable) in favor of one that allows for the presence of "fiction." That is, history as a form of literature does not simply recount events in a disconnected or uninterested way but *organizes* them in a form that seeks coherence. Equally, fiction can be *truthful* in that, while not slavishly tied to the mechanical details of an event, it is capable of addressing something equally important about reality—the realms of possibility and of the "universal." History and fiction are both narratives that seek to describe either what reality *is* or *is like* with the purpose of making human existence meaningful.

Ricoeur may be said to be attempting to retrieve history as something more than merely a disconnected set of cold, objectified "events" emptied of the warmth of human stories. "History" once again has something to do with people's vision. It is an act of interpretation, and all interpretation is necessarily an act of *commitment*. History implies continuities, and continuities in turn imply responsibilities. Commitment and responsibility point to the important fact that history is not merely about the past but also about the present and future. A historical consciousness opens us to possible action rather than to a passive acceptance of "the way things are." In this way of understanding, "history" becomes a critical spiritual issue.

Augustine's Theology of History

It is not surprising that Ricoeur's preoccupation with time and history draws him to engage with the theology of St. Augustine. Augustine's theology of history, expounded mainly in his *City of God*, has probably been the single most influential historical theory in Christianity.[13] Augustine's thought has also been pervasive in a more implicit way in Western culture in general. The particular context for the work was the sack of Rome by the Visigoths in 410 CE. This event critically undermined a perception current among many Christians after the conversion of the emperor Constantine that the Roman Empire was a divinely willed, and even divinely guided, framework for human existence. In terms of Richard Niebuhr's classic typology of relations between religion and culture, *Christ and Culture*, there had been a shift from a pre-Constantinian conflict between Christianity and public history to the absorption of the faith by the political and social reality of the empire.[14] This corresponded to the type Niebuhr refers to as "The Christ of Culture" and about which he was highly critical. The origins of early monasticism undoubtedly lie in a variety of motivations and influences; however, there can be no doubt that the rapid expansion of monasticism in the fourth century CE was partly a prophetic, spiritual, and social reaction to the perception that the Church was becoming overidentified with public imperial history.

In the context of a fragmentation of empire in the first part of the fifth century CE, Augustine redefined the relationship between the Kingdom of God and human history in terms of two communities or forces, the City of God and the Earthly City. Like the tares and the wheat of the gospel parable, the two cities cannot be perfectly differentiated within time. Ultimate meaning and stability cannot be found in the Earthly City, which is a context of incessant change. Nevertheless, states and empires may be said to have a "historical role" in that they have an impact on the advance of the City of God. Thus, the Roman Empire may be said to have had a "mission" to unify people in order that the Gospel might spread more easily. In itself, however, the Empire had no eternal significance, and its historical decline was inevitable.

Augustine's distinction between the City of God and the Earthly City threw into sharp relief a tension at the heart of Christian spirituality. If the origins of Christianity involve an affirmation of history, there has always been a siren voice that suggests that what is fundamentally important spiritually lies *now* in a parallel dimension alongside or outside historical events and *ultimately* in an eternity on the far side of time. Augustinian theology and spirituality may be a reaction against a dangerous and theologically dubious association between God and the State. But is there a place in Augustinian thought for the Kingdom of God to grow *within* human history? Does human history in time and space have meaning?

Because Augustine believed that the full explanation of "history" lay in the ultimate "event" (the consummation of God's Kingdom), his history belongs in the eschatological category. This concept of divine control of history continued among Christian writers in a fairly uninterrupted way until relatively modern times. In the course of the last two hundred years or so this became absorbed into a post-Enlightenment belief in the god of "Progress"—that the world was inexorably moving toward greater rationality, greater justice, greater civilization, and greater economic development. Augustine himself must be exonerated from such confusions. He did not identify divine control of history with the concept of social, political, or economic success. No historic age grew closer to God, perfection, or eternity than any other. In that sense, the City of God operates in a realm distinct from everyday history. Conversely, a providential understanding of history does not involve a triumphalistic theology but a theology of hope glimpsed through tragedies and failure.[15] This is just as well because the Enlightenment interpretation of history as the triumph of progress died on the Somme and at Auschwitz.

An important key to Augustine's theology of history is that his *City of God* is based on his own experience. Indeed some see it as an application on a wider canvas of Augustine's sense of God's providence in his own life as expressed in the pages of the *Confessions*.[16] Fundamentally, the lesson of Augustine's checkered career and of world history is that out of all things comes good. Although the City of God operates on a level distinct from the events of ordinary history the distancing is far from absolute. True, Rome (or any other human *imperium*) is not the Kingdom of God in human form. The Earthly City, and thus human history, is always contingent. But human history is God's creation and is not, therefore, to be condemned as merely evil, or treated as an illusion. For Augustine, the lessons of history lead him to be calmly confident about the future even *in and through* the ambiguities and darkness of human events and experiences. If contingent "time" and "history" are to end, it is the ending of fulfillment, not of destruction and therefore of ultimate meaninglessness.

Even if Augustine rejected a progress model of human history, and no age could be said to be closer to God than any other, he also possessed a deep sense that *each and every moment in time* was equally filled with God's presence and activity. Augustine's theology of history essentially describes two dimensions of history: the history of contingent events and, running through it, the thread of sacred history that alone tells us what God is *really* doing.[17] Therefore, every moment is significant even if that significance is presently mysterious. Such a view seems close to Paul Ricoeur's understanding of "narrative" which is not descriptive of the time-space world as it is, and therefore of "history" in a positivist sense. Narrative *re*describes the world rather than describes it. Narrative brings together and harmonizes the otherwise discordant and disparate elements of the experience of time and history.

In an important sense, Augustine's distinction between sacred and secular history does not render the history of time and space meaningless. Rather it liberates it in its contingency from any need to be tidied up. It is only when a Divine Providence version of history collapses into an Enlightenment version of "history-as-progress" that we end up with a reediting of human history that becomes exclusive and sanitized and therefore oppressive and dysfunctional. I have taken pains elsewhere to describe how the history of Christian spirituality has been edited in this unhealthy way.[18] What we can nowadays detect in studies of Christian spirituality is the effort to take its history seriously *precisely as history*. This is not purely a pragmatic or methodological point. It has theological and spiritual resonances because such an attitude recognizes that Christian spirituality is not a perfect seamless robe but is associated with contexts, viewpoints, worldviews, and experiences. The history of spirituality is a record of attempts, and no more, to live out the Gospel, by fits and starts, in the complexity of human events.

Eschatology and History

An eschatological model of history is not per se bound to empty the history of human events of significance by suggesting that meaning is to be found only in some indefinable future after the death of time. There are indeed over–future-oriented eschatologies just as there are over-realized ones. To suggest blandly that God *has* redeemed the world despite visible evil, or to suggest that God's redemptive love merely awaits us on the other side of history, leaves us with a God cruelly detached from the here-and-now realities of human suffering and violence. In terms of Niebuhr's typology, interpreted in terms of eschatologies, it is perhaps his fifth type, "Christ the Transformer of Culture," that approaches an ideal balance. This type, as Niebuhr himself suggests, would seem to come closest to Augustine. This eschatology suggests that the beginnings of the Kingdom lie in history, through the process of spiritual transformation. Yet the process is always to be completed and so there is perpetually an impulse to press on toward a final completion.

A balanced eschatology opens every "present moment," and indeed history as a whole, to what is beyond it or more than the present instant. History and the 'present moment' are thus not reduced in importance, let alone annihilated, but actually *expanded and enhanced*. Every moment contains not only the presence of the past but also the hope of the future. Every moment is also decisive. An eschatological perspective makes chronological time also *kairos* time. Each historical moment is an "end moment" that makes whatever we do now an act of commitment to what is final or decisive. One might say that every moment is "eucharistic" in a broad sense. The Eucharist is the characteristic action of the Christian community. We give thanks. We remember the saving events of Jesus Christ. We anticipate in joyful hope our ultimate destiny. Theologically and spiritually, celebrations of the Eucharist are moments of concentration and intersection that both gather all time—past, present, and future—into the here and now and also bring human time into transforming contact with the "epoch-making event of Jesus Christ in its once and for all character."[19]

Spirituality and Historical Interpretation

Despite contemporary misgivings, historical consciousness is a fundamental element in the interpretation of spiritual texts and traditions and reminds us of the irreducibly contextual nature and particularity of spiritual values. Serious consideration of the complexities of history has been a major development in the academic study of spirituality over the last thirty years or so. Before that time, spirituality tended to pay little attention to context, whether of historical texts and traditions or of the contemporary interpreter. Studies of classic traditions did not reflect on the contingency of their theological or cultural assumptions. In the case of classical writings, problems of interpretation were not a major issue in a world where Christians had little sense of historical distance from the perspective of ancient authors.

One reason why the study of spirituality in theological circles now pays greater attention to the complexity of historical interpretation lies in an important shift provoked by a change of language associated with the Second Vatican Council in the early 1960s. The use of the phrase 'signs of the times' by Pope John XXIII, and its repetition in the Council documents, was effectively a recognition that history was not incidental to but the context for God's redemptive work. Every historical moment has a dynamic of its own where the presence and power of God may be perceived. Consequently, faith is not opposed to history, and no separation is possible between religious history and world history.[20]

Spirituality and Context

Spiritualities do not exist on some ideal plane outside the limitations of history. The origins and development of spiritual traditions reflect the specific circumstances of time and place as well as the psychological state of the people involved. They consequently embody values that are socially conditioned. To take one example, the emphasis on radical poverty in the spirituality of the thirteenth-century mendicant movement was not simply a "naked" scriptural value but a spiritual and social reaction to particular conditions in society and the Church at the time—not least to what were seen as their prevailing sins.[21]

This does not imply that spiritual traditions and texts have no value beyond their original contexts. It does mean, however, that to appreciate their riches we must take context seriously. The concept of "context" was imported from the fields of history and the social sciences. It has become a primary framework for the study of spiritual traditions. All spiritual experience is determined to some degree by culture—that is, a system of meaning or a worldview in the sense used by anthropology. Culture "denotes an historically transmitted pattern of meanings embodied in symbols, a system of inherited conceptions expressed in symbolic forms by means of which men [sic] communicate, perpetuate, and develop their knowledge about and attitudes toward life."[22] Spiritual traditions, and the texts that are their 'products,' are cultural expressions.

Spirituality is thus never pure in form. "Context" is not something that may be added to or subtracted from spiritual experiences or traditions but is the very element within which these find expression.[23] This contradicts an older conception of Christian spirituality as a stream of enduring truth in which the same theories or images are simply repeated in different guises. Even spiritual theologians as sophisticated as Karl Rahner and his brother Hugo appeared at times to place a figure like Ignatius Loyola essentially outside the limitations of history. His spirituality was "not really an event in the history of ideas that could be inserted, if we were so to choose, in the 'Tridentine' or 'Baroque' periods....It is something of exemplary value in a quite fundamental way, for an age that is only just starting." In a footnote, Karl Rahner developed this thought further by suggesting that "Ignatius has something almost of the archaic and archetypal about him....He has nothing that really belongs to the Baroque or the Renaissance about him."[24] The writings of the Rahner brothers led the Catholic Reformation historians Outram Evennett and John Bossy to point out the danger of making spiritual experience or teaching "a region of certainty transcending any historical or psychological conditions."[25]

These comments about culture and context in relation to spirituality would now be widely accepted. However, a comparison of three classic histories of spirituality written during the twentieth century soon reminds us of how substantial the changes have been over the last fifty years.

Pierre Pourrat's four-volume *La Spiritualité Chrétienne* was published shortly after the First World War. His unified approach to spiritual doctrine led him to suppose that the same theology of prayer, virtue, or spiritual growth could be found in all spiritual traditions. Different "schools" of spirituality or different national "types" of spirituality differed only in presentation. The cultural dominance of the Greco-Latin forms was unquestioned. Pourrat effectively ignored the existence of other spiritual "cultures" (e.g., Celtic in the West or Syriac in the East). He also limited his attention to monasticism and mysticism with virtually no reference to lay or "popular" spirituality.

Louis Bouyer's three-volume (in the English edition) *A History of Christian Spirituality* was published in the early 1960s around the time of the Second Vatican Council. Bouyer was still preoccupied with the essential unity of spirituality and often lacked an awareness of differences between or even within "schools" of spirituality. In other respects, however, his volumes were a considerable advance on Pourrat. The cultural perspective was broader (e.g., Syriac and Celtic traditions do get a mention), lay spirituality has more substantial treatment, and his third volume offered, for its time, a relatively sympathetic treatment of Orthodox, Protestant, and Anglican spiritualities. Women were, however, still relatively invisible.

Finally, the three Christian volumes within the Crossroad series World Spirituality: An Encyclopedic History of the Religious Quest appeared in the late 1980s. These differ vastly from Pourrat and Bouyer. Most significantly, they are collections of specialist essays by teams of international and ecumenical scholars rather than grand surveys by single authors. The history of spiritual traditions is to be seen as inherently plural, linked to specific social, cultural, and theological contexts. We can no longer expect a single person to have the detailed knowledge to write a multivolume history. While by no means perfect, the volumes offer a much better balance between Eastern and Western Christianity and make other efforts to express the cultural plurality of spirituality beyond a Greco-Latin hegemony. The spirituality of lay Christians and women's perspectives are better represented and there is an acceptance that earlier condemnations of dissenting spiritualities need to be revised.[26]

While pluralism and context are now accepted as the unquestioned background to the study of historical spiritualities, the way in which contextual studies developed raises questions for people who are concerned with the specifically religious themes of spirituality. For example, the history of spirituality has come to mean the study of how religious attitudes and values are conditioned by surrounding culture and society. This brings historical spirituality close to the study of *mentalités*, or worldviews, so beloved of French historians in the second half of the twentieth century. This "social" version of history is informed by anthropology and religious sociology. The limitation of such an approach to spirituality, if it is exclusive, is that it tends to abandon theological sources and the questions raised by theological theory. We need a middle way between the older (exclusively theological) approach to spirituality and the newer stress on changing social contexts.[27] One case study is the recent treatment of early Christian asceticism and monasticism. A contextual approach tends to resituate asceticism in a broader world than monasticism or even patristic Christianity and approaches its history with questions drawn from a wide range of disciplines. This raises many new and interesting questions. The problem is that such an approach *in isolation* often leaves little room for the theological goals that were the active horizons of Christian asceticism.[28]

The contextual nature of spiritual traditions means that the process of historical analysis must nowadays address a number of critical questions.[29] First, in any given tradition or text how was holiness conceived? Which categories of people were thought of as holy? What places or things were deemed to be particularly sacred—and, negatively, who or what was excluded from the category "holy" or "sacred"? For example, close association with sexual activity (marriage) or with physical reality (manual labor) was for many centuries difficult to connect with ideas of holiness. Second, who creates or controls spirituality? For example, to what degree does the language of spirituality

reflect the interests and experience of minority groups (who nevertheless controlled spiritual resources) such as clergy or monastic person-
nel? Third, what directions were not taken? In other words, to what
degree has it been assumed that the choices made were in some
absolute way superior to those that were rejected? For example, what
were the real motives for the condemnation as heretics of the medieval
women's spiritual movement, the Beguines? Was it a genuine concern
for the spiritual welfare of laypeople or a suspicion of laypeople not suf-
ficiently under clerical control? Finally, where are the groups that did
not fit? For example, why was it that, within the Western Catholic tradition, the experience of lay Christians and women especially was
largely ignored until recently in the formulation of spiritual theory?

Following from these questions, we should note that all historical
studies involve choices, and this affects our understanding of what
counts as "spirituality" as well as our interpretation of spiritual traditions. First, *time limits* are chosen. In other words, writers decide on the
appropriate boundaries within which to date spiritual movements and
thus to understand them. For example, our sense of the continuity or
discontinuity between the spirituality of the Middle Ages and that of
the Protestant Reformation will be affected by an apparently simple
matter of how and where authors choose to divide a multivolume history.[30] Second, traditional histories reveal a *geographical bias*. We make
assumptions about where "the center" and "the margins" are in a history of spiritual traditions. For example, until recently, the spirituality
of Celtic Christianity was usually treated in terms of its absorption into
a homogenized Latin tradition around the eleventh and twelfth centuries rather than on its own terms. Third, we choose *certain evidence
as significant*. So, for example, if studies concentrate exclusively on
mystical texts or monastic rules, the impression is given that spirituality is essentially literary, is to be found exclusively in privileged contexts, and may be distinguished from the merely devotional or
"popular" religion. Devotion is generally associated with feelings rather
than ideas, and, in spiritual cultures that value the mind above the body
or emotions, religious devotions are often underestimated. Particular
spiritual practices that engaged the affective side of religion were char-
acteristically excluded from consideration in histories of Christian
spirituality. I am thinking of such practices as pilgrimage, processions,
the veneration of devotional objects, and so-called devotional practices

such as the rosary or the stations of the cross. There is a sense in which this was, and sometimes still is, thought of as "popular piety" rather than "spirituality." Studies that give no attention to these practices and sentiments, however, offer a very one-sided approach to the history of spirituality. Equally, a rigid distinction between "high" mystical spirituality and popular devotional spirituality is unhelpful. As the medieval Franciscans and the Beguines both clearly showed, devotional themes and practices were often an important backdrop to complex mystical-theological writings.

Conclusion

The contemporary climate of postmodernity may suggest that we have reached the end of history in the sense that "history" has become fatally associated with ideology, structures of control, and the dominance of certain elites whether in society or in the Church. In its more extreme forms, postmodernist theory is indeed antihistorical. More moderate voices do not reject a historical consciousness and its positive values, however, but seek to refine it. If history (and its wisdom) has been oppressive because associated with dominant economic, social, or even spiritual groups, it must now be reconstructed as a liberating force by giving space to the stories of forgotten or rejected minorities. History becomes truly wise when it is a narrative that is capable of including women as well as men, the whole of humanity as opposed to merely the economically powerful nations, the material earth as well as humankind. As Augustine may still remind us, "history" is also truly wise when, by opening every contingent moment to infinite possibility, it offers a holistic spiritual vision rather than a limited vision of fulfillment conceived in terms of purely material enhancement.

2
INTERPRETING TEXTS AND TRADITIONS
Understanding and Appropriation

The study of Christian spirituality involves critical issues of interpretation both of spiritual traditions as a whole and of specific texts. In this context, the word *text* may refer to the scriptures, viewed as spiritual wisdom documents, to other written works in the tradition, or it may be understood more broadly. While biblical texts are obviously accorded a special revelatory status, to approach other texts as bearers of spiritual wisdom raises similar interpretative issues. I take interpretation to be essentially a quest for understanding. This is a complex matter because understanding is associated with "meaning" rather than purely with gathering factual information and data.

The fundamentals of Christian spirituality as a field of study, its object and methods, are considered elsewhere in this book. At this point I merely wish to summarize some key points that relate to the question of "interpretation." First of all, I am going to assume, rather than develop, the widely accepted notion that spirituality is a self-implicating discipline. This suggests that the study of spirituality is not only *informative* but also *transformative*. When we approach particular traditions or texts, we clearly seek information. This is likely to include historical data, a detailed analysis of texts, an understanding of theological frameworks, and a determination of the kind of spiritual wisdom or practice that is being represented. Beyond *information*, however, lies a quest for the "truth" or wisdom embodied in a tradition or text and how this may be accessed. This aspect of coming to understand a tradition or text confronts us with the questions "What difference does this make?" and "What could or should our response be?" This is the transformative dimension of the study of spirituality and involves *judgment* (this makes sense, is important and of value) and *appropriation* (we seek to make this wisdom our own). I will return to this point later.

This rich approach to "understanding" in the field of Christian spirituality inevitably means that the Enlightenment ideal of a single method, appropriate to a free-standing field of study, has to be abandoned. Indeed, in the academic world more broadly the notion of internally consistent but mutually exclusive disciplines separated by hard boundaries is breaking down. The identity of an area of study is no longer to be found in maintaining sharp distinctions of method. This shift has been characterized as "a centrifugal, rather than centripetal sense of disciplinary identity."[1] In this context, Christian spirituality is generally agreed to be an *interdisciplinary* field (albeit with a special relationship to theology) that draws on a range of methods and thus demands a sophisticated rather than simple approach to interpretation.

In the first instance, an interdisciplinary approach expands the disciplines on which the process of interpretation draws. Depending on the nature of the tradition or text under consideration, the classical approach drew on historical, linguistic, and literary methods. Because of the religious nature of what is being interpreted, theological tools were also necessary as aids to analysis and evaluation.[2] To these must now be added an engagement with the methods of modern philosophy, social sciences, and psychology, along with critical fields such as feminist or liberationist theory.

The more complex approach to interpretation, however, nowadays implies more than a mere expansion of the methods employed. Precisely because the spiritual traditions and texts to be interpreted are viewed as likely sources of *wisdom*, interpretation has shifted beyond which methods might provide the best data to hermeneutical theory—in other words, to a much deeper consideration of the very nature of interpretation itself. This approach asks what "world of meaning" is presented in a tradition or text and what kind of wisdom is available. Such an approach to interpretation recognizes that what is present in spiritual wisdom traditions and texts is not reducible to what we can know cognitively. Because such wisdom is profoundly challenging and is likely to change us if we pursue it, a contemplative approach must be added to an intellectual one.[3]

Context and Choices

While spiritual traditions and texts may have value beyond their original contexts, to appreciate their riches fully we must take that context seriously. While scriptural values clearly play an explicit role in the development of all Christian spiritualities, critical investigation inevitably reveals two things. First, these values are appropriated in different ways in different contexts. Second, other forces also control the development of traditions and the ways they are recorded.

The concept of "context" was originally imported from the fields of history and the social sciences. It has become a primary framework of interpretation in the study of spiritual traditions. All spiritual experience is determined to some degree by culture. By "culture" I imply a system of meaning or a worldview in the sense used originally by anthropology but now borrowed by other disciplines. This approach emphasizes that culture itself is a "text," potentially with many layers of meaning. It demands sophisticated interpretation rather than straightforward classification and explanation. The symbols, rituals, attitudes, and perspectives about life that constitute a culture enable human societies to cohere and function. Culture regulates how people assign meaning and allocate value in terms of the key elements of human living. It defines their social, economic, political, and religious behavior. Spiritual traditions, and the texts that are their products, are cultural expressions.[4] Spirituality is thus never pure in form. "Context" is not really something that may be added to or subtracted from spiritual experience or practice but is the very element within which these find expression. Even though religions claim a transcendent dimension, all faiths throughout history have been embedded in specific cultures.[5]

Equally, as already noted, all historical studies involve choices that affect our interpretation of spiritual texts and traditions. First, our time limits establish the appropriate boundaries within which to date spiritual movements and thus to understand them. Second, a geographical bias tends to reinforce assumptions about where the center is and where the margins are in a history of spiritual traditions. Third, certain evidence is prioritized as significant—for example, classical histories tend to give predominant attention to texts, or to traditions that have produced written texts, thus giving the impression that spirituality is essentially literary and is to be distinguished from the mere devotions and pieties of popular religion.

Interpretation and Commitment

The question of choices, even in the context of purely historical study, already suggests that every act of interpretation is value-laden and involves various kinds of commitment that are far from simple. Because, for many Christians, certain important spiritual texts (or "classics") have been accorded the status of wisdom documents, there is a particular edge to the scholarly question of interpretation. With both scriptural texts and spiritual wisdom documents, similar basic questions arise. If our interest in such texts is not purely literary or anti-quarian, the question of *why* we read such texts and what we read them *for* are particularly central. How we proceed to read texts is thus intimately related to why we read them. Fundamentally, we cannot unlock the depths of a spiritual wisdom document, any more than the depths of a scriptural text, except through a process of interpretation that draws the reader into a particular world of meaning.

In this context, a number of scholars now refer to what has been called an "appropriative method" in relation to interpreting Christian traditions and texts, whether scriptural or spiritual. By this, scholars mean that the purpose of interpretation is not merely accurate knowledge but *application*, and the purpose of application is *appropriation*. That is, "understanding" a spiritual text fully is transformative rather than purely informative.[6] Understanding is concerned with meanings but also with purpose and values. To be appropriated, texts need to be understood from the inside out, as it were.

In his introduction to a collection of essays on the theological interpretation of scripture (but with considerable relevance to reading texts of spirituality), Stephen Fowl outlines such an approach. Both the fragmentation of theological disciplines and the separation of theology from praxis are, he argues, products of modernity, with its particular understanding of the process of knowing and the content of knowledge.[7] The modern era promoted historical-critical methods that tended to separate a way of reading directed at historical reconstruction from the theological purpose a Christian reading of scripture was intended to serve. Throughout Christian history, however, it has been normal for the majority of Christians to read the scripture *theologically*, at least implicitly. That is, they read scripture "to guide, correct, and edify their faith, worship and practice as part of their ongoing struggle to live faithfully before the triune God."[8] This same understanding of textual reading may be applied to spiritual classics. The transformative approach to interpretation and knowledge has also been endorsed in recent decades by philosophical theologians such as the Roman Catholic David Tracy and the Anglican Rowan Williams.[9]

Spiritual Classics

The presentation of the history of spirituality and the interpretation of texts are of general as well as scholarly concern. Many people associate themselves with historic spiritual traditions in ways that affect their present sense of identity. Equally, other people seek spiritual wisdom through the medium of classical texts. Even those people who have departed from conventional religious traditions paradoxically draw upon traditional wisdom in such classic Christian mystical figures as Hildegard of Bingen, Meister Eckhart, or the anonymous author of *The Cloud of Unknowing*. The interpretation of classic texts for contemporary use is therefore a live and critical one.

While spiritual texts are historically conditioned, some cross the boundaries of time or place and retain their popularity and importance in contexts very different from their own. This is what is implied by the term *classics*.[10] Such texts disclose something that remains compelling. They continue to challenge readers and bring them into transforming contact with what is enduring and vital in the Christian tradition. The nature of a text's literary genre often influences its popularity and effectiveness.[11] In general, the strength of classics is that they do not merely offer information but are capable of persuading and moving a reader to a response.

A vital aspect of the special power of spiritual classics is the fact that they are *committed texts*. Spiritual classics, rather like scriptural texts, offer a particular interpretation of events, people, or teachings. Every spiritual classic has a specific take on the tradition it promotes. In interpreting a spiritual classic, we unavoidably engage with this commitment. We cannot bypass the claims to wisdom—indeed, to a vision of "truth"—embodied in such texts.

David Tracy suggests the following in exploring the notion of what he calls a "classic text":

> First, there exists a qualitative difference between a classic and a period piece; second, there exists an assumption that a classic, by definition, will always be in need of further interpretation in view of its need for renewed application to a particular situation; third, a classic, again by definition, is assumed to be any text that always has the power to transform the horizon of the interpreter and thereby disclose new meaning and experiential possibilities.[12]

In a genuine classic there is always what Tracy calls a paradoxical tension between its particularity and its universality. The "universality" of the classic is its capacity to disclose a world of meaning and to evoke transformation in a potentially infinite succession of readers. Interestingly, for Tracy the category of "a classic" is not limited to written texts but may be extended beyond books to events and persons that have some form of revelatory status. As we will see later, I would add to this list artefacts, buildings, visual arts, and poetry.[13] Thus, a personality such as Francis of Assisi or a Gothic cathedral may be as much a "classic text" as the *Showings* of Julian of Norwich.

Process of Interpretation

We are inevitably aware of different cultural and theological perspectives when we read a classical spiritual text from another time or place. If interpretation is meant to serve appropriation, we cannot avoid the question of how far to respect a text's conceptual framework, structure, or dynamic in relation to contemporary practice. Certain responses would be naive. We may ignore the author's intention and the text's structure entirely and simply pick and choose from the text as it suits us. The opposite danger is to assume that only the author's intention is normative. Even assuming that we can accurately reconstruct this intention, such an approach subordinates our present horizons to the past and ignores entirely the context of the contemporary reader. Both approaches assume that the meaning of a text is a straightforward matter. A more fruitful, while more complex, approach to interpretation is to engage in a receptive yet critical *dialogue* with the text. Such a dialogue allows the wisdom of a text to challenge us while at the same time according our own horizons their proper place.[14]

If there is to be a dialogue between the horizons of a text and our own, the text's historical context is certainly an important starting point. Spiritual classics were written for clearly identified audiences and addressed specific concerns. The insights of literary criticism also remind us that however familiar words may seem to be in the first instance, the experiences and assumptions that lie behind them are different from our own and consequently give particular words a new significance. We also need to recall that, in reading a text, we are not dealing with two quite disconnected moments (our own and that of the author) but also with what comes between: that is, how a text has been transmitted from its origins to the present and the history of its interpretation. The tradition of interpretation and use of a text over centuries affects our own moment of reading. I will return later to the question of how we are to define the "community of capable readers" across time.

While historical knowledge has to some extent a normative role in interpreting texts, there are limits to its value. For example, what we encounter in a text is not direct experience of another time but what the text *claims* about it, for all texts employ the conventional categories of their age. In other words, all texts are themselves interpretations of experience, not merely records of it. Some, such as the Long Text of the *Showings* of Julian of Norwich (the fourteenth-century English mystic), were written many years after the experiences that gave rise to them and are explicitly based on hindsight. To allow for the interpreted nature of texts, however, is not to reject the value of the results. Indeed, subsequent reflections by the author may be more relevant to those who seek to *use* a text than the original unique experience on its own. For example, *the* classical Christian texts, the Gospels, are creative reworkings of earlier oral or written traditions about Jesus of Nazareth that the Gospel writers allowed to interact with the contexts and needs of their audiences. This creative approach is part of the value of the Gospels for readers in subsequent ages.

However, the conventional approach to textual interpretation inherited from the nineteenth century, and used until fairly recently, had as its basic principle that the values or experiences that a modern reader brings to a classic text are a problem for correct understanding.[15] Recent developments in hermeneutics seek a broader approach where the possibilities of a text, beyond the author's original conception, may be evoked in a creative way by the new religious world in which such a text finds itself.

While Sandra Schneiders' approach to a scriptural text "as locus of revelatory encounter" may be extended to spiritual classics, we should bear in mind certain cautions expressed by Rowan Williams.[16] For example, in his *On Christian Theology* Williams takes the French philosopher and theologian Paul Ricoeur to task for concentrating too much on the revelatory nature of a *text* in isolation without giving sufficient weight to the revelatory character of the process of interpretation.[17] Thus "God 'speaks' in the response as in the primary utterance." Or, as he puts it elsewhere, "the locus of *revelation* is the text as it stands *in interaction with the reader*."[18] Implicitly at least, both Schneiders and Williams understand the interpretation of religious texts to be best served by a process that is personally engaged as well as intellectually rigorous. Interpretation in the fullest sense creates a world of meaning in which people come to see and act differently.

The interpretation of spiritual classics is not the preserve of scholars but also takes place (usually implicitly and occasionally ignorantly) in the practical *use* of texts (for example, Ignatius Loyola's *Spiritual Exercises* in retreat work). Therefore, the example of the performing arts is helpful in understanding the new approach to interpretation. Musicians interpret a text, the score. They may be technically faultless in reproducing the notes and the composer's instructions. A "good" performance is certainly true to the score because performers cannot do simply anything with a score and still call it a Beethoven symphony. Yet, a good performance is more than this. It will also be creative because the composer did not merely describe how to produce sounds but sought to shape an experience. Thus, there is no single, definitive interpretation of a text because new aspects are revealed whenever the text confronts new horizons and questions.[19] This image of performance leads us to the core of the interpretative process. Without ignoring the original historical context of a text, or the intention of the original author(s), we reveal new and ever-richer meanings that the author never knew every time we read it. The pursuit of meaning undoubtedly demands that we understand something about the technicalities of a text. A real conversation with it, however, expands our vision rather than merely extends the pool of data. We interrogate the text, but our questions are, in turn, reshaped by the text itself. This process is what is sometimes referred to as the "hermeneutical circle." One of the most influential figures in the development in religious circles of a broader interpretation theory has been the German philosopher Hans-Georg Gadamer. He stressed that a text must "break the spell" of the reader's presuppositions which initially gave the reader an entry point. The text corrects and revises our preliminary understanding.[20] Gadamer's theory of interpretation assumes that texts have an "excess of meaning" beyond the subjective intentions of the author. This is what enables a spiritual classic to come alive in the present. The present situation, as experienced by the reader, affects the meaning of the text and a text alters the reader's understanding of the present. Gadamer further concluded that understanding, interpretation, and application were not self-contained moments but a unified process. In Gadamer's view, the weakness of earlier theories of interpretation was that they detached the practical application of a text (for example, in preaching) from technical analysis. In fact we come to a deep understanding of a text *only* by applying it to the present.[21] In the dialogue between text and reader the aim is to fuse the horizons of both in an interpretation that is always new. A classic may allow a genuinely new interpretation, yet the reader is also provoked (sometimes by what is initially strange or even shocking) into new self-understanding because of the encounter. Thus a spiritual classic is not a timeless artefact that demands mere repetition. Understanding the text implies a constant reinterpretation by people who question and listen from within their own historical circumstances. A concrete example would be the way the Rule of St. Benedict has, over the centuries, regularly inspired reforms in monastic community that, while retaining a common core, have produced strikingly different lifestyles.

Gadamer's theory is complemented by the somewhat different approach of the equally influential Paul Ricoeur. Ricoeur emphasizes that once wisdom has been fixed in a written text there follows a radical "distanciation" of the discourse from its original production. First, the text is distanced from its author, who effectively loses control. The text takes on a life of its own as a medium of meaning. Second, the text is distanced from the original audience. A written text inherently becomes available to whoever cares to read it. Third, the text is distanced from its original context (decontextualization), which makes the text able to function in relation to later and different situations (recontextualization). In summary, Ricoeur's emphasis on distanciation enables the text to transcend the limitations of its origins in order to function potentially in any context.[22]

What Kind of Meaning?

What kind of meaning is reached through this process of interpretation? From a theological point of view, interpretation does not, indeed cannot, produce a form of discourse that offers a definitive and total perspective. In practice, religious accounts operate less as an exhaustive interpretation of how the universe operates and more as, in the words of Rowan Williams, "*strategies* [his italics] for responding consistently and intelligibly to the world's complexity."[23] Interpretation is not "an exploratory reduction, but the gradual formation of a 'world' in which realities can be seen and endured without illusion."[24]

Hermeneutics of Consent and Suspicion

Contemporary approaches to interpretation suggest the need for what are nowadays referred to as a "hermeneutics of consent" and a "hermeneutics of suspicion." In the first case, we "consent" to a text in the sense that its origins, the author's intention, and the consensus of interpretation over time within the "community of capable readers" continue to exert some kind of normative role that prevents us from exploiting the text ruthlessly for our own ends.[25] In the second case, however, we recognize that the questions provoked by our contemporary situation may well be critical of aspects of the text and its theological or cultural assumptions. For example, we are nowadays more aware of the *social* conditioning of texts and of the need to expose the hidden biases against certain ideas or groups of people within the Christian tradition, not least within the history of spirituality, particularly ones that continue to influence us.[26] We need to examine not merely the surface of the text but its silences—what lies behind the text, what is assumed, what is not said, what is excluded.[27]

For some theologians, all interpretations of Christian texts or history are radically interrupted by the Holocaust. Thus David Tracy suggests that the very historicity of Christianity inevitably involves "a frightening disclosure of the real history within which we have lived."[28] Every attempt to retrieve the tradition "must today include a radical hermeneutics of suspicion on the whole of Christian history."[29] The same judgment, it may be argued, applies with more or less force to other painful elements of the history of Christianity, and of Christian spirituality in particular. I am thinking especially of various forms of Eurocentrism or theological colonialism, the undermining of women's spiritual wisdom, and the dominance of clerical forms of spirituality over an everyday spirituality of work and of sexuality.

Some Issues in Contemporary Interpretation

After addressing important general aspects of the theory and process of interpretation, I want to turn attention to a number of specific issues concerning the contemporary interpretation of texts and traditions. The first concerns the importance of appreciating what lies behind the surface of the texts we see. The second concerns a wider understanding of the word *texts* beyond purely written forms. The third concerns whether classic texts may in principle become unusable. The final issue concerns the related questions of who constitutes a "community of capable readers" and who has the right to access the wisdom of spiritual texts.

1. What Lies Behind the Text

The text we see and seek to use sometimes shields a hidden text that is critical to our interpretation. This may apply, for example, to related written texts. If we were to examine the *Constitutions* of the Jesuit Order, they appear on cursory reading to be essentially a practical and legal document.[30] Contemporary scholars agree, however, that the intelligibility of the text depends heavily on the more foundational text that lies behind the *Constitutions*, that is, *The Spiritual Exercises*. In the light of this hidden text, the *Constitutions* are revealed not so much as a legal document but as a flexible attempt to offer a way of living out the experience of the Ignatian Exercises in a communitarian and ministerial form.[31] Reciprocally, the *Constitutions* then become of interest to people seeking to deepen their understanding of the Ignatian Exercises but without any particular interest in male clerical community.

The famous *Canticle of the Sun* by Francis of Assisi provides a different example of how the interpretation of a written document vitally depends on understanding something behind the text. On its own, it is possible to reduce the sentiments of the *Canticle* to a bland, romantic love of the natural world. The underlying meaning of the *Canticle* is more radical, however. The key to it is that all our fellow creatures (animate or inanimate) are brothers and sisters and reflect the face of Christ. Francis of Assisi experienced each particular element of creation, not merely creation in the abstract, as arising from the same source, the Trinity revealed in the Incarnate Jesus. The corollary is that each created particularity is a revelation of God. The foundation of Franciscan respect for all created things is that God, through whom everything was created, has come among us to be a creature.

The first nine verses of the *Canticle* speak of the cosmic fraternity of all elements of creation. For example,

> Let everything you have made
> Be a song of praise to you,
> Above all, His Excellency the Sun (our brother);
> Through him you flood our days with light.
> He is so beautiful, so radiant, so splendid,
> O Most High, he reminds us of you.

This uplifting doctrine of cosmic fraternity, however, conceals a sharp prophetic message. For one thing, the text does not simply celebrate God's goodness expressed in the world as God's gift. Verses 10–11 celebrate the peace that comes from mutual pardon or reconciliation. It is generally thought that the verses were written as part of a campaign to settle a dispute between the mayor and bishop of Assisi.

Be praised, my Lord,
Through those who forgive for your love,
Through those who are weak,
In pain, in struggle,
Who endure with peace,
For you will make them Kings and Queens,
O Lord Most High.[32]

Thus the created world shifts from being merely a beautiful place to a "reconciled space" because of the fraternity of all things in Christ. There is no room for violence, contention, or rejection of the "other."

Here we face a critical question. What does Francis understand by the "other"? For this we have to recall one of Francis's foundational experiences. The "other" for Francis had a particular meaning. Behind the text of the *Canticle*, and underlying his whole theology of creation and incarnation, is another "text"—that is, Francis's early encounter with a leper that changed his life. In the first three verses of *The Testament* dictated shortly before his death in 1226 Francis actually identified the first moment of his spiritual life with his encounter with the leper.[33] The meeting with the leper was not merely the encounter with human suffering. In medieval terms, Francis was led to embrace the excluded "other." Lepers were not simply infected with a fearful disease. In medieval society they symbolized the dark side of existence onto which medieval people projected a variety of fears, suspicions, and guilt that must be excluded from the community not merely of the physically healthy but also of the spiritually pure. Lepers were outcasts banished from society. They joined the criminals, the mad, the excommunicated, and the Jews.[34] Through the encounter with the leper, Francis came to see that participation in human experiences of suffering and of exclusion was at the heart of God's incarnation as revealed in the face of the Crucified Christ.

2. Can Texts Become Unusable?

Precisely because many people approach spiritual texts or traditions in search of wisdom, we face the problem that the language and some of the presuppositions present in a classic are not only strange but positively alien to anyone seeking to appropriate the wisdom in the twenty-first century. An interesting example is the fourteenth-century English mystical text *The Cloud of Unknowing*. This has become amazingly popular in recent times—in fact it has been reprinted almost annually since its initial publication by Penguin Classics in the mid-1960s. Yet what are we to make, for example, of the statement that we are to view the self as a "foul, stinking lump of sin"?[35] More detailed study reveals that the text appears generally suspicious of the body and of the material world. It also seems to be highly individualistic compared to contemporary spiritual sensibilities. It clearly assumes that contemplation is only open to a small elite.

It may be possible to argue that in a contemporary rereading of the text apparent clashes of culture can be understood differently or interpreted as of merely secondary importance compared to the fundamental spiritual wisdom of the text.[36] Yet the question remains. In principle, may people eventually be forced to say that a text is now, practically speaking, unusable because it is riddled with assumptions radically out of tune with modern knowledge or values?

Any even tentative answer depends on the foundations I have already described. The first is that meaning does not reside solely in a fixed text but is also established in the dynamic conversation between the text and the contemporary reader. As I see.it, the very notion of the classic text, as put forward by theorists such as David Tracy, presupposes that certain wisdom documents have shown a capacity to break free from the constraints of their original contexts. This means that they can no longer be seen as tied absolutely to the assumptions and horizons of the original author or of his or her anticipated audience. Such texts have thus already proved capable of being persistently reinterpreted in every act of reading.

In the case of a text that explicitly exists to be *performed*, such as Ignatius Loyola's *The Spiritual Exercises*, the imperative of adaptation to the needs of retreatants is built into the text itself and is reinforced in the earliest practical interpretations of it.[37] Thus the meaning of the Exercises is, according to the text's own logic, not simply the written document but is also what emerges in every use of the Exercises as a medium of spiritual development—and every use is a unique reinterpretation.

David Tracy extends the idea of "classic text" beyond literary ones. In the final chapter I will explore in detail the idea that religious build-

ings are spiritual texts. For our present purposes, if we think of buildings as texts, we face the same questions of reinterpretation and adaptation. One refreshing aspect of recent scholarship on medieval
cathedrals is the way it seeks to integrate art history and medieval studies with theology and spirituality. The result is a move away from the
idea that buildings are simply fixed monuments of pure architecture.
The spirituality implicit in cathedrals is *not* based on a purely abstract
notion of sacred place. It is critical to their theological interpretation
that cathedrals are places of social connection and of community definition. To put it another way, a building without performance is merely
a piece of abstract styling, and, whatever else is true, that is not the
meaning of Gothic space. Cathedrals are repositories for the memory
and the aspirations of the community that are constantly renewed and
changed across time. Indeed, the moment a building like a cathedral
becomes *fixed*, rather than continually mobile and changing, it is a
museum rather than a living symbol of human community living.

Today, medieval religious buildings are experienced by a completely different audience from their original one. There is no way back
to "real" cathedrals or a "real" medieval audience. Nor should we try to
re-create artificially the ambience of a past age. A historic religious
building is a text whose meaning is forever revealed anew as it is interpreted and reinterpreted through shifting patterns of usage. However
fixed such buildings seem, there seems to be little evidence that their
ability to transmit spiritual wisdom has come to an end even in a relatively post-religious age.

Thus the meaning of classic texts is never definitively *fixed*. In
this sense, it does not seem likely, *at least in principle*, that we will reach
the limits of possible interpretations and therefore of the "usefulness"
of a classic text. Obviously there are changes of taste that result in certain texts receding into the background, perhaps to be rediscovered in
another age. In itself, however, this does not imply the loss of classic
status. I may well believe, following David Tracy once again, that texts
can be judged according to criteria of adequacy, that is, the text meets
the basic demands of human living, and criteria of appropriateness,
that is, the text is faithful to a specifically Christian understanding of
existence.[38] The precise way these criteria are interpreted, however, is
also a matter of context. We can apply them only within the limits of

our present time, but we also have to admit that our judgments are not eternally conclusive.

3. What Is a Community of Capable Readers?

The fluidity of texts, and their capacity to reveal new levels of meaning, relates closely to the question of *who* is assumed to be capable of interpretation. In practice, what is sometimes referred to technically as "the community of capable readers" necessarily changes across time.

For example, in the case of the Ignatian Exercises, interpretation is no longer understood to be limited to the perspectives of a male, Roman Catholic clerical religious order, the Jesuits. Women, not least religious communities of sisters founded in the same tradition, are no longer passive recipients of an interpretation established elsewhere but are inherent to the very process of interpretation and the establishment of meaning.[39] The same point can be made of vast numbers of laypeople more generally. Even more radically, given the Reformation origins of the Exercises, the "community of capable readers" nowadays includes people beyond the boundaries of Roman Catholic Christianity who have benefited from making the Exercises and have joined the ranks of those who guide others through the process.[40]

In the case of religious buildings, does a hermeneutical process of "conversation" leave open the possibility that today's visitors to a European medieval cathedral may, in principle at least, become part of an expanded community of capable readers? Such a thought is deeply problematic for those who believe that cathedrals exist only to serve the Christian worshipper. Today's visitor may just as easily be a tourist with no sense of what the cathedral originally expressed and how they are used liturgically today. My point is that this does not necessarily imply an inevitable abandonment of cathedrals as social and spiritual texts by the non-Christian majority. If true, this raises interesting issues when there are plans to reorder a medieval cathedral for contemporary use. Whose needs take priority? What understanding of spirituality is modeled in the changes—a purely liturgical one or one that invites a much broader range of people to gain access to spiritual wisdom in and through the building? Are nonworshipping visitors merely an "add-on" from the heritage industry? Are they perhaps passive targets for new strategies of Christian evangelism? Or, potentially, may they become active participants in a new hermeneutical conversation that is in process of exploring previously unanticipated layers of meaning in buildings such as cathedrals?

Conclusion

Much of this chapter has been concerned with the role of historical consciousness and with the *process* of interpreting texts and traditions. The final question reminded us, however, that the nature of the "community of capable readers," in other words *who* interprets and offers authoritative readings of texts and traditions, is at least as interesting and important a question, theologically and spiritually.

What this final question also illustrates is that the history of interpretation, even in the field of spirituality, involves issues of power.[41] Of course power is not inherently a bad thing or we would not speak of the *empowerment* of people, for example, through a more equitable distribution of skills and information. Within the context of Christian spirituality, the reality of power cannot be avoided in how it is defined, who merits a place in its "official" history, and who is enabled to become an effective interpreter of texts and traditions.

It may seem that the emphasis in this essay on the complexity of the issues surrounding interpretation and appropriation involves a kind of mystification or an elitism that denies access to spiritual wisdom to the non-scholar. My response is that the reverse should become the case. It is vitally important to offer as wide an audience as possible a slice of the hermeneutical cake. Scholars or others with technical knowledge of traditions and texts are not "stewards of private mysteries," neo-gnostics with privileged access to understanding. The task of translation is a theological *duty*. This point touches both on our philosophy of education and on our theology of Christian and human communion. My belief is that even popular courses and workshops on spirituality are severely limited in value if they confine themselves to practical questions rather than seek to mediate a deeper understanding of spiritual texts and traditions in a way that is not only practically relevant but also accurate and intelligible.

3
SPIRITUALITY AND THEOLOGY
Belief and Practice

Paradoxically, the progressive decline in religious practice in Western societies has been accompanied by an increasing hunger for spirituality. One sign of this is the availability of an extraordinary variety of books and courses on popular spiritual psychology, science and religion, mysticism, ritual and meditation. For example, in general bookstores in the United States and the UK, popular editions of Christian mystics such as Meister Eckhart or Hildegard of Bingen sit alongside books about Sufism and the occult. In both North America and the British Isles, Celtic spirituality (often an uncritical pagan, Christian, and invented mix) has been enthusiastically "rediscovered." Music too plays its part in the spirituality renaissance as recordings of monastic chant appear in music best-seller lists. Many people who are interested in spirituality are also suspicious of religious dogma. A coherent belief system is no longer assumed to be necessary for a fruitful spiritual journey. There has been a privatization of spirituality and a concentration on the interior life. "Spirituality" in popular understanding is often eclectic and antirational. This reflects a wider Western cultural fragmentation popularly known as postmodernity.

The Culture of Postmodernity

For better or for worse, the impact of postmodern culture (as well as theory) on the developing field of spirituality has been significant.[1] Postmodernity is too complex to discuss fully, but a brief summary might go as follows. Its roots lie in the experience of loss that, theorists suggest, characterized the late twentieth century. What has been lost is the spirit of optimism and certainty associated with an apparently stable social, religious, intellectual, and moral order. The decisive breakdown began with the 1914–1918 war and reached an appalling climax in the Nazi death camps and the bombing of Hiroshima and Nagasaki.[2]

Theorists support broadly one of two versions of postmodernism. The first is essentially deconstructive. It is radically suspicious of attempts at normative interpretations of culture. The second form is less extreme. It recognizes the reality of social and cultural fragmentation but seeks to reconstruct a strategy that enables some kind of authoritative interpretation of events. Both versions of postmodernism have something in common, however. They reject the optimism of post-Enlightenment "modernity" about the capacities of human knowledge. In other words, postmodernism criticizes overconfidence in the powers of reason to establish definitive meaning. Postmodernism recognizes that all human attempts to grasp "truth" are culturally conditioned, contingent, and morally flawed as well as intellectually partial. Contemporary culture is suspicious of total systems, whether moral, philosophical, or theological, that seek to escape from the limitations of context. It is a short step from this suspicion to a rejection of conventional religious institutions.

Spirituality and Belief

Christianity has traditionally sought to speak about God revealed in Jesus Christ, yet, in the West at least, it currently exists in an intellectually fluid and uncertain culture. For contemporary Christians, spirituality is no longer necessarily the practical application of a theological belief. There is a kind of doctrinal vacuum even inside Christian communities. Beyond the boundaries of the Christian Church, the situation is even more uncertain. Yet, we cannot entirely escape theological questions. Our worldview is framed by the beliefs we carry with us. Christianity's fundamental doctrinal frameworks, for example, the language of Trinity and incarnation, act as the boundaries within which we come to understand ourselves, other people, and the world around us. While the characteristic question of the contemporary spiritual seeker is more likely to be "Who am I?," the question at the forefront of the great Western spiritual classics was "What or who is God?" To some extent, the instinctive separation of theology from the practice of everyday life that still characterizes much Western Christianity came about because believers internalized a post-Reformation, post-Enlightenment opposition between the "secular" and "sacred" spheres of existence.

The study of spirituality is slowly finding a place within the theological academy but continues to be viewed with suspicion in some circles. Some of this suspicion is rooted in the long tradition of separation between theology and spirituality. This has led to the two words being interpreted as concerned, respectively, with the intellectual and devotional dimensions of Christian religion. Nowadays, however, spirituality demands to be taken seriously as a scholarly field in its own right. This raises difficulties for theologians especially when spirituality refuses to see itself simply as an optional and subordinate area of study. Spirituality appears to outside observers to want to cross the disciplinary boundaries that were previously considered "hard." It also seems to lay claim to almost unlimited tools (for example, historical, biblical, theological, philosophical, psychological, and social scientific methods). Spirituality has been accused of not defining its own methodology precisely. In fact, significant attempts have been made by scholars in recent years to provide a coherent definition and methodology from both theological and historical standpoints.[3] Spirituality is beginning to take shape as a substantial field with a special, but not exclusive, relationship to theology.

Historical Developments

In the West, the subject we now study as spirituality began as part of an undifferentiated reflection on Christian sources and their application. From the patristic period until the development around the twelfth century of the "new theology" of the cathedral schools and eventually the universities theology was a unified enterprise.[4] To say this does not simply mean that later distinctions between the *intellectual* divisions within theology (for example, biblical studies or philosophical theology and so on) were not present. The unity of theology

56

implied that intellectual reflection as a whole, contemplation, worship, and the Christian life were, ideally speaking, a seamless whole.

To be a theologian meant that a person had contemplated the mystery of God revealed in Christ and possessed an experience of faith on which to reflect. Knowledge of divine things was inseparable from the love of God deepened in prayer. For Augustine (*De Trinitate*, books 12–14), God is known not by *scientia* but by *sapientia*—that is to say, not by analysis but by a contemplative "knowing" through love and desire. Patristic theology was not an abstract discipline separated from pastoral theory and practice. The unifying feature was the Bible and the patristic approach to scripture ultimately developed, in the West, into a medieval theory of exegesis.[5] Thus, theology was a process, on different levels, of interpreting scripture with the aim of deepening the Christian life in all its aspects.

Doctrinal theology arose from this biblical base and attempted to provide a language to express an essentially mystical apprehension of God revealed in Christ and as Spirit within every Christian. The very heart of patristic theology was "mystical"—not "mysticism" in the later Western sense of subjective religious experiences, but reflection on how every baptized Christian was drawn into the divine mystery through belonging to the "fellowship of the mystery," that is the Church, by exposure to scripture and by participation in the liturgy. In the sixth century this insight fused with Neoplatonic elements in the writings of an anonymous Syrian theologian known as Pseudo-Dionysius or Dionysius, to produce a more explicit "mystical theology."[6] The unity between knowledge and contemplation found its supreme expression in the West in the golden age of monastic theology. This stretched from Gregory the Great in the sixth century through Anselm of Canterbury in the eleventh century to Bernard of Clairvaux in the twelfth century.[7] The Eastern Orthodox tradition, unlike the Western tradition, continues to this day to follow the patristic model of "mystical theology."[8]

It is difficult to be precise about the date when a more rational or scientific approach to theology in the West was born. This is because change is always an extended process rather than a single event. From approximately 1100 onward, however, scholars such as Peter Abelard (1079–1142) began to understand theology as a process of intellectual speculation. In the construction of the new theology, philosophical categories (especially those of Aristotle) began to rival biblical ones. The "new" theologians treated scripture and patristic writings in a more propositional way.

Not surprisingly, there were serious conflicts between those who espoused this new approach and those who continued to oppose it.[9] During the twelfth century, the centers of theological enquiry increasingly moved from the monasteries to new cathedral schools that gave birth to the first European universities. This involved not merely a geographical shift from the countryside to the new towns but also an ideological shift in that theology was no longer focused in places dedicated to a holistic religious way of life. The new scholarship existed primarily to foster teaching and learning. The new theology gradually gave birth not only to distinctions between disciplines such as biblical theology, doctrinal theology, and moral theology but also produced a belief that the discipline of the mind could be separated from the discipline of an ordered lifestyle or *ascesis*.

It is true that the greatest figures of the theology of the new schools (Scholasticism) such as Thomas Aquinas and Bonaventure still sought to unite theological reflection with contemplation. Yet the new theological method with its more "scientific" approach led to a slow but sure separation of spiritual theory from the hard core of theology. This was a tragedy for both. Secular reason has traditionally been considered the child of the Reformation and the Enlightenment. Its intellectual origins lie, however, in the theological developments in the High Middle Ages where "thinking" came to be understood as a mastery of facts rather than attention to a vision of truth expressed in symbols.

By the end of the Middle Ages, the spiritual life had increasingly moved to the margins of theology and culture as a whole. Although late medieval religion was not completely individualistic (the growth of lay confraternities is evidence of the importance of collective experience), there is no doubt that religious practice became more personal and internalized. It also began to demand a new specialized language, mystical theology, distinct from theological discourse as a whole and capable of expressing its separate existence.

By the sixteenth century the relationship between mystical theology and theology in general was at best ambiguous and at worst antagonistic. The divisions in Western Christianity after the Reformation encouraged theology to concentrate on doctrines in order to become the guardian of the prevailing orthodoxy, Catholic or Protestant. Equally, much mainstream Protestantism tended to be suspicious of a turn inward to the human heart, deemed to be corrupted by sin and selfishness. Mysticism and contemplation also appeared to claim that through practice, through effort, one could reach out toward union with God. In contrast, *the* fundamental mark of Reformation piety was the principle that God alone initiates and accomplishes everything in the work of salvation.[10] The Reformation traditions, therefore, became somewhat suspicious of attention to the spiritual life with the exception of some elements within the Church of England.

The period of the Enlightenment in the seventeenth and eighteenth centuries saw the growth of empirical and scientific enquiry as a way to truth and certainty. This further aggravated the split between theology and the Christian life. Theology tended to espouse a defensive intellectual positivism and emphasize that it was a "scientific" discipline. That is to say, faith was increasingly expressed in propositional and conceptual terms. The value of abstract intelligence was overestimated. Consequently the experiential dimension of human life was to be questioned continuously throughout an analytical journey toward what could be proved. The notion that theology was a science became linked to the belief that scientific enquiry could generate value-free knowledge.[11]

During the next hundred and fifty years a vocabulary of Christian life and prayer stabilized in isolation from doctrinal theology, particularly in Roman Catholic circles. There were, of course, Anglican and Protestant mystical writers who produced works of spiritual guidance or meditation. Among Anglo-Saxon Protestants (not least the Puritans) and Lutheran Pietists there was a vocabulary of "piety," "Godliness," "holiness of life," and "devout life." A genre of devotional literature developed to correspond to this.[12]

Toward the Contemporary Era

At this point, it is helpful to sketch how the contemporary reintegration of theology with spirituality gradually came about. First, in the late nineteenth and early twentieth centuries there was a revival of a purer form of Thomist theology after centuries of second-rate

Scholasticism. This encouraged some reengagement between the subject matter of spirituality and theology. Numerous manuals of ascetical and mystical theology appeared in Roman Catholic circles throughout the twentieth century until the Second Vatican Council in the 1960s. Texts such as those by A. A. Tanquerey and R. Garrigou-Lagrange became the handbooks of ascetical and mystical theology in Roman Catholic seminaries and theology faculties. Attempts were made in Anglican circles in the 1930s to produce something comparable. These were also based to some degree on Thomist principles.[13]

This form of reintegration had severe limitations, however. The starting points for the new "spiritual theology" were the same principles that governed dogmatic theology. That is to say, the overall approach was one of precise categories, distinctions, and definitions. Despite the experiential and practical subject matter, "spiritual theology" was fairly static and the method was essentially deductive, moving from first principles to practical application. Divine revelation and rational knowledge were the major sources because a "scientific" study of the spiritual life needed universal principles. "Spiritual Theology" first appeared in the official Roman Catholic theological curriculum in 1919 and by 1931 was included in an official Vatican document on ecclesiastical education, *Deus Scientiarum Dominus*.

One classic definition of how spiritual theology related to the wider theological field appeared in Pierre Pourrat's influential three-volume history of spirituality, *La Spiritualité Chrétienne*, which appeared in the 1920s.

> Spirituality is that part of theology which deals with Christian perfection and the ways that lead to it. *Dogmatic Theology* teaches what we should believe, *Moral Theology* what we should do or not do to avoid sin, mortal and venial, and above them both, though based on them both, comes *Spirituality* or *Spiritual Theology*. This, again, is divided into *Ascetic Theology* and *Mystical Theology*.[14]

For Pourrat, spirituality was subordinated to both dogmatic and moral theology.

Immediately prior to Vatican II, writers such as Louis Bouyer moved away from the style of the older writers. His work espoused a more scriptural, liturgical, and even ecumenical approach.[15] Bouyer was concerned to define spirituality as a theological discipline but one that was distinct from dogmatic or systematic theology. Spirituality was not concerned with abstract ideas (although that way of understanding systematic theology is revealing in itself). Rather, it examined the way in which the objects of faith arouse reactions in religious consciousness. Bouyer departed from Pourrat's classic statements in another significant way because he suggested that moral theology concerned more than obligations, the dos and don'ts of human action. For Bouyer, moral theology was also concerned with ideals and with understandings of perfection. It therefore overlapped with spirituality although the latter focused more directly on the human search for God. Overall, in Bouyer the boundaries between the various theological disciplines are much more blurred than was the case with earlier writers such as Tanquerey or Pourrat. Bouyer was more aware than his predecessors that all theology has the potential to be spiritual if it does not limit itself to scholastic rationalism.

In addition, the history of spirituality and spiritual theology taught in Roman Catholic and some Anglican circles until recent times primarily referred to various forms of monastic or clerical life such as Benedictine, Franciscan, Carmelite, or Jesuit. This approach emphasized the priority of those people who sought a life of perfection away from the world and distinct from lay life. It contrasted this with the "ordinary life of faith" of the vast majority of Christians who lived in "the world." The initial impetus of the Second Vatican Council in the 1960s with regard specifically to spirituality was to endorse a *ressourcement*, a return to original sources, directed once again at members of religious orders. This process was essentially "in house" and therefore still marginal to the wider theological project.

In recent decades several major shifts in the relationship between spirituality and theology have taken place. First of all, what is understood by "spirituality" has changed significantly. It is no longer limited to monastic-clerical elites and has also broadened beyond attention to prayer and contemplation to include reflection on the values and lifestyles of all Christians. The term *spirituality* has gained considerable ecumenical acceptance and so studies of it tend to draw on the riches of a shared Christian heritage rather than limit themselves to sectarian understandings of life in the Spirit.[16]

Second, Christian spirituality is no longer concerned with defining "perfection" in the abstract. Rather it surveys the complex mystery of human transformation in the context of a dynamic relationship with God. These days, spirituality seeks to integrate all aspects of human experience and existence. The British theologian Rowan Williams, now archbishop of Canterbury, rejects an understanding of spirituality as the science of spiritual and private experience: "it must now touch every area of human experience, the public and social, the painful, negative, even pathological byways of the mind, the moral and relational world."[17] Perceptions of spirituality came to give priority to the inner life over external action and public engagement. How and why this needs to be replaced by a tension between interiority and exteriority will be addressed in chapter 5. At this point it is sufficient to affirm that I believe a tension between the mystical and the prophetic should be characteristic of Christian spirituality in our contemporary world.

Third, spirituality has once again become more fruitfully associated with theology and biblical studies, and theology itself has changed in significant ways. Theologians are now more likely to take experience and practice seriously as subjects for theological reflection. Theology has moved from a deductive, transcultural approach to reflection on the experience of God and the practice of discipleship in cultural particularity. In some cases, reflection on "experience" and/or "practice," and the question of the relationship between experience/practice and the tradition, has become the heart of theological method.

Among the major late-twentieth-century theological thinkers who have engaged with spirituality were the Roman Catholics Karl Rahner, Hans Urs von Balthasar, Edward Schillebeeckx, and Bernard Lonergan; the Protestants Jürgen Moltmann and Wolfhart Pannenberg; and the Anglican Rowan Williams. In addition, attention should also be paid to two theological movements as a whole, liberation theology and feminist theology. In what might be thought of as the second wave of each of these, a fundamental connection between theology and spirituality has become axiomatic.

Twentieth-Century Theologians

Bernard Lonergan (1904–84), the Canadian philosophical theologian, has been described variously as the greatest English-speaking theologian since Newman and a giant of modern Roman Catholic theology capable of standing alongside Karl Rahner.[18] Lonergan directed a great deal of his attention to theological method. His "transcendental method" suggested that religious experience, and particularly conversion, was the heart of theological enquiry. For Lonergan, there is an invariable movement within human consciousness which begins with experience. All of us move from attention to our experience to an understanding of what has been experienced and then to judgment in the light of that understanding. Finally we reach a point of choice or decision in terms of what has been understood. In other words, human intentionality moves from desire to knowledge and finally to action. All this takes place within a process that involves personal consciousness being drawn toward the Ultimate, Love, God. This process of growth or conversion is an integrated one that finally involves the affective, imaginative, intellectual, moral, and religious dimensions of our lives. Lonergan's language frequently sounds empirical. This may be explained by Lonergan's mathematical and scientific background—unusual in a theologian. Its self-actualizing emphasis (albeit self-actualization for the sake of others) also brings us close to the world of psychology. While Lonergan was concerned for a new language to mediate faith to a world of cultural pluralism, he was in all respects doctrinally conventional. His emphasis on experience as the first moment of conversion is, in practice, influenced less by modern psychological insights than by the classic tradition of patristic and early medieval theology. This tradition emphasizes that love precedes and is the foundation of knowledge.[19]

Perhaps more than other Western theologians of any tradition, Karl Rahner (1904–84) has made acceptable the language of "openness to mystery" and "self-transcendence." Both of these concepts had long been familiar to students of spirituality. The mystery, of course, is God in whom is our origin, within whom we live and toward whom we are drawn in a continual movement of self-transcendence. In other words, simply by being human we are fundamentally oriented toward the mystery of God. Rather than starting with the idea of God, Rahner begins his theological enquiry with our shared human experience. In this sense he represents a theological response to modernity's emphasis on the human subject. There is a kind of knowledge that is acquired simply by being in existence. This is experiential knowledge. Because we are social beings, this knowledge is not isolated but reaches the level of reflection and communication in us. One aspect of this existence and our experience of it is a sense of responsibility and a realization of our freedom to choose. To this extent we exist beyond the world and its causes and in this sense we transcend it. The questions that arise, therefore, concern where we come from (if not solely from the world) and where our transcendence is leading us (if the world cannot define our limits). It is this ultimate question, or transcendental experience, that confronts us at every turn. It is this question that Rahner reflects upon as a starting point for speaking of God.

Despite this way of proceeding, at a more fundamental level Rahner understands that God is always the starting point. It is God's free communication of self (grace) that actually *is* this capacity for transcendence within us. God's grace encompasses the whole of our human existence in such a way that our consciousness, our intellect, and our will are illuminated and guided. Thus God is both beginning (initiator) and end (gift). Because Rahner's approach to self-transcendence applies to every human without exception, he offers a balanced incarnational theology and spirituality. Rahner rejects any dichotomy between sacred and secular, private and public, "extraordinary" and "ordinary" religious experience. By stressing both the mystery of God and an incarnational vision, Rahner united the *via negativa* with the *via positiva* in his theological language.[20]

Hans Urs von Balthasar (1905–88) in his later years became famous (perhaps notorious) for his opposition to liberal theologians. In particular he espoused a theology "from above" and a traditionalist ecclesiology. Whatever our theological standpoint, however, it is impossible to ignore the power of his synthesis of classical theology and spirituality.[21] Von Balthasar understood all theology to be potentially "spiritual theology" in that it should transcend purely rationalist thinking. Equally, all spirituality is theological in that its "meaning" is necessarily associated with revelation. This view found classic expression in an article by von Balthasar in one of the early editions of *Concilium*, "The Gospel as Norm and Test of All Spirituality in the

Church." For von Balthasar, revelation is the key to defining spirituality. He argued that "within the Church it is the Gospel that is the standard and touchstone of all spirituality." All human forms of spirituality are rooted in the revelation of a loving triune God. For Christians, no spirituality can be authentic if it is disconnected from Christ's revelation and the "ultimate meaning" that is communicated and realized through that revelation.[22]

Unlike Lonergan and Rahner, von Balthasar was profoundly suspicious of the turn to experience and to the human subject as the basis for theology and spirituality. In his view, this tended to make faith too subjective and detached from its fundamental roots in revelation. Constructively, von Balthasar placed greatest emphasis on the importance of the visible form of Jesus Christ as the expression of God's inner-trinitarian reality. The centrality of this idea pushes both theology and spirituality in an incarnational and sacramental direction. It also opens up a rich emphasis on beauty and aesthetics that became von Balthasar's hallmark.

We have already noted that continental Protestantism was at one time extremely suspicious of the language of spirituality or mysticism. In recent decades, however, a number of significant Protestant theologians have begun to give attention to religious experience or to a theology of the spiritual life. Some people would suggest that all the major writings of Jürgen Moltmann bring together questions of Christian living with the great themes of Christian doctrine. Moltmann has also written one or two essays explicitly in what would these days be called the field of spirituality. The most notable is his little book *Experiences of God* and especially the chapter "The Theology of Mystical Experience." There are some brief but interesting remarks concerning the distinction between mystical and doctrinal theology. Moltmann also comments on the ethical dimension of the "experiential wisdom" (*sapientia experimentalis*) that is associated with spirituality or mysticism. This concept is similar, of course, to Luther's own emphasis and is also close to Tillich's idea of "participative knowledge."

The most interesting aspect of Moltmann's essay, however, is his approach to the dynamics, or stages, of the spiritual journey. Moltmann's theology of the cross enables him to express the purpose of 'mystical union' in terms that avoid any sense of separation from the world or of a necessary transcendence of material existence. On the contrary,

Moltmann perceives mystical union as a preparation for action, for radical political commitment, and for a deepened discipleship *in the world*. This is the pattern for Christian life determined by the cross of Jesus. Moltmann also pursues the theme of the relationship of mysticism to the theology of the cross in another, little known, essay on Teresa of Avila.[23]

Another German Protestant theologian, Wolfhart Pannenberg, has addressed questions of spirituality in more detail. He is particularly critical of the kind of academic theology that appears to be uninvolved with questions of application and practice or that intentionally separates itself from the experiential roots that underlie doctrinal issues. Clearly there is a reciprocal relationship between spiritual experience and doctrinal reflection. Equally clearly it is perfectly valid for Pannenberg to say that, in a certain sense, the contours of any Christian spiritual tradition will be determined by prior theological assumptions. However, Pannenberg also accords a certain priority to spirituality in the otherwise endless hermeneutical circle. Thus he suggests that every major historical form of spirituality implies a complete interpretation of the world. This will relate to whatever aspect of doctrine is central to the religious consciousness of the time. Yet at the same time, "in the more important forms of Christian spirituality we encounter the substructures of theology."

Pannenberg astutely notes that the Reformation was a response to a *spiritual* crisis rather than a purely intellectual one. When he describes medieval spirituality, he may be open to the criticism that he indulges in some historical oversimplification. Doubtless there was a profound sense of distance from God and of sinfulness in much (but not all) medieval piety. This is unlikely, however, to have been the product merely of the development of auricular confession and penitential literature, as Pannenberg appears to suggest. The spiritual climate was in practice the product of a much more complex mixture of factors. This included changes in religious practice over time, socioeconomic realities, and a general sense of human vulnerability that arose from regular cycles of plague, war, and famine. Whatever the causes, the consequence was an urgent concern for immediacy with God and the cultivation of every form of mediation that might serve to bridge the divine-human divide. Thus the classic doctrines of Reformation theology, such as justification by faith alone, responded to profound spiritual needs and then themselves gave birth to a new spirituality. Pannenberg is concerned, however, that subsequent Protestant spirituality failed adequately to protect the Reformers' theological emphases. This is especially the case with the freedom of the Christian person brought about by grace. According to Pannenberg, Protestant piety tended to perpetuate the familiar medieval guilt-consciousness and penitential piety in new forms. More recently, as a response to this problem, Pannenberg has suggested the need to renew Protestant spirituality through a reengagement with sacramental, especially eucharistic, theology.[24]

If we turn to the Anglican tradition, a number of recent writers have given explicit attention to the relationship between theology and spirituality. Arguably the most important contributions to the relationship between theology and spirituality come from the writings of Rowan Williams. A concern for the reengagement of theology with spirituality is implicit in everything he writes and in the totality of his approach to theology. It is therefore difficult to select particular works as "spiritual" in contrast to other writings. However, the book *The Wound of Knowledge* has become something of a classic in the field of spirituality. While the book's framework is broadly chronological from the New Testament to the sixteenth century where it ends, it is not intended to be a full narrative history of spirituality. Rather, it is a rich essay concerning ways in which some central themes of Christian theology intersect with particular moments or traditions in the history of spirituality. In a later study of Teresa of Avila, Williams also has many important things to say about the relationship of theology and spirituality, not least concerning how mysticism is a way of knowing that is important and real yet distinct from the rational discourse of speculative theology.[25]

Liberation and Feminist Theologies

Apart from individual theologians, two contemporary schools of theology demand attention. Perhaps more than any other recent school of theology, the liberation tradition is concerned to affirm the spiritual roots of all theology. The theological method involved in the liberationist approach is fundamentally inductive rather than deductive—that is to say, it consists of reflection on human experience in a general sense. However, it is reflection on the quite *specific* daily experiences of Christian communities in Latin America, Asia, and elsewhere that exist in conditions of overwhelming poverty, suffering, and oppression. Liberation theology is also a form of reflection that focuses on the experience of *a people*, a collective experience rather than that of isolated individuals. In this tradition, theology and spirituality are inherently intertwined from the start and at all points. There is no question of needing to bridge a gap or of bringing two discrete disciplines together. Gustavo Gutiérrez may be taken as the leading exponent of Latin American liberation theology, who, particularly in *We Drink from Our Own Wells* and *On Job*, suggests that the kind of reflection that the theology of liberation represents is conscious of the fact that it was, and continues to be, preceded by the spiritual experience of Christians who are committed to the process of liberation.[26] Finally, it is important to note that liberation theology reflects on explicitly *spiritual* experience rather than merely on a sociopolitical one. Equally, it is the case that valid theology is *lived* (orthopraxis), and so the actual following of Jesus Christ in concrete circumstances, not merely reflection on "discipleship," is an essential theological "moment."

Another contemporary movement, feminist theology, also suggests the need for a profound reintegration of experience and reflection. Anne Carr suggests, "As the experience of God's salvation in Christ and the response of individuals and groups to that salvation, spirituality can be understood as the source of both theology and morality."[27]

Again, this relationship is dialectical because theology and morality also work upon spirituality. This means that they may critique and transform spirituality which is often an unconscious pattern of convictions and behavior in relation to God. All generalizations are hazardous. It seems reasonable, however, to suggest that a critical element in much feminist theology is the desire to move theologies of the human person (theological anthropology) away from a dual-nature theory to a single-nature one.[28] For feminist theology there may be observable differences between the sexes regarding styles of understanding and relating to self, others, and God. Yet these result from the power of historical conditioning. Thus, it is argued, *feminist* theology and spirituality does not consist essentially in reflection on distinctively female ways of relating to God in contrast to male ones. That focus is more appropriately termed "women's spirituality." In contrast, feminist spirituality has intellectually sought to integrate a critique of the impact of patriarchal tradition on both women and men and, in its application, lives out of this consciousness.[29]

The work of feminist scripture scholars sensitive to spirituality such as Sandra Schneiders has been an important tool.[30] In theological terms, Elizabeth Johnson and Catherine LaCugna have offered sophisticated and spiritually rich rereadings of the theology of the Trinity with a clear sense of the implications for a more adequate spirituality.[31] In terms of rereadings of classic spiritual texts from a theological point of view, the works of Grace Jantzen and Dorothee Sölle on Christian mysticism are important examples.[32]

How Do Theology and Spirituality Relate?

In addressing how theology and spirituality relate to each other, there have been broadly two schools of thought among scholars. The first seeks to promote spirituality as an autonomous discipline, distinct from theology although related to it. The second prefers to treat spirituality simply as a subdivision of theology.

The most significant representative of the first position is the biblical scholar Sandra Schneiders.[33] Schneiders believes that spirituality and theology are close partners that mutually assist, but are autonomous from, each other. Spirituality should not be seen as a subdivision of one of the traditional theological disciplines such as systematics, historical theology, or moral theology. Theology cannot ultimately *contain* spirituality because the latter is inherently interdisciplinary and, even in a Christian context, is no longer limited to a practical expression of doctrines.

The second viewpoint is represented by the eminent American historian of mysticism Bernard McGinn. In that he believes that spirituality has a priority in its partnership with theology, he rejects the old-fashioned view that spirituality was simply derived from dogmatic theology. Nevertheless, he is concerned that the concrete nature of religious experience should properly be the concern of theology as a whole and is nervous of separating spirituality from it in any way. Consequently, McGinn believes that spirituality is best taught within a combination of theological disciplines: systematics, historical theology, ethics, and the history of Christianity. Following von Balthasar, he believes that the particularity of Christian spiritual experience demands that theology be the primary criterion of its interpretation.[34]

Several British and American theologians have tried to move away from a sharp contrast between these two positions.[35] It seems possible to argue that a relationship between spirituality and theology is central without denying that spirituality has a distinct identity. The important word is "distinct" rather than "autonomous." In different ways, these scholars suggest the need for a "turn to spirituality" within the overall theological enterprise. Theology must come to realize more effectively its own, essential spiritual core. It must also seek to enter into dialogue with spirituality in a way that is radically different from its more familiar conversations with philosophy or other intellectual disciplines. This involves allowing theological discourse to be questioned by the deeper insight that the reality of God is beyond the "God" of theological systems. The reality of God is more likely to be encountered by the ways of "knowing" espoused by mystical texts that are, at the same time, ways of unknowing from the perspective of conceptual thinking.

Theology Evaluating Spirituality

What use are spirituality and theology to each other? A number of writers offer useful theological criteria for evaluating spirituality. Theologians commonly approach the question on two levels. The work of David Tracy may be taken as a typical example. First, it is important to show that a spiritual tradition meets the basic demands of modern knowledge. This approach is termed "criteria of adequacy." Beyond this basic, human level lies a further level concerning issues of faithfulness to a specifically Christian understanding of existence. This approach is termed "criteria of appropriateness."

The application of criteria of adequacy should not be interpreted as a reduction of Christian theology and spirituality to purely secular norms. What it implies is that neither spirituality nor theology can be innocent of generally accepted developments in human knowledge. Nor can they ignore the ways in which previously overconfident views of human progress have been undermined by the painful historical events of the twentieth century. To put it simply, we have to take into account the new worlds opened up since the nineteenth century by evolutionary theory, psychology, and the social and political sciences, and more recently by cosmology and quantum theory. Equally, theology and spirituality can never be the same after Auschwitz and Hiroshima.

Tracy suggests three broad criteria of adequacy. First, every religious interpretation of experience needs to be meaningful. That is, it must be adequately rooted in common human experience. Second, the religious understanding of experience should be intellectually coherent. Third, any spiritual tradition needs to throw light on the underlying conditions of life. Does it have anything to say about whether our human confidence in life is actually worthwhile?[36]

In terms of criteria of appropriateness, in general terms any spirituality ought to relate us to a God worthy of our loving commitment.[37] An adequate understanding of Christian spirituality must relate in some way to the classic Christian doctrines. Far from being irrelevant, the language of Trinity and incarnation acts as a critique of distorted spiritualities that are preoccupied, in a narcissistic way, with "self-realization" or self-improvement.[38] Within the limits of legitimate diversity and of valid emphases, spiritualities should be inclusive of the *whole* gospel rather than unbalanced. What models of holiness are presented? Is the view of human nature dualistic with a low theology of the human body? Is there a balanced and healthy evaluation of sexuality? Understandings of prayer and contemplation are central in Christian spirituality. Does a spiritual tradition view Christian life as rooted in a common baptism? Is there a balance between contemplation and action? Christian spirituality of its nature cannot avoid the question of tradition. What is the role of scripture and tradition? Finally, an important question is whether a spirituality has a developed eschatology and specifically one that encourages an appropriate balance between "the now" and "the not yet."

Spirituality Evaluating Theology

Spiritual traditions in their turn offer criteria to judge the adequacy of theological systems. A fundamental question must always be borne in mind. This concerns whether a theology offers not merely an attempt at knowledge of the presence of God but a knowledge that enlivens the *practice* of the awareness of the presence of God. Intellectual coherence is not sufficient. As the Orthodox theologian Andrew Louth suggests,

> Spirituality [is] that which keeps theology to its proper vocation, that which prevents theology from evading its own real object. Spirituality does not really answer the question, Who is God? but it preserves the orientation, the perspective, within which this question remains a question that is being evaded or chided.[39]

Equally, Karl Rahner's theological method reminds us that spirituality provides solid foundations for judging the adequacy of theological explanations. For example, he suggested that classical "spiritual texts" may be true sources of theology as both Rowan Williams and Jürgen Moltmann have argued specifically for Teresa of Avila.[40] Such texts frequently contain wisdom that philosophical theology has not taken seriously. If we were to push Rahner's basic stance to its logical conclusion, spirituality is the unifying factor that underlies all attempts to "do" theology or, more properly, to *be* a theologian.

If you like, spirituality reminds theology that the theological enterprise is fundamentally practical and needs to be practiced. In the context of academic study, this view implies that what is sometimes called "practical theology" should not be an optional extra within the theological core curriculum. However, the place of practice in theology means something more. Theology is not merely concerned with content or resources. To do theology means becoming a *theological person*, not merely using theological tools.

Being a theological person implies more than intellectual exploration. The ancient meaning of *theologia* is a much broader concept than theology as a modern academic field. It inevitably involves what Eastern Orthodox Christianity has called *theoria*. At first sight, this word is misleading to Western eyes. It is more accurately translated as "contemplation" rather than "theory."[41] The committed believer is one who *lives* theology rather than does it as an activity detached from who he or she is. Sadly there is still a tendency in Western thought to think and act as if knowledge means something purely objective and rational.

But theology in its richest sense is essentially performative as well as informative; it is concerned with action as well as ideas. Consequently, the title "theologian" does not imply someone who provides specialized analysis and information while standing at a personal distance from the object of reflection. "Being a theologian" involves a quality of presence to the reality we reflect upon as much as a concern for the techniques of a specific discipline.

The ancient meaning of a theologian as a person who sees and experiences the content of theological reflection connects well with contemporary understandings of the self-implicating nature of study. Theology and spirituality in their fullest sense are self-implicating. This does not imply anti-intellectualism. There needs to be a critical approach to both theology and spirituality, but critical analysis is the servant of good theology not, surely, what theologians do or live theology for. In both theology and spirituality a kind of transformation is implied by the search for knowledge. As David Tracy reminds us, "'Saying the truth' is distinct from, although never separate from, 'doing the truth'....More concretely, there is never an authentic disclosure of truth which is not also transformative."[42]

Spirituality also offers a vital critique of any attempt by theology to launch itself into some stratosphere of timeless truth, abstract distinction, or ungrounded definition. The way that spirituality "speaks" of God is radically different from the approach of old-fashioned systematic or fundamental theology. If theology turns to spirituality and allows its systems to be questioned, it will find that spirituality recognizes that what is implied by the word *God* cannot ultimately be spoken completely.

One of the most fundamental aspects of the Christian doctrine of God is that the human quest for God demands a paradox of both knowing and not knowing. This has particular force in the context of a conversation between spirituality and theology. The words *cataphatic* and *apophatic* have often been used to describe the two sides of human relations with God. The cataphatic element emphasizes the way of imaging. It is a positive theology or a theology of affirmation based on a high doctrine of creation and of human life as contexts for God's self-revelation. The apophatic element, in contrast, emphasizes "not knowing," silence, darkness, and the absence of imagery. It is a negative theology, or a theology of denial. A sixth-century pseudonymous Eastern writer known as Dionysius (or Denys) the Areopagite was one of the most influential exponents of the concepts of apophatic and cataphatic theologies.[43] He had a major impact on Western theology and mysticism. In Dionysius' approach to God, knowing and unknowing are mutually related rather than mutually exclusive. For Rowan Williams, apophatic or negative theology is ultimately normative. This is because it should be seen not simply as a way of correcting an unbalanced positive theology. "Apophasis is 'not a branch of theology', but an attitude which should undergird *all* theological discourse, and lead it toward the silence of contemplation and communion."[44]

It is worth noting that a number of modern theologians have been fascinated by the theological possibilities of mystical writings. David Tracy, for example, suggests that in our present era "we may now learn to drop earlier dismissals of 'mysticism' and allow its uncanny negations to release us."[45] This reflects Tracy's own journey toward a belief that the apophatic language of the mystics is where theologians must turn in our present times.

> As critical and speculative philosophical theologians and artists learn to let go into the sensed reality of some event of manifestation, some experience of releasement and primal thinking, a sense of the reality of mystical experience can begin to show itself in itself. Even those with no explicit mystical experience, like myself, sense that thinking can become thanking, that silence does become, even for an Aquinas when he would "write no more," the final form of speech possible to any authentic speaker.[46]

In the West we have inherited a tendency to believe that knowledge means only abstract intelligence and objective analysis. The problem with theological "knowledge" is that while we may be impelled to speak of God, we cannot in the end speak definitively *about* God in the sense of capturing the divine. The problem with a purely intellectual search for God is that it necessarily regards what is sought as an object or an objective that can be reached. Insofar as we can, in Christian terms, speak of the human search for God, it will be a search that continually fails to capture or find God in any definitive sense.

4

TRINITY AND
ANTHROPOLOGY
The Self and Spiritual Transformation

Our theology of God-as-Trinity engages directly with how we define human identity and human transformation. Some people may question the appropriateness of taking the Trinity as the main theological theme in the study of spirituality. It is often assumed that theologies of the human person provide the best starting point. These at least have the merit of beginning with "the human condition." This contextual, bottom-up inductive approach to theology of course reflects the new theological currents that emerged after World War II, were not fully embraced until the Second Vatican Council, and even today are questioned by some traditionalists—reflection on history, the world, human existence, experience, and progress.

I suggest, however, that to take the doctrine of God as a primary area of reflection need not involve a retreat into abstraction. Understood correctly, our theologies of God are not "scientific" definitions. The doctrine of the Trinity places at the heart of our theology not a potentially soluble equation but a *mysterium* that we can know through love rather than detached analysis (what Paul Tillich referred to as participative knowledge). While the Trinity is often discussed in terms of "distinctions" whereby we can know something of God, behind these is a unity that is ultimately incomprehensible. The theology of the Trinity affirms something about God, yet, because the affirmations we make move us beyond what we can grasp, the Trinity reveals God as ultimately unknowable.

All Christian theology revolves around a particular understanding of God—but a God who engages with and changes the human condition in general and each person in particular. So the nature of what it is to be human, what humans are called to become, and the

75

process and means of transformation cannot be divorced from our understanding of God in Christ. While it may be said that *the* fundamental human experience is of one's self, it may also be said (following Karl Rahner's thought) that at the heart of this experience lies the Absolute. Put in more explicitly Christian terms, human beings experience themselves most completely as recipients of God's self-gift. There may then be a movement from the human self as gifted to the nature of God as the giver of gifts and as one who communicates to the world in self-giving love. The way Christians name this God, whose very life is to give and to reveal, is Trinity.

First of all, I want to offer some comments about how we understand "the self," particularly to question an excessive emphasis on interiority and individuality. Then I will make some remarks about trinitarian theology in relation to human existence, and finally the connections between trinitarian theology and a theology of the self will be illustrated by reference to the writings of the fourteenth-century English theologian and mystic Julian of Norwich.

Human Identity—The Problem of Inwardness

Rowan Williams notes, "Common to a good deal of contemporary philosophical reflection on human identity is the conviction that we are systematically misled, even corrupted, by a picture of the human agent as divided into an outside and an inside—a 'true self', hidden, buried, to be excavated by one or another kind of therapy."[1] For Williams, this version of the "self" is both a fiction and morally problematic. It suggests that our deepest interests are individual and preordained and undermines any notion that the human situation fundamentally embodies a common task. Such a view privileges the search for an authentic inner identity "unsullied by the body or history," as Williams puts it.[2] For Williams there is no complete, a priori identity to be unearthed by peeling away various layers of outer existence; rather, the real self is found or, better still, made from the very beginning in human communication and interaction.

I agree with Williams that a dangerous *rhetoric* of interiority, creating a dichotomy between inner and outer life, gradually affected spirituality over the last hundred years. This resulted from the combined influence of aspects of Enlightenment thinking and late-nineteenth-century psychology. For Augustine and other classic theologians, however, interiority did not imply the same thing as it does in the modern era.

Interiority in Augustine and Descartes

The earliest approaches to the Christian life inherited from late classical Judaism demonstrated an intense sense of vital solidarity between the individual and the community. Following this tradition, Augustine adopted the symbol of the heart as a way of expressing the self. As Augustine so often takes the blame for pushing Christian thought in the direction of a protected inner world, it is worth examining briefly how he understands interiority. In book 10 of his *Confessions*, when discussing how well other people may know the truth of a person, Augustine refers to "my heart, where I am whatever it is that I am."[3] The use of the word *heart* suggests that the Christian journey takes us toward the interior self, the true self, where God dwells. This is away from what Paul refers to as the outer man: "Even though our outer nature is wasting away, our inner nature is being renewed day by day" (2 Cor 4:16). In context, outer nature is to be understood as the life that is transitory. The notion of "outer" refers to a temptation to live *superficially* on the surface of life, mistaking what is transitory for what is fundamental.

For Augustine, God created humans with the divine image in their heart. This *imago Dei* is the true self and sin disconnects us from it. In his *Tractates on the Gospel of John* Augustine invites us to reconnect with this real self: "Return to your heart! See there what perhaps you perceive about God because the image of God is there. In the inner man [*sic*] Christ dwells; in the inner man you are renewed according to the image of God."[4] The context is again important. Earlier in the same section, Augustine suggests that in leaving the heart we leave ourselves: "Why do you go away from yourselves and perish from yourselves? Why do you go the ways of solitude? You go astray by wandering about....You are wandering without, an exile from yourself." It is not the journey into the heart that is solipsistic, but leaving the true self. By this, Augustine implies an experience of fragmentation linked to "the senses" which have many parts, offering different kinds of information. Each sense experiences reality only *in part*. Yet senses are nevertheless important. Augustine describes them as the "assistants" of the heart. Thus "the heart" stands for "the whole self." It brings together sense impressions and is the principle of unity and the interpretation of reality as a whole.

René Descartes' "*Cogito, ergo sum*" (I think, therefore I am) is perhaps the best-known philosophical dictum of all time, and its implications have had, at least implicitly, a profound influence on Western theology. The philosophy of Descartes (1596–1650) has often been described as Augustinian, although Descartes himself was not so convinced of his intellectual connections to Augustine. Whatever the case, what emerged from Cartesian thinking has been identified as the modern self. Descartes sought to establish what could be trusted as being absolutely certain. To this end, he peeled everything away until he reached what he saw as the foundational bedrock—individual consciousness or the rational self. This gave birth to a literally self-centered perspective on identity. From this arises a dominant Western intellectual understanding of personhood as self-conscious, self-reliant, self-transparent, and all-responsible. The individual self comes first and social communication comes second. I suggest, however, that Augustine's inner self is not of this kind. His was a spiritual project rather than Descartes' epistemological one. Augustine, unlike Descartes, did not seek to separate mind and body but sought salvation for both. In fact, Augustine might have suggested to Descartes that the more dangerous deception is possible *in the mind* rather than through the senses. The fundamental human sin, after all, was not concupiscence but pride—the desire to grasp a definitive and independent knowledge of good and evil!

While some versions of spirituality display a split between mind and body, between interior and exterior, and strongly privilege subjective interiority in so doing, this cannot be blamed on Augustine. He would not have understood such a dichotomized, lonely self. The truly interior person, by becoming more deeply drawn into the trinitarian mystery of God, is able to transcend such categories as "exterior" and "interior."

The Significance of Trinitarian Theology

Catherine Mowry LaCugna wrote a significant book in the retrieval of Trinity theology as practical theology. "The doctrine of God is ultimately a practical doctrine with radical consequences for Christian [and I would add "human"] life."[5]

The doctrine of the Trinity in the West sadly became in large measure disconnected from the theology of salvation and of human existence until relatively recently. The consequence was a separation between doctrine and "practical" theology of any kind, not least spirituality. The theological frameworks employed both in post-Reformation Catholicism and within the churches of the Reformation suffered from the same problem. In contrast to this trinitarian void, the 1980s and 1990s witnessed an extraordinary reassessment of the doctrine of the Trinity. The Trinity once again became the center of theological debate.

The foundation for much contemporary thinking lies in some version of Karl Rahner's dictum that "the 'economic' Trinity is the 'immanent' Trinity and the 'immanent' Trinity is the 'economic' Trinity."[6] To put it more simply, the inner life of God is to be understood not as essentially other than but as inherently bound up with the whole economy of salvation. Many of the attempts to draw out the practical implications of trinitarian belief, for example, the work of Catherine LaCugna quoted above, often base themselves on the theology of Rahner. While Rahner's approach to the Trinity has found wide acceptance, it has sometimes been criticized for appearing to suggest that there is no more to God than God's action in history. This risks a kind of reductionism that compromises God's freedom in the process of revelation.[7] Although Rahner's dictum should be nuanced, it serves to exclude idle speculation about the "being" of God apart from God's action in salvation. The freedom of God does not imply the utter *arbitrariness* of God's action. This would imply a kind of divine dysfunctionality where there was no congruence between what God does and what God is. God can only be free to do what God *is*. This, however, is not the same as to suggest that God is reducible to the processes of human history.

It is worth recalling that Rahner's theology owes a great deal to the spirituality of the Ignatian *Spiritual Exercises*. So, in Ignatius'

"Contemplation on the Incarnation," what Ignatius refers to as "the Three Divine Persons" look on the world and on humanity "in Their eternity" and resolve from that eternal perspective that "the Second Person" should become human "to save the human race."[8] Thus, in Ignatian thought, God's trinitarian being, creation, and incarnation-salvation form a single process. One might say that this process is inherent in who God is. God's "being" is identical with a trinitarian act of communion but also with a triadic dynamic of loving action vis-à-vis humanity.

If we wish to understand the doctrine of the Trinity, with its newly recovered dynamism, we need to understand it to be more than merely one doctrine among many. In reality, to affirm God as Trinity touches every aspect of Christian belief, attitudes, and living.[9] There have been a variety of proposals concerning how trinitarian theology has implications for Christian life. To some extent these themes group around the idea of "relationality" and its implications for ethics as well as for a theology of the Church and for prayer.

The concept of "relationality" has become a popular focus for contemporary reflections on the Trinity. The problem is that such a concept is capable of being reduced to a rather simplistic equation: "God is social therefore human life is social." Despite the dangers of reductionism, the concepts of relationship and community offer especially fruitful connections between doctrine and spirituality. To put it in other ways, while a great deal of Christian theology has been concerned with personal salvation, the theology of the Trinity reminds us that to be personal is necessarily also to be interpersonal. This shift is understandable as relatedness stands in sharp contrast to inherited images of God as essentially distinct from the world, free from the limitations imposed by change and by time and disengaged from human events. In a relational model, the doctrine of the Trinity reveals a different understanding both of the nature of God and of human personhood in the image of God. The fundamental truth of existence is that to be human is to be rooted in mutual self-giving love. To exist consists of being-in-relationship.

One approach to the implications for spirituality of a relational model of God has taken what is often called a "social" direction. This approach has strongly political and ethical overtones but is limited by its rather functional nature. Jürgen Moltmann rejects a hierarchical approach to God's nature and its implications for the ordering of human existence. The cardinal point of the doctrine of the Trinity is that no divine person is more complete or more significant than any other. Moltmann prefers the traditional image of mutual interrelationship (*perichoresis*) as more fruitful for approaching the reality of God. He argues that, as a consequence, "superiority" and "subordination" have no place in the social order either.[10]

Both liberation theology and feminist theology have also contributed to the social model of the Trinity. Not surprisingly, both share with Moltmann a strong antipathy to hierarchical relationships. The equality of relations within God is the basis for nonhierarchical relationships more generally. This is not merely by way of example but also through God's concrete action within human lives.[11] Within the liberationist tradition, the Brazilian theologian Leonardo Boff also moves beyond a purely exemplary approach to God's social nature in relation to human equality. To be "social" is the very goal of our existence, collectively as well as individually. The purpose of human history is to become "society" in a true sense. Thus our duty is to protest against all structures of domination that inhibit this fundamental vocation of humanity.[12]

Other contemporary theologians go beyond a primarily functional approach to the "relational" Trinity. God's relational quality is fundamental—it is an "ontological" category. God can only be understood as "persons-in-communion."[13] Attempts to develop a "communion" model for God's nature owe a great debt to the work of the Greek Orthodox theologian Metropolitan John Zizioulas, who in turn bases himself on the fourth-century Cappadocian Fathers.[14] According to a communion-*koinonia* model, God is not to be thought of as absolutely simple but as "being-in-communion." Communion makes things be and nothing exists without it. God's unity consists in the interrelationship of persons in free and loving relationships. This understanding of God is particularly rich in possibilities for a theology and spirituality of personhood and community. "A person" is not a self-relational category. Both particularity and interrelationship are structured into the very nature of all created reality including human persons.

In the course of discussions like this, we must beware of making conceptual prisons for God. "Relationality" has its place in our thinking about God but can easily become something that we begin to say conclusively about God. The French philosopher Jean-Luc Marion prefers the language of God as Love. This enables us to move beyond the limitations of the language of Being in reference to God. In what Marion calls the "trinitarian game of love," God is inherently giver. God loves by definition. "No condition can continue to restrict his initiative, amplitude, and ecstasy. Love loves without condition, simply because it loves; he thus loves without limit or restriction."[15] Marion's idea of God's "ecstasy" is a reminder that the name "Love" for God implies an overflow, an outpouring that is pure gift. The outpouring of God enters human history precisely as mystery, not as intelligible definition. This outpouring is enfleshed in Jesus of Nazareth who loved to the end, to the cross and beyond, and thereby expressed God's excessive love.

The contemporary emphasis on community, love, and relationship at the heart of God clearly points to the practical and ethical consequences of believing in the Trinity. Yet we need to avoid the danger of reducing the Trinity to a question of relevance. The validity and strength of the doctrine do not consist simply in sanctioning contemporary social ethics or a spirituality of justice, however important and admirable these may be. In the end, the doctrine of the Trinity is necessarily autonomous from our needs. In other words, it is not an extrapolation from values such as "community" or "equality." We know God as Trinity because of the life and work of Jesus Christ and the gift of the Spirit.

Several contemporary trinitarian writings emphasize the centrality of praise, or "doxology," in Christian living.[16] A trinitarian perspective brings spirituality and theology together because doxology is central to the doctrine. The doctrine of the Trinity does not merely seek to speak *about* God (indeed emphasizes a certain reticence in speaking) but underpins a *desire for* God. From the earliest days of the Christian community, the life of the community and of individuals within it has been understood as a journey to God, through Christ and in the Spirit. Prayer does not merely express such a belief but is actually part of the journey itself. Thus, praise, doxology, is not simply a way of stating things but is actually instrumental in drawing us into the relational mystery of God.

The Trinity and Humanity in Julian of Norwich

The mutual indwelling of God in us and us in God permeates the theology of the English mystic Julian of Norwich. Julian lived sometime in the period between c. 1343 and c. 1417, an anchoress or possibly a Beguine, in Norwich, which was at the time one of England's wealthiest cities and a port with close trade connections to Flanders. In the midst of her politically, economically, socially, and religiously fractured fourteenth-century world, Julian's teaching does not represent a retreat into interior spiritual delight accessible only to a mystic elite. In her two texts of the *Showings* or *Revelations of Divine Love* (a Short Text [ST] and a more theologically dense Long Text [LT]) she describes what she writes down as a "blessed teaching" for others.[17] Her purpose is to emphasize a single revelation of divine love, in order to liberate her fellow Christians from all that prevents them growing into the life of God—especially the barriers of sin and despair.[18] Her teaching is for all who seek to love God, whatever their social position. "In all this I was greatly moved in love towards my fellow Christians, that they might all see and know the same as I saw, for I wished it to be a comfort to them, for all this vision was shown for all men."[19]

The Passion as Measure of the Trinity

Julian's foundational experience, on which she bases her theological reflection, consisted of sixteen visions spread across roughly a twenty-four-hour period in 1373 while she was seriously ill. The visions, "showings" or "revelations," focused primarily on the Passion of Jesus. Julian recognizes that everything she was taught was grounded in the first revelation.[20] That is, the whole of Julian's theology finds its focus in the Passion. Her teaching on God as Trinity, on creation, and on the incarnation is ultimately measured by the standard of the cross. The Passion is understood fundamentally as the supreme revelation of the love of God. Love is God's nature, and this love is directed outward toward creation and humanity.

God's love is not an emotion nor is it simply related to God's action. For Julian, Love is God's reality. Julian does not provide simple definitions or a systematic structure to help us to understand what this means. Her pedagogical approach is to begin with the Passion, expressed in visionary form, and then to proceed by means of other images and stories. In this way, Julian is able to teach a deeper wisdom beyond the language of logic. The *Showings* begin with an overwhelming image of self-giving love in the face of the crucified Jesus.

The *point* of the visions was to find in this broken figure the reality of God. Yet, at the same time, to see God only mediated through the flesh of Jesus or through God's "working" also paradoxically serves to preserve the otherness of God—transcendence in the immanence. "I perceived, truly and powerfully, that it was he who just so, both God and man, himself suffered for me, who showed it to me without any intermediary."[21]

Thus in Jesus Christ all humanity, creation, life, and eternal future are caught up into the very life of God as Trinity. "And in the same revelation, suddenly the Trinity filled my heart full of the greatest joy, and I understood that it will be so in heaven without end to all who will come there. For the Trinity is God, God is the Trinity. The Trinity is our maker, the Trinity is our protector, the Trinity is our everlasting lover, the Trinity is our endless joy and our bliss, by our Lord Jesus Christ and in our Lord Jesus Christ."[22]

On the cross, the relationship of God to humankind is shown to be identical with the love relationship of the Trinity—a dynamic and mutual indwelling in which each person of the Godhead is constantly giving to and sharing with the others. This way of being is also revealed as afflicted love, united through suffering to all humanity.

From the vision of Christ on the cross Julian learned that everything is filled with God and enclosed by God. Through the cross, God offers intimacy, "familiar love." Julian does not suggest directly that God suffers. Yet there are hints that God is not untouched by our condition. In the incarnation, God is indissolubly joined to the human condition and longs for us.

Julian regularly employs paradoxical language. As second person of the Trinity, as God, Christ is impassible. And yet, as united to the human condition, Christ is still said to have the thirst and longing that he had upon the cross. This will remain the case "until the time that the last soul which will be saved has come into his bliss." Then Julian is bolder still. There is longing and desire *in God*, and this quality is part of God's everlasting goodness. "For as truly as there is in God a quality of pity and compassion, so truly there is in God a quality of thirst and longing....And this quality of longing and thirst comes from God's everlasting goodness."[23]

Because of God's indwelling, this notion of God's thirst explains our own desire. God in Christ thirsts, and because of our union with God we also thirst. Just as Christ's spiritual thirst is God's painful longing for us, so the longing and yearning we feel is our unsatisfied desire for God or God's desiring in us. "God's thirst is to have man, generally, drawn into him, and in that thirst he has drawn his holy souls who are now in bliss. And so, getting his living members, always he draws and drinks, and still he thirsts and he longs. I saw three kinds of longing in God, and all to the same end, and we have the same in us, and from the same power, and for the same end."[24]

For Julian the simple fact is that, in her understanding of the Passion, the Trinity as a whole participates in all activities relating to salvation, which is part of the eternal "economy" of God even if only the "virgin's Son" may be said to suffer. "All the Trinity worked in Christ's Passion, administering abundant virtues and plentiful grace to us by him; but only the virgin's Son suffered, in which all the blessed Trinity rejoice."[25] The participation of the Trinity in salvation is also strongly implied in the eleventh chapter of the Long Text, where she sees God "in a poynte."[26] Here God is seen to be in all things, doing all things and bringing them to their ordained conclusion.

> And therefore the blessed Trinity is always wholly pleased with all its works; and God revealed all this most blessedly, as though to say: See I am God. See, I am in all things. See, I do all things. See, I never remove my hands from my works, nor ever shall without end. See, I guide all things to the end that I ordain them for, before time began, with the same power and wisdom and love with which I made them; how should anything be amiss?[27]

Julian uses a range of triads in reference to the Trinity. She especially and classically links power or might with the Father, wisdom with the Son, and goodness or love with the Spirit. Yet these qualities are not to be limited to specific persons of the Trinity. They are "properties" *in God*. Equally, in her teaching on God as Mother (imaging

85

generativity and loving-kindness) she is radically trinitarian. Jesus as Mother is not distinguished from the Father as Ruler or Judge—ultimately, the Trinity is our Mother. Julian maintains a delicate balance between distinguishing the persons of the Trinity from each other and, on the other hand, depersonalizing matters so as to deal only with abstract "attributes." Thus, as Julian "contemplated the work of all the blessed Trinity"[28] she saw the three "properties" of fatherhood, motherhood, and lordship "in one God." Our essential human nature (substance) dwells equally in each person and in all the persons together. "And our substance is in our Father, God almighty, and our substance is in our Mother, God all wisdom, and our substance is in our Lord God, the Holy Spirit, all goodness, for our substance is whole in each person of the Trinity, who is one God." Julian is clear about the fundamental unity of God as Trinity. "For the Trinity is God, God is the Trinity. The Trinity is our maker, the Trinity is our protector, the Trinity is our everlasting lover, the Trinity is our endless joy and our bliss, by our Lord Jesus Christ and in our Lord Jesus Christ."[29] This early statement is further underlined in chapter 23 concerning our salvation: "All the Trinity worked in Christ's Passion, administering abundant virtues and plentiful grace to us by him."

The mutual indwelling of the persons of the Trinity one in the other (*perichoresis*) is affirmed at a number of points, including at the end of the famous parable of the Lord and Servant. "Now the Son, true God and true man, sits in his city in rest and in peace, which his Father has prepared for him by his endless purpose, and the Father in the Son, and the Holy Spirit in the Father and in the Son."[30] We are drawn into this mutual indwelling, into an intimacy with God that is Julian's version of deification. She expresses this as a mutual enclosure. We are enclosed in God and God is enclosed in us:

And I saw no difference between God and our substance, but, as it were, all God; and still my understanding accepted that our substance is in God, that is to say that God is God, and our substance is a creature in God. For the almighty truth of the Trinity is our Father, for he made us and keeps us in him. And the deep wisdom of the Trinity is our Mother, in whom we are enclosed. And the high goodness of the Trinity is our Lord, and in him we are enclosed and he in us. We are enclosed in the Father, and we are enclosed in the Son, and we are enclosed in the Holy Spirit. And the Father is enclosed in us, the Son is enclosed in us, and the Holy Spirit is enclosed in us, almighty, all wisdom and all goodness, one God, one Lord.[31]

Reality Seen through God's Eyes

Julian seeks to articulate not only something of what God is but also, as with Ignatius Loyola cited earlier, something of how God sees. Because of this, she offers a radically alternative vision of created reality, including human existence. This results in two striking assertions. First, there is neither blame nor wrath in God.[32] Second, and related to it, sin is "nothing"[33] or "no deed."[34] In seeing God in everything[35] Julian also sees all things in God and therefore "in all this sin was not shown to me." Later, as she considers how sin hinders her longing for God,[36] she is taught that she could not see sin as she contemplated the Passion because "it has no kind of substance, no share in being, nor can it be recognized except by the pain caused by it." Sin is the cause both of human pain and of the Passion and yet "sin is necessary" (or in Middle English, "*behovely*"—that is, appropriate or suitable). In an echo of the Easter Vigil, sin is the *felix culpa* that reveals so great a redeemer or, in Julian's teaching, enables us to experience the depths of God's being as love.

In the end, God does not "see" sin but only the bliss that will be ours. In God's vision this is the ultimate truth of human existence and so Julian, in her God's-eye view, cannot see sin even though she knows its effects within human life and experience. This is not to deny the reality of human sin; but it is to say that the centrality of sin in human experience is not reproduced on the level of God's essential relationship with humanity. Julian expresses this in terms of paradox at the end of chapter 34: "When I saw that God does everything which is done, I did not see sin, and then I saw that all *is* well. But when God did show me about sin, then he said: All *will* be well" (italics mine). One might say that in her God's-eye view Julian has a realized eschatology but that from the point of view of experience she necessarily has a proleptic eschatology. This redeems her teaching from the accusation that it is unrealistic and overoptimistic about the reality of sin and evil.

The two assertions are based on God's "great endless love."[37] "God is that goodness which cannot be angry, for God is nothing but goodness."[38] As the famous parable of the lord and the servant makes clear,[39] however, it all depends on a difference of seeing. The parable is a response to Julian's questions about sin and why she cannot see it when she contemplates all reality in God. God looks on human beings and their failings with compassion and not with blame.

In the parable, the fallen servant sees neither his loving lord "nor does he truly see what he himself is in the sight of his loving lord." We do not see ourselves truly. Indeed, as Julian suggests in the next chapter (52), "God sees one way and man sees another way." Essentially God cannot but see humanity in the light of his Son. "When Adam fell, God's son fell [into Mary's womb]; because of the true union which was made in heaven, God's Son could not be separated from Adam, for by Adam I understand all mankind."[40] Julian finally understands the parable when she begins to see matters from God's perspective.

From this standpoint, the stories of Adam (the Fall) and of Christ (the incarnation) are somehow a single event. The moment of Adam's fall becomes the moment of salvation as well. The parable is an exposition of salvation history from God's viewpoint. God looks upon us as we are in Christ and sees us in our final integrity: healed, sinless, and glorified. In the light of eternity we are ever in union with God and always have been. This has already been implied in the phrase, "I saw God in a point [or instant of time]."[41] All that is in both time and place is but a single "point" to God. "And for the great endless love that God has for all humankind, he makes no distinction in love between the blessed soul of Christ and the least soul that will be saved."[42]

Julian's anthropology (echoing that of St. Augustine to some degree) is complex and depends on understanding two dimensions to human existence, "substance" and "sensuality."[43] These are not easy to define because the words have a number of connotations.[44] One aspect of them, however, is to describe "substance" not simply as that dimension of ourselves that is by nature united to God but also as the self that God sees. "Sensuality," therefore, may stand not merely for our contingent, particular selves but for the self that we are aware of in our historical, contingent lives. Neither is exclusively true and neither is untrue. The paradox of the self is somehow caught in the image of "the crown." We are God's crown. That is a crown of thorns as Jesus Christ suffers for our sins[45] and a crown of glory "which crown is the Father's joy, the Son's honour, the Holy Spirit's delight, and endless marvellous bliss to all who are in heaven."[46]

Conclusion

I have ended this chapter with Julian of Norwich because her theology of the Trinity is entirely "practical," as is the totality of her theological perspective. The Trinity, as it were, is the "answer" to the question of whether and how God is engaged with the world and what being human means. The God of Julian's *Showings* is joyfully and purposefully involved in human history, in the smallest of human events, and in the lives of all of her "even [fellow] Christians." While the freedom of God demands that this involvement be by choice, it is nevertheless, for Julian, God's happiness and fulfillment. In that sense, God's salvific action in the world is not simply a *revelation* of God's inner nature as a trinitarian community of persons. It is also the *vehicle* for mutual trinitarian inter-action. In this way, Julian draws together the immanent Trinity and the economic Trinity. God's action in creation and transforming of human existence and identity *is* God's trinitarian way of being.

Part Two

SPIRITUALITY
AND SOCIAL
TRANSFORMATION

5
PRAYER AND SOCIAL ENGAGEMENT
Interiority and Action

My purpose in this chapter is to explore some of the theological issues that arise as we consider the relationship between prayer and social engagement. To begin with, however, it is important to establish some general points about how we define prayer and then to outline two general theological issues that critically affect the relationship between Christian life and our engagement with the outer, public, social world.

Prayer

A basic question is how we actually define "prayer." What do we mean by prayer? And *how* does "prayer" work? Most writing on prayer (usually devotional and only occasionally theological)—whether it concerns personal prayer or common worship—assumes that what is primarily under consideration is a set of distinctive "practices" and "methods." These practices are to be distinguished from "the practice of everyday life" or even "the practice of Christian discipleship" in the broad sense. We are then left with the difficult task of relating prayer practices, which largely take place aside from everyday existence, to everyday life. This is the classic challenge of bridging a presumed gap between contemplation and action.

My starting point is simply to suggest that this approach to prayer begins in the wrong place. Of course, "prayer" involves practices—whether extended or brief, complex or simple. Practices, however, only make theological as well as spiritual sense as explicit realizations of something much more basic—a relationship with God that is fundamental to human existence and permeates every aspect of it. Theologically, prayer in a Christian perspective is based on a sacramental view of the created order. Christian spirituality in its broad conception is founded on a belief that God reaches out to human beings and equally invites us to seek God in return. A "sacramental view" presumes that we are opened to God's grace and to God's transformative Spirit *in and through* human history and *in and through* human affairs. By implication, the sacred, the divine, is to be discerned not merely within explicitly religious contexts but within all aspects of everyday life—not least in social and political life. Karl Rahner once defined prayer "dogmatically," as he put it, as:

> the explicit and positive realization of our natural and supernatural relationship with the personal God of salvation. It realizes the essence of the religious act. It is man's [*sic*] entry into the transcendence of his own being, in which he allows himself to become receptive, humble and reverent, gives himself in a positive response, and is totally available and subjectively concerned *in his whole existence* [my italics] with the mystery of God as a person.[1]

In the same essay, Rahner further notes: "All positive religious acts which are directly and explicitly related, both knowingly and willingly, to God may be called prayer." As we shall see, Karl Rahner has had a particular influence on theologians concerned to bring together contemplation and social or political engagement. You will notice that Rahner still refers to "positive religious acts" and uses words such as "directly," "explicitly," "knowingly," or "willingly."

Two American theologians, however, Lawrence Cunningham and Keith Egan, who have written extensively on the field of spirituality, offer other useful pointers in their book *Christian Spirituality: Themes from the Tradition*.[2] They begin by discussing prayer as an *activity* but see this activity as "a fundamental gesture of belief, faith, dependence and connectedness."[3] In their section on methods of prayer there is a subsection entitled "Making Ordinary Life a Prayer,"[4] but this, as with Rahner, is still a *conscious act* of placing oneself in the presence of God in the midst of action. Finally,[5] in a subsection on "Prayer as Activity," they move beyond "prayer as methods" to a sense that, if prayer is a gesture that links us to God, then all that we do as disciples is also a form of prayer.

> In other words, it is possible to think of our lives as Christians as a form of prayer and the moments when we formally stop to pray either individually or in common as "summing up" or "articulating" our larger, less-consciously-prayerful acts which make up the business of living.

Christian Life and Social Engagement

My second background point is to note that how we approach a relationship between the Christian life and social engagement obviously depends on our theological evaluation of the outer, social, "public" world. Unfortunately, our Western culture is deeply polarized. The private sphere (inwardness, family, and close friends, an idealization of home and domesticity) tends to be privileged as the backstage where the individual is truly him/herself, relaxing unobserved before putting on various personae that the "self" needs to play out different roles on the stage of social life.[6] Living in public is not, however, really a matter of *a role* that it is possible to shed. If there were a preexistent self prior to all roles, then social life would be detached from identity. The Christian theological tradition, however, underlines the fact that there is not an *absolutely* private self. Human existence, and Christian discipleship, inherently embody a social task. "The social realm" is better thought of as a dimension of identity, an aspect of who I am, rather than something I enter or choose not to enter.

It is important to note the intimate link between Christian discipleship, including the association between social life and human identity, and our trinitarian theology of God. The core of the Christian life is to be united with God in Jesus Christ through a Spirit-led communion with one another. God's own relational nature is fundamental to this life. God *is* "persons-in-communion," a mutuality of self-giving love. Communion underpins existence. Nothing *is* without communion, including human life.[7] The mission of God, *missio Dei*, is the divine activity of self-disclosure in creation, salvation history, and the incarnation, drawing all things into the limitless embrace of God's unifying love. The life of discipleship is to participate ever more deeply in this *missio Dei* through a faithful following of the way of Jesus, the bearer and expression of God's mission.

Our Theology of Human History?

How we interpret the "world" and "human history" as theaters of God's action and of Christian response and human transformation is the first of two important theological themes that relate to our fundamental perspectives about prayer.

As a previous chapter has noted, Augustine's theology of history, expounded mainly in his *City of God*, is probably the single most influential historical theory in Christianity.[8] Augustine's thought has also been pervasive in an implicit way in Western culture more broadly. We may note, for example, the power of the much later, but related, Two Kingdoms theology of Martin Luther. Martin Luther, especially in his *The Freedom of a Christian*, appears to have built a neo-Augustinian radical chasm between a realm of freedom and a realm of unfreedom.[9]

Such a Two Kingdoms theology is to some extent reproduced in modern theological affirmations of Christianity's countercultural role, such as that of Stanley Hauerwas[10] and rejections of secularity, such as that of John Milbank.[11] Both writers are anti-assimilationist with regard to Christianity's position in society and view the Church as an alternative "politics." In its extreme forms, such a viewpoint risks losing the public, outer world as a place where God is experienced and redemption is offered and received. It is worth bearing in mind Wolfhart Pannenberg's note about the limitations of a Two Kingdoms theology in relation to social-political engagement:

> The Lutheran separation of the spiritual from the secular kingdom may contribute not more than a cautionary note concerning the difference between the ultimate reality of the kingdom of God, which the Church is ultimately concerned with, and the provisional character of every institutional form, that of the secular state as well as the organisation of the Church.[12]

The particular context for Augustine's work was the collapse of the Western Roman Empire in the fifth century CE. Augustine defined the relationship between the Kingdom of God and human history in terms of two forces, the City of God and the Earthly City. Like the tares and the wheat of the gospel parable, the two cities cannot be perfectly differentiated within time. Ultimate meaning cannot, however, be found in the Earthly City, which is a context of incessant change.

Augustine's distinction between the two cities highlights a perennial tension in Christian spirituality. If Christianity's belief in God's incarnation involves a positive understanding of human history, there has always been an alternative anti-historical voice that suggests that what is fundamentally important spiritually lies outside history (in some parallel spiritual dimension) or beyond history in an eschatological future. Augustine clearly underlines the dangers of theological associations between God and the State. There is, nevertheless, a place in Augustine's thought for the Kingdom of God to grow within historical processes and events. The most important conclusion to be drawn from this is that no historic age could grow closer to God than any other age. Yet Augustine possessed a deep sense that *each and every moment* was equally filled with God's presence and activity. A further conclusion is that Augustine's understanding of history and how we live within and respond to its processes embodies a theology of hope glimpsed through tragedies and failure.[13] Augustine's theology of history in the *City of God* is based upon a wider canvas of his own experience of God's providence in his own life as expressed in the *Confessions*.[14] Fundamentally, the lesson both of Augustine's checkered career and of world history is that out of all things comes good. Human history is God's creation and is not, therefore, to be condemned as evil or an illusion. For Augustine, the lessons of history lead him to be calmly confident about the future even *in and through* the ambiguities and darkness of human events and experiences. If contingent history is to end, it is an ending that speaks of fulfillment rather than of ultimate meaninglessness.

Augustine's theology of history essentially describes two dimensions of one history: the history of contingent events in the world and, running through it, the thread of sacred history that alone tells us what God is really doing.[15] Therefore, every moment is significant even if that significance is presently mysterious.

Do We Give Priority to Interiority?

A second key theological theme related to prayer is whether and to what degree we prioritize interiority within Christian spirituality. "Interiority" is not a straightforward concept. For Augustine and other classic spiritual teachers, it did not imply the same thing as it might do in our era. In his contribution to *A History of Private Life* Peter Brown reminds us that the earliest approaches to the Christian life inherited from late classical Judaism demonstrate an intense sense of vital solidarity between the individual and the community. Individual human existence was intrinsically related to the common good. The perceived danger was for people to retreat into privacy rather than give themselves wholeheartedly to the task of serving their neighbors. Hence, Jewish writers turned their attention to the "thoughts of the heart"—the supposed core of motivation and intention. Human destiny was a state of solidarity with others, expressed in the image of the undivided heart.[16]

Following this tradition, Augustine, like the early desert fathers and mothers, adopted the symbol of the heart as a way of expressing the self. As I have suggested in an earlier chapter, Augustine's language of the heart is not necessarily evidence of a privatized spirituality. What is interior to me is, for Augustine, where I am also united with the whole of creation. The *imago Dei* in which we are created and which is imprinted on the heart must be read alongside Augustine's doctrine of creation. In his *Commentary on Genesis*, Adam's sin was to please himself and to live for himself (*secundum se vivere, sibi placere*). Thus communion is ruptured—whether our unity with God, solidarity with others, or harmony with our own true self. In other words, sin is a withdrawal into privacy, which is distinctly different from interiority. Self-seeking pride is the archetypal sin.[17] Original Eden, the monastic life, the ideal City of God are all based on "the love that promotes the common good for the sake of the heavenly society."[18] In fact, the most insidious sin was privacy or self-enclosure. The private is seen as the opposite of common or public. For Augustine, the Heavenly City was the community in which there would be the fullness of sharing.[19] Within Augustine there is a tension that should not be resolved between a striking sense of the personal self and an equally striking sense of the fundamentally social nature of human existence. "The heart" for Augustine is where true integration of interior and exterior, spiritual and fleshly happens. Equally, Augustine is clear that if anything is claimed to be in the heart or inside us but does not show itself outwardly in love and community, it is illusory. "The return to the heart is but the first step of a conversion process that proves itself in universal and unrestricted—catholic—love."[20]

Prayer and Social Engagement

Within a positive view of history and a sense of the profound and necessary connection between interiority and outer action, I now want to outline how a number of theologians discuss the ways in which prayer, or the mystical-contemplative dimension of life, is a vital ingredient in social engagement.

A number of theological writers over the last thirty years or so have argued that the mystical-contemplative way is a necessary dimension of social engagement. Interestingly, the Spanish theologian Gaspar Martinez has recently suggested that what he calls "worldly theologies," those modern Catholic theologies engaged explicitly with the public dimensions of life, are simultaneously the ones that focus most sharply on the mystery of God, with a greater rather than a lesser emphasis on spirituality and mysticism. He notes in particular Johannes Metz, Gustavo Gutiérrez, and David Tracy—significantly, all of them inspired in different ways by Karl Rahner (although we should also note the writings of Edward Schillebeeckx in this regard).[21]

Because the so-called political and liberation theologies are overtly concerned with social engagement—indeed, with the prophetic role of Christianity in relation to social *transformation*—it is particularly instructive to see the degree to which the connections between prayer and social action are integral to such theologies. Again I can do no more than sketch out a few examples in a nonsystematic way.

The Chilean theologian Segundo Galilea has written more than anyone else concerning the mystical or contemplative dimensions of political and social responses to injustice. Galilea suggests that there needs to be a movement away from the notion that an effective response is purely ethical or structural (this, Galilea suggests, may merely become a new form of oppression) toward a truly spiritual experience of discovering the compassion of God incarnate in the poor. Humans are not able to find true compassion, or to create structures of deep transformation, without entering contemplatively into Jesus' own compassion. Only contemplative-mystical practice, allied to social action, is capable of bringing about the change of heart necessary for a lasting solidarity and social transformation—particularly a solidarity capable of embracing the oppressor as well as the oppressed. Thus, according to Galilea, social engagement must be accompanied by a process of interior transformation and liberation from self-seeking. This is the heart of what he terms "integral liberation."[22] Galilea's position reminds us that if we need to reflect on how social-public life informs and forms our spiritualities and prayer, we also need to cultivate a *critical* attentiveness to social and political realities rather than risk an uncritical absorption of spirituality into social forms.

Galilea calls for a reformulation of the idea of contemplation and of the mystical. At the heart of the Christian tradition, he suggests, has always been the notion of contemplation as a supreme act of self-forgetfulness rather than a preoccupation with personal interiority. In the teachings of the great mystics, contemplation has always been related to the classic Christian themes of the cross and death.

> This implies the crucifixion of egoism and the purification of the self as a condition of contemplation. This crucifixion of egoism in forgetfulness of self in the dialectic prayer-commitment will be brought to fulfilment both in the mystical dimension of communication with Jesus in the luminous night of faith, and also in the sacrifice which is assumed by commitment to the liberation of others. The 'death' of mysticism and the 'death' of the militant are the two dimensions of the call to accept the cross, as the condition of being a disciple....The desert as a political experience liberates [the Christian] from egoism and from the 'system', and is a source of freedom and of an ability to liberate.[23]

The Brazilian theologian Leonardo Boff has sharply criticized the traditional spiritual and monastic formula of *ora et labora* (prayer and work) on the grounds that it espouses a kind of parallelism. At best the *et* has stood for an alternation of interior prayer and external engagement. Classically, contemplation was thought to be the source of all value. Social engagement was not a direct mediation of God but was only of value to the extent that it was "fed" by contemplation and thus "redeemed" from its secular, profane associations.[24] Boff notes that in some contemporary Christian approaches to engagement, overdominated by social and political theory, a parallelism continues to exist but is reversed. Thus, social engagement predominates over contemplation so that contemplation becomes another, subsidiary, form of social practice. Boff argues for an equal, dialectical relationship "treating them as two spaces that are open to one another and imply each other."[25] This dialectic produces a unity in what Boff calls the "mysticism-politics relationship." Boff coins a new phrase to describe being contemplative while engaged fully in the public spaces of political transformation—*contemplativus in liberatione.* This unity of prayer-liberation is based on a living faith that "defines the 'from where' and the 'towards where' of our existence, which is God and his design of love, that is communicated through, and materialised, in all things."[26] Thus the contemplative and mystical "is not carried out only in the sacred space of prayer, nor in the sacred precinct of the church; purified, sustained and nurtured by living faith, it also finds its place in political and social practice."[27]

Gustavo Gutiérrez' book *On Job: God-Talk and the Suffering of the Innocent* has been described as a breakthrough in his theology.[28] Gutiérrez' interpretation of Job underlines clearly that prayer and contemplation are paramount in his approach to theology, and to the connections between theology and social engagement. In Gutiérrez' interpretation of Job, the difference between Job and his friends is that the latter base their reflections on abstract principles rather than on an encounter with the limitless love and compassion of God. In contrast, Job seeks his "answer" face to face—one might say "head to head." This moves Job beyond purely social or ethical reasoning to spiritual reasoning—a realization that God acts out of gratuitous love. Such an insight can come only from a kind of *confrontation* with God. This reminds us of Johannes Metz's point that prayer is a special kind of limitless language that takes us beyond the reasonable. "In this sense, everything can be said to God in prayer, from rage, frustration and accusation, to downright denial of God's existence."[29] Contemplation and confrontation are closely linked. Inevitably this reminds us of the power of the imprecatory psalms. Job does not receive an answer to his precise questions but what he does receive is much deeper than what he sought. Contemplation widens perspectives. Silence, prayer, and listening to what God has to say are central to Gutiérrez' approach to social engagement. But contemplation does more. In Gutiérrez' commentary, Job's encounter with God enables him to abandon himself into God's unfathomable love, beyond an abstract notion of ethics or justice. This abandonment is not the same as *fatalistic acceptance*. It is an abandonment that results from deeper realization. In terms of social engagement, to speak of abandonment into God's unfathomable love *beyond* justice does not imply a suspension of the ethical dimension of life. Rather it situates the ethical within the broader and deeper scope of God's gratuity. "Prayer and contemplation are not separate moments from practice, but an inner element of that practice."[30] Rowan Williams makes a related point in his essay "Sacraments of the New Society," where he argues that the solidarity in God expressed by and facilitated by the sacramental order (especially baptism and Eucharist) outpaces our concept of human rights in that "we are caught up in solidarities we have not chosen," let alone defined legally or philosophically. In a sacramental perspective "we confront something we cannot plead with." So, "fundamental equality is established by the indiscriminate regard of God."[31]

From a different theological tradition, Jürgen Moltmann in his short (and often overlooked) book *Experiences of God* writes of the ethical dimension of the mystical *sapientia experimentalis*—close to Martin Luther's own understanding of spirituality and to Paul Tillich's related concept of "participative knowledge." The most interesting aspect of his approach to contemplation, however, is the delineation of a fivefold process to replace the more traditional patristic-medieval "threefold way." This process is really a continuous circular movement. It begins with our social engagement with the ambiguities and pains of the outer world. The instinctive response to injustice, for example, is to want to change things. Action for change, however, inevitably leads to a realization that a truly Christian response has to be embedded in contemplation. In this there is an echo of the liberation theologians I have already mentioned. Contemplation, which in Moltmann is focused on the history of Jesus Christ in the Gospels, leads to a movement away from self and from false images of God toward the classic Reformation dictum, "God alone." The encounter with the living God, purified of selfishness, is what has been described in classic Western mysticism as "union." But this union is not an end in itself. The purpose of mystical union is not to remain in a kind of pure spiritual experience beyond our responsibilities in everyday life. What is encountered at the heart of God is the cross. Union, therefore, leads to a deeper identification with the person of Jesus who moves out of himself in kenotic love. So, the mystical journey leads the believer through union, which now becomes a new point of departure, to a renewed practice of everyday discipleship and social engagement. "As long as we do not think that dying with Christ spiritually is a substitute for dying with him in reality, mysticism does not mean estrangement from action; it is a preparation for public, political discipleship."[32] The icon of mysticism therefore becomes the political martyr as much as the monk. Here we are reminded of Dietrich Bonhoeffer, whom Moltmann explicitly mentions.

> The place of mystical experience is in very truth the cell—the prison cell. The "witness to the truth of Christ" is despised, scoffed at, persecuted, dishonoured and rejected. In his own fate he experiences the fate of Christ. His fate conforms to Christ's fate. That is what the mystics called *conformitas crucis*, the conformity of the cross....Eckhart's remark that suffering is the shortest way to the birth of God in the soul applies, not to any imagined suffering, but to the very real sufferings endured by "the witness to the truth."[33]

Conclusion: Transformation and Integrity

If we are to draw a single overall conclusion about the relationship of prayer and social engagement from what has been mentioned in the chapter, it would be in terms of *purification* or the *transformation of practice*. For Dorothee Sölle, the Protestant theologian and political activist deeply inspired by the mystical tradition, resistance and changing the world *must* have mystical roots.[34] For her there are three dimensions or levels to what might be called "mystical consciousness." She speaks first of "amazement," which is not only wonder or praise of God but something that "tears the veil of triviality" because it is to be touched by the spirit of life. "Without reinspiration, nothing new begins." At this first level, "we do not embark upon the path of our journey [the spiritual journey] as seekers, but as people who have been found; we are preceded always by the goodness we have experienced."[35] Then, on the second level, there is leaving oneself, letting go or, as she puts it, "missing God"—a purification born of realizing "how distant we are from a true life in God."[36] This is a process of "dis-education" [her term], freedom, especially in our world a freedom from "the addictive and compulsive mechanisms of consuming"—I have/I choose, therefore I am! Finally, the third level is "a living in God"—a *via unitiva*.[37] This level involves healing—a healing that is also the birth of true resistance. For we become capable of healing others only insofar as we are healed.

Finally, in a brief but pregnant essay, "Theological Integrity," Rowan Williams has provocative things to say about the power of contemplation—admittedly in the context of theological speech. It seems to me, however, that what he has to say equally sums up something critical about Christian praxis—our processes of social engagement. It is that word *integrity*. For Williams, contemplation is about honesty and integrity in what we say *about* God and what we seek to do *in the name of God*. If our engagement with the social world involves speech—speaking out—our words must have integrity. "Having integrity then, is being able to speak in a way which allows of answers. Honest discourse permits response and continuation; it invites collaboration by showing that it does not claim to be, in and of itself, final."[38]

This notion is a difficult lesson for people who, in speaking the language of religion, make claims about the right way to lead a human life. The point, however, is that religious speech in the public arena does not merely expound political or social theory. It speaks ultimately of what God seeks, desires, *wills*. Thus, such religious speaking out must be rooted as much in encounters with God, "praise of God," as in analysis.

Williams suggests that this kind of speech involves "dispossession"—a "dispossession of the human mind conceived as central to the order of the world, and a dispossession of the entire identity that exists prior to the paschal drama, the identity that has not seen and named its self-deception and self-destructiveness."[39] At the heart of this necessary dispossession is contemplation—a waiting on God, an *apophasis* as the process of giving place to the prior actualities of God. "The fruition of the process [of contemplation] is the discovery that one's selfhood and value simply lie in the abiding faithful presence of God, not in any moral or conceptual performance."[40] Contemplative union is a state in which "the self acts out of an habitual diffused awareness that its centre is God."

> To act from its centre *is* to give God freedom in the world, to do the works of God. The self, we could say, has attained integrity: the inner and outer are no longer in tension; I act what I am, a creature called to freedom, and leave behind those attempts at self-creation which in fact destroy my freedom. As Teresa [of Avila] puts it, Martha and Mary unite: truthful, active and constructive love issues from and leads into patience and silence, or, better, is constantly *contemporary* with patience and silence.[41]

6
MYSTICISM AND
SOCIAL PRACTICE
The Mystical and Michel de Certeau

Judging by the religion or Mind-Body-Spirit sections of large book-stores in the United Kingdom and the United States, there is a peculiar fascination with mysticism these days. The word is often used to refer to anything esoteric, particularly if it promises special insight, wisdom, or the key to life. The notion of "mysticism" generally implies that one can have an immediate encounter with, perhaps immediate knowledge of (but not in an analytical-conceptual sense), the mystery of God. In other words, mysticism seems to imply some kind of direct and personal *experience* in contrast to the way people usually think about religion—that is, structures, rituals, doctrines, morals, laws. Indeed, mysticism is, like its associated word "spirituality," sometimes contrasted favorably with "religion" in this structural sense. Sometimes it is seen as the essence of all true religion behind the different religious languages we use about God—a common stream running through all great religions, from Roman Catholicism to Tibetan Buddhism but in a way that is not ultimately dependent on their differences.

Reasons for Current Interest

In my estimation, the reality is less dramatic. Yet why is there such a fascination with mysticism these days? I detect two main and closely related reasons. Both have to do with what I would call the crises of our modern world and also with a consequent and intense emotional need. First of all, many people desire to transcend boundaries and to experience union with other people or with the natural order. They want to

106

overcome the divisions of humanity, whether these are political, religious, or cultural, because they experience them as deeply destructive. So people look for something "common" on a spiritual level. But because the first port of call, organized religion, appears to be riven with mutual suspicion, they look for contexts of the spiritual that bypass these deeply unattractive realities.

Second, a variety of social, economic, and political factors make many people suspicious about the capacity of purely material enhancement to fulfill human aspirations. Thus, the existential crisis of meaning, fears for the future of humanity, a certain cynicism about humanly created structures (politics or the Church), may be assuaged by an appeal to a level of consciousness that is available *intuitively* rather than by more intellectual, rationalist, and moralistic means. Mysticism therefore seems to offer an essentially noncognitive connection with the very depths of human existence.

The Problem of Definition

The legitimacy of the term *mysticism*, however, which, as we shall see from the work of Michel de Certeau, first appeared in France ("*la mystique*") in the seventeenth century, has been frequently questioned in Christian circles. To some observers the notion of mysticism seems to create a separate, eccentric sphere of religion. Indeed, when we examine the concept, we immediately face problems of definition.[1] Is it that "strange things happen to peculiar people" or does it, as the nineteenth-century English Benedictine Cardinal Gasquet (no friend of the mystical) once said, "begin with mist and end in schism"? Despite the large body of modern writing on the subject—in philosophy, history, theology, and studies in comparative religion—mysticism is notoriously controversial and difficult to define.[2] In popular parlance, the word is often taken to refer to anything in the field of religion that is strange or nonrational.

Until relatively recently, most writings have concentrated on mysticism simply as a category of religious *experience*. This approach results in several problems. First, it tends to separate mysticism from theology—the ways we attempt to think or speak about God. Second, it removes mysticism from the public world into the realm of private, individual, interiority. The result is that it is difficult to know how mysticism could be of great importance to society or the wider Church. Third, it tends to concentrate on phenomena or states of mind and emotions experienced by a limited number of people as the result of intense meditative practices or ascetical disciplines. This effectively separates mysticism from ordinary human existence and from the Christian life in general.

If mystical impulses are detected in all world religions, is there "mysticism as such" which we can define apart from specific belief systems? That would broadly be the view of the still influential thinking of the American philosopher and psychologist of religion William James, particularly as expressed in his 1902 Gifford Lectures, *The Varieties of Religious Experience*.[3] His emphasis was on interior religion rather than on external forms. Interior religion for James was understood to be a global, universal phenomenon—a "pure consciousness event" prior to interpretation and specific doctrines. There are at least three problems, however. First, attempts at inclusive definitions are open to the criticism that they fail to do justice to the riches and complexities of specific religious traditions such as Christianity, Islam, or Buddhism. They are highly abstract and are not what the so-called mystics say about their understanding of the spiritual path. The point is that any adequate theory of mysticism must begin not with an abstract "essence" but with reflection on specific personalities, historical moments, or cultural-religious contexts.[4] Second, we cannot distinguish *absolutely* experience from interpretation, nor should "mystical" be confined to autobiographical accounts of special experiences. In fact they are interdependent because we can only experience within our overall frameworks of meaning or worldviews. In other words, when we experience anything, we know that it is an experience of this or of that. In fact, the moment we name an experience as an experience of *something*, we do so as an act of interpretation. Third, mysticism, especially in Christianity, is as concerned with *language* as it is with *experience*. That is, the mystical dimension of Christianity questions the ultimate adequacy of all conventional definitions of God. The great medieval Dominican Meister Eckhart loved to cite or paraphrase Augustine on speaking about God: "If I have spoken of it, I have not spoken, for it is ineffable."[5]

Christian mystics may be said to be those who believe in and practice their faith with particular intensity. The great mystical writers are adamant that what they are concerned about fundamentally concerns a process or way of life rather than altered states of consciousness.[6]

The Basis of Christian Mysticism

While the noun *mysticism* is relatively modern, the use of the word *mystical* as a qualifier for elements in Christian practice and thought is ancient.[7] The Greek adjective *mystikos* with its implications of silence or the unseen was used by ancient writers in reference to the mystery cults, but by the second century CE, beginning with Clement of Alexandria, the word began to be adapted by Christians to signify the hidden realities of the Christian life. It was primarily employed in relation to the deeper spiritual meanings of the Bible, but it was also used to point to the inner power of Christian rituals and sacraments. Then, in the third century, a biblical scholar but also catechist, Origen (d. 254), developed a biblically based program for the way the Christian was to be purified from sin, and, especially through a spiritual, deeper, approach to reading and interpreting scripture, the Christian was lifted up to the point where she or he was not just immersed in love of God but united to the God who *is* love.[8] Around the beginning of the sixth century the anonymous Syrian monk who adopted the pseudonym Dionysius (after St. Paul's convert, Acts 17:34) used the term *mystical theology* to indicate the kind of knowledge that engages with the unknown God. Dionysius was also among the first to use the term *mystical union*.[9]

The main point to emphasize, however, is that Christian mysticism is rooted in the baptismal call of all Christians to enter ever more fully into the "mystery" of God through exposure to, and response to, the scriptures, liturgy, and sacraments. This, rather than an interest in people's experiences, was the understanding of "mysticism" in the early Church. Thus, Pseudo-Dionysius, whose works had such an influence on medieval Western mystical theology, sums up this early tradition rather than contradicts it. This underlines that mysticism, in its deepest sense, is potentially a dimension of every Christian's life. It also emphasizes that mysticism is a *gift* rather than something achieved through individual effort.

Mysticism and Visions

Yet, having said all this, some people have intense visionary experiences that are popularly described as "mystical." The key, however, is that such experiences relate to a deep communion with God (or an immediacy of presence). On their own such experiences are not reliable indicators of the mystical. They may result from psychosis or be induced artificially by drugs, by sleep deprivation, or by fasting. Some modern writers on mysticism, for example, Bernard McGinn, are uncomfortable with the notion that visions are mystical. This leads McGinn to question the mystical credentials of some leading medieval women writers (for example, Hildegard of Bingen).[10]

If there are dangers in overemphasizing paranormal phenomena, however, there is an equal danger in rejecting them entirely. Many authorities agree that a truly Christian understanding of mysticism involves transformation of *life* in both a religious and social sense and not merely altered consciousness. Phenomena may sometimes be indicators of authentic transformation, however. A number of commentators also point out that visionary experience may be a source of authority or a validation of spiritual teaching for those people such as medieval women mystics who lacked official status or recognition in the Church.[11] In the fourteenth century it is not insignificant that someone such as Julian of Norwich used her visions not as ends in themselves but as the basis for her sophisticated theological reflection and spiritual teachings.[12]

Mysticism and Union

The word most frequently used by mystics and commentators to describe the heart of Christian mysticism is "union." In a more fundamental theological sense, however, union with God is the precondition of *all* human spiritual development rather than simply its most advanced stage. In addition, in nontheological studies of mysticism, union has sometimes been characterized in terms of passivity and by absorption into the divine where individual identity is lost. Apart from the difficulty of relating this, without qualification, to theological understandings of how God relates to people in freedom and love, such a notion does not correspond, despite some ambiguities, to what we know of the great Christian mystics. Rather, the deep union with God of, say, a Bernard of Clairvaux, a Francis of Assisi, or a Catherine of Siena led them into greater activity and service of others rather than toward the opposite. Having said this, we cannot bypass entirely the ambiguity of some mystical language, particularly in that greatest exponent of fourteenth-century Rhineland mysticism, the Dominican Meister Eckhart. Particularly in his radically paradoxical and intentionally contradictory vernacular German sermons, he appears to make daring assertions of mystical identity between humans and God. This led to suspicions of heresy and the condemnation of some of his teachings. At the same time, however, Eckhart preached the absolute abyss separating us from the mysterious transcendent God and the necessary negation of all human concepts of "God" in our quest to reach out toward a transcendent and mysterious God's *grunt* or "ground."[13]

Mysticism and Social Transformation

The mystical dimension of Christian practice has profound social implications.[14] One of the greatest of Western mystical writers and theologians of the Trinity, the fourteenth-century Flemish priest John Ruusbroec, saw the mystical life of contemplation in terms of "the life common to all." This life joined human beings to one another in the service of all and also harmonized action and contemplation into a single whole. So, the "spiritually elevated" person never ceases to be the "common" person. The elevated person "owes himself to all those who seek his help" and seeks to share the "life common to all" that is God's own life within us.[15]

> A person who has been sent down by God from these heights is full of truth and rich in all the virtues....He will therefore always flow forth to all who need him, for the living spring of the Holy Spirit is so rich that it can never be drained dry....He therefore leads a common life, for he is equally ready for contemplation or for action and is perfect in both.[16]

Elsewhere, Ruusbroec writes:

> Thus this man is just, and he goes towards God by inward love, in eternal work, and he goes in God by his fruitive inclination in eternal rest. And he dwells in God; and yet he goes out towards all creatures, in a spirit of love towards all things, in virtue and in works of righteousness. And this is the supreme summit of the inner life.[17]

Ruusbroec was quite clear that those people who practiced the attainment of a peaceful contemplative inwardness as their fundamental goal and disregarded the demands of charity or ethics were, of all people, most guilty of spiritual wickedness.[18] Evelyn Underhill in her classic work *Mysticism* described Ruusbroec as one of the greatest Western mystics precisely because she believed that selfless service of others was characteristic of specifically Christian mysticism and marked it out from mysticism in other world faiths.[19]

A number of theological writers in the late twentieth century have also argued that the mystical way is a necessary part of social engagement rather than separate from it. The Chilean theologian Segundo Galilea has written arguably more than anyone in the liberationist tradition concerning the mystical dimensions of political and social responses to injustice. He suggests that if responses to poverty and injustice in the world are purely structural, the new structures on their own may simply become new forms of oppression. Structural change needs to be complemented by a truly spiritual experience of discovering the compassion of God present in the poor. Humans are not able to find true compassion, nor create structures of real transformation, without entering contemplatively into God's own compassion. Only contemplative practice, allied to social action, is capable of bringing about the change of heart in us that is necessary for a lasting solidarity. Thus, according to Galilea, social engagement must be accompanied by a process of inner transformation and liberation from self-seeking. Galilea calls for a reformulation of the idea of the mystical. At the heart of the Christian mystical tradition, he suggests, has always been the notion that true contemplation is a supreme act of self-forgetfulness rather than a preoccupation with personal experience.[20]

Michel de Certeau

The French Jesuit Michel de Certeau (1925–86) was one of the most creative interdisciplinary intellectuals of the late twentieth century as well as a highly original writer on Christian mysticism. At the same time, his writings are difficult to summarize or to interpret definitively. This difficulty lies partly in the way he wrote and partly in the enigma of his own life. To begin with, de Certeau's writings consciously resist systematization. He also brought an extraordinary range of intellectual interests to every subject he examined. He drew brilliantly and extensively upon history, theology, Christian spirituality, cultural theory, philosophy, psychology, politics, social sciences, semiotics, and linguistics. There was also an inherent ambiguity to de Certeau's life. In his later years he appeared to abandon institutional Christianity and to have moved to the margins of religious belief yet never formally resigned as a Jesuit or priest and continued to be driven in strange and important ways both by Christian themes and by what might be called the "Ignatian project." Increasingly, de Certeau was preoccupied with exploring the idea that human identity and existence was a form of fluid and mobile "practice" rather than a matter of being able to define the nature of an abstract "self."

Interiority and Desire

Michel de Certeau's interdisciplinarity and eclecticism are readily apparent in his study of mysticism. His originality has stimulated people to think of mysticism in new ways. True, his interest focused predominantly on sixteenth- and seventeenth-century Spanish and French mysticism, and on his perception that the period saw a significant move inward. There was a growing preoccupation during that period with the experiential and with the autobiographical. This conformed to de Certeau's own fascination with modern psychoanalysis, which drew him, along with another Jesuit writer on Ignatian spirituality, François Roustang, into the circle of Jacques Lacan. De Certeau's understanding of the meaning and role of "mysticism" cannot, however, be reduced to sheer subjectivity, interiority, or individual experience in isolation. For one thing, he wrote in the context of a Western European culture that had lost faith in the bedrock of an autonomous, clearly defined human subject—whether grounded in "the soul" or in the Cartesian rational "mind." At the same time, de Certeau's interest in mysticism as a social practice rather than simply as subjective experiences brought him close to the emphasis on mysticism as a process or way of life present in other recent commentators such as Bernard McGinn.[21]

For de Certeau, mysticism was bound up with *desire*. "Desire" is a key word in his writings—one that he shared with such French post-modern philosophers as Michel Foucault and Jacques Derrida but which also summarizes the heart of the Ignatian spiritual tradition to which de Certeau was so indebted. For both the mystic and the post-modern person, "desire" expresses a certain kind of drivenness, an intensity and movement ever onward inspired by what is *not* known, *not* possessed, *not* fixed or final.

> They are, she [Hadewijch, the Beguine mystic] said, "drunk with what they have not drunk": inebriation without drinking, inspiration from one knows not where, illumination without knowledge. They are drunk with what they do not possess. Drunk with desire. Therefore, they may all bear the name given to the work of Angelus Silesius: *Wandersmann*, the "wanderer."[22]

Desire is also expressive of embodiment in which an unstable and incomplete "self" is continually being constructed in a movement outward and in encounters with what is other than itself. For de Certeau, mysticism is inherently engaged with the public world and is a form of "social practice." Indeed, one of de Certeau's central views was, like that of Galilea and some other liberation theologians, that Christian mysticism is essentially radical and disruptive, both religiously and socially.

The Concept of "A Mystical Tradition"

In his early work and researches on "mysticism" or "mystics" (*la mys-tique*—his word for the study of the mystical life), Michel de Certeau can be more or less credited with establishing that, as a distinct category associated with subjective religious experiences, it originated in early seventeenth-century France.[23] Although de Certeau admitted that the remote origins of "mysticism" in this subjective sense lay much earlier in the late thirteenth century, especially with Meister Eckhart and the Beguines, he believed that the key point in its formalization was between the mid-sixteenth century and the mid-seventeenth century.[24] This paradigmatic period of mysticism proliferated in the context of what de Certeau refers to as "a loss." The various movements and writings were born (to use de Certeau's words) "with the setting sun." This sunset was the gradual demise of a previously dominant Christian religious worldview.[25] De Certeau asserted that the "dark nights" expressed in various mystical texts refer not merely to interior, subjective states of spiritual loss and absence but also to the global situation of religious faith in Western culture.[26]

De Certeau was a first-class historian. Consequently, he was fully aware that the change in mystical writings during the late sixteenth century and the seventeenth century toward an emphasis on interior experiences, apparently detached from doctrine or Church life, eventually *created* the very concept of "mystical tradition." The notion of a specific mystical tradition, stretching back from the post-Reformation period through the Middle Ages to the early Church, is in that sense an artificial construct. It involved a retrospective recruitment of earlier spiritual writings into a particular experiential framework—or what de Certeau referred to as "experimental knowledge." On the heels of the construction of a mystical "tradition" followed the gradual psychologization of the study of mysticism where private insights and special experiences became the criteria for the presence and validity of "the mystical." As already noted, this would reach its height in the late nineteenth century with the work of William James.

Mysticism as Subversion

The classic sixteenth- and seventeenth-century mystical texts that de Certeau studied did not attempt to replace an ailing intellectual system of theology by setting up new systems of knowledge or alternative fixed places of power. For de Certeau, mysticism subverted this very way of thinking. Rather, mysticism pointed toward a quite different approach to the Christian tradition. This was to be not a set of structures or a body of doctrines but a practice, an action. The language of movement implies a continual transgression of fixed points. This approach to Christianity as a journey, practice, action, with its emphasis on variety rather than on organization or a dogmatic order, would seem to be drawn from de Certeau's membership in the Jesuit order and original immersion in Ignatian spirituality.[27] In de Certeau's use of the phrase "way of proceeding" there are clear echoes of Ignatius Loyola's language for the Jesuit way of life as *nuestro modo de proceder*.[28] Precisely because mystic language tentatively engages with the absolute, it can only "say" what is absolute or unbounded by, in de Certeau's words, "erasing itself."[29] Because the object of mystical texts is infinite, such a text is "never anything but the unstable metaphor for what is inaccessible." So, for de Certeau, the modern discipline of "mystics" "only assembles and orders its practices in the name of something that it cannot make into an object (unless it be a mystical one)."[30]

For de Certeau, the subversive quality of mysticism is represented by the theme of perpetual departure or transgression. There is a close relationship between the post-Enlightenment modernist emphasis on objective knowledge and issues of power. In this context de Certeau suggested that those people (the mystics) whose lives witnessed to the otherness of an essentially mysterious God were outsiders to the modernist project.

> Unbeknownst even to some of its promoters, the creation of mental constructs…takes the place of attention to the advent of the Unpredictable. That is why the "true" mystics are particularly suspicious and critical of what passes for "presence." They defend the inaccessibility they confront.[31]

> As early as the thirteenth century, that is, since the time when theology became professionalised, spirituals and mystics took up the challenge of the spoken word. In doing so, they were displaced toward the area of "the fable." They formed a solidarity with all the tongues that continued speaking, marked in their discourse by the assimilation to the child, the woman, the illiterate, madness, angels, or the body. Everywhere they insinuate an "extraordinary": they are voices quoted—voices grown more and more separate

from the field of meaning that writing had conquered, ever closer to the song or the cry.[32]

De Certeau's interest in sixteenth- and seventeenth-century mysticism arose from the parallels he perceived between this period and his own late twentieth-century world when words, especially those of scripture, could no longer be spoken to believers in the old ways. The world was increasingly seen as opaque and unreadable. In response to this spiritual disenchantment the people we refer to as mystics sought to invent a different kind of place, one that was not a fully formed or complete place at all. As de Certeau says himself, this "is only the story of a journey" that is necessarily fragmented and ultimately defies conclusive investigation. In his somewhat opaque words, "it overpowers the inquiry with something resembling a laugh."[33] Mystical literature offers routes to whoever paradoxically "asks directions to get lost" and seeks "a way not to come back."[34]

> The various strains of *mystics*, in their reaction to the vanishing of truths, the increasing opaqueness of the authorities and divided or diseased institutions, define not so much a complementary or substitutive knowledge, topography, or entity, but rather a different treatment of the Christian tradition....[T]hey institute a "style" that articulates itself into *practices* defining a *modus loquendi* and/or a *modus agendi*.... What is essential, therefore, is not a body of doctrines (which is the effect of these practices and above all the product of later theological interpretation), but the foundation of a field in which specific procedures will be developed.[35]

Mysticism and Social Practice

The initial impression is that the writings of de Certeau concerning mysticism not only make it marginal but also privatize it. Indeed it is precisely an act of withdrawal from social "space" that gives rise to a definable "mystic" in the sense defined by de Certeau. "A prophetic faith organised itself into a minority within the secularised state."[36] In de Certeau's words, any ambition by the Roman Catholic Church after the Council of Trent to "reconstitute a political and spiritual 'world' of grace" ultimately failed. While de Certeau describes the movement of spirituality to the cultural margins and its redistribution among mystic groups utilizing new kinds of discourse, his understanding of "mysticism" is always as a social rather than purely personal, interior reality. In fact de Certeau differs from many other twentieth-century commentators on mysticism precisely by *not* stressing individual mystical experiences in isolation but treating them as social phenomena. Mysticism is social not merely passively (that is, by being a reflection of a particular historical context) but also *actively* in that it affects and transforms the world and even self-consciously in that the major mystics set out to create new forms of discourse and new religious groups.[37]

While the overall location or "site" of mystic literature in this period should not be oversimplified, Michel de Certeau suggested that there were "privileged places" for the development of mystical insight and practice within certain social categories. These categories comprised people with little or no power in the public world. De Certeau noted that mysticism seemed to be closely related to forms of instability or social disinheritance. Thus the rise of mystic literature often reflects the decline of a society based on various ideologies of stability— social, economic, and religious. Mystics tended to appear in the

> social categories which were in socio-economic recession, disadvantaged by change, marginalised by progress, or destroyed by war....Aside from a few mystics on the road to social promotion...the majority of them...belonged to social milieux or "factions" in full retreat. Mysticism seems to emerge on beaches uncovered by the receding tide.[38]

In de Certeau's analysis, mystics were people who existed socially, culturally, or religiously on boundaries. He noted especially the sixteenth-century Spanish mystical movement where an unusual proportion of the most significant figures came from the marginalized social class of *conversos* or Christianized Jews. These include Teresa of Avila, Luis de Leon, and two figures central to the early Jesuits, the second General, Diego Lainez, and Ignatius Loyola's secretary, Juan de Polanco.[39]

Sometimes mystics actively associated themselves with contexts of "nothing." This was a radical response to a fundamental situation of loss. De Certeau mentions two features. First, some mystics made the symbolic gesture of entering a corrupt religious community to seek the birth of a new beginning within the "nothing" or, as de Certeau put it, "a repetition of a founding surprise." Thus Teresa of Avila entered a decadent Carmel and Ignatius Loyola committed himself to religious life even though overall it was an institution in decline. Second, some members of the spiritual and social elite (for example, the circle of Bérulle in seventeenth-century France) actively sought to associate themselves with the poor, the simple, and the illiterate. As de Certeau put it, they sought to leave behind traditional sources of authority in order "to turn to the exegesis of 'wild' voices."[40]

Mysticism and Christian Discipleship

We should remember the relationship between de Certeau's interest in mysticism and the way he understood himself to be attempting to speak as a Christian in a twentieth-century world where institutional Christianity was no longer seen as a context of definitive meaning. A critical question for de Certeau concerned how we can continue to believe when Christian faith no longer has a distinctive place. In the end, after examining various models, he suggested that there is no *theoretical* construct available to describe Christian identity definitively. What is left is the age-old tension between discipleship (following), and conversion (change). The believer is one called to follow faithfully, almost in blind faith.

> As the ecclesial "body of sense" loses its effectivity, it is for Christians themselves to assure the articulation of this "model" with actual situations. This "model" refers to the New Testament combination of "following [Jesus]" and "conversion."…The first term indicates a going beyond which the name of Jesus opens up, the other a corresponding transformation of consciousness and of conduct.[41]

For de Certeau, Christians are called to wander, to journey with no security apart from a story of Jesus Christ that is to be "practiced" rather than objectively asserted.[42] This Christian practice is profoundly disruptive of all social systems. De Certeau characterized the whole Christian tradition, as well as specifically mystical withdrawal, as a "way of proceeding"—in other words, not as an institution but rather as movements or pilgrimages across fixed locations of power. Indeed, Christian spirituality must avoid the temptation to settle down into a new and definitive "place."

> The temptation of the "spiritual" is to constitute the act of difference as a site, to transform the conversion into an establishment, to replace the "poem" [of Christ] which states the hyperbole with the strength to make history or to be the truth which takes history's place, or, lastly, as in evangelical transfiguration (a metaphoric movement), to take the "vision" as a "tent" and the word as a new land. In its countless writings along many different trajectories, Christian spirituality offers a huge inventory of difference, and ceaselessly criticises this trap; it has insisted particularly on the impossibility for the believer of stopping on the "moment" of the break—a practice, a departure, a work, an ecstasy—and of identifying faith with a site.[43]

In de Certeau's terms, the particularity of the event of Jesus Christ is the measure of all authentic forms of Christian discipleship in the sense that they presuppose that event but are not simply identical repetitions of it. In a sense, the particularity of the event of Jesus Christ "permits" the contextual nature and the particularity of all subsequent discipleship. There, too, God may eternally say "yes" to us without condition. For de Certeau, however, the primary symbol of discipleship is now an empty tomb.[44] "He is not here; for he has been raised, as he said...indeed he is going ahead of you to Galilee" (Matt 28:6–7). God in Jesus cannot be pinned down to any here and there, to this and that. The place of Jesus is now perpetually elusive. He is always the one who has gone before us. To be in the place of Jesus, therefore, is literally to be "disciples," that is, to be those who "follow after" in the direction of Jesus' perpetual departure.

Again, to adopt the language of de Certeau, discipleship simultaneously demands a "place" and an "elsewhere"—or a "more." It is impossible to grasp the heart of de Certeau's perspective without detailed attention to his Jesuit roots and lifelong preoccupation with the Ignatian mysticism of "practice" especially through the medium of his work on the life and writings of the seventeenth-century Jesuit mystic Jean-Joseph Surin. This mysticism of practice offered de Certeau among other things the language of a quest for the *magis*, the *semper maior*, the "always more," the greater glory of God that is always beyond where we are at any moment. Hence the spiritual value of journey and the transgression of boundaries, always exceeding limit in search of "what is more."

> Within the Christian experience, the boundary or limit is a place for the action that ensures the step from a particular situation to a progress (opening a future and creating a new past), from a being "there" to a being "elsewhere," from one stage to another....A particular place—our present place—is required if there is to be a departure. Both elements, the place and the departure, are interrelated, because it is the withdrawal from a place that allows one to recognize the enclosure implicit in the initial position, and as a result it is this limited field that makes possible a further investigation. Boundaries are the place of the Christian work, and their displacements are the result of this work.

And again:

> In order to pass from one place to another, something must be *done* (not only *said*) that affects the boundary: namely, *praxis*. It is this action which transcends, whereas speeches and institutions circumscribe each place successively occupied.[45]

Thus, paradoxically, the radical social role of both Christian practice and specifically of mysticism is to become non-places, disruptive acts of resistance at the heart of all systems and attempts at definitive statements about the nature of reality.

Mysticism as a Fable

De Certeau wrote in terms of the "mystic fable." This implies that mysticism is a "fable" in the sense that it cannot claim the status of defin-

121

itive truth. It is a language without obvious power. Yet paradoxically, that is its strength. It calls into question strategically defined, and apparently definitive, systems of meaning. Christian believers are called in this postmodern age to become wanderers once again who are always departing from a temptation to remain static and fixed in response to the call of Christ to follow, without power, authority, or even secure identity. The Christian community carries the "fabled" tale of Christ, which subverts all human fixities, across an alien territory toward the unnameable reality that we call "God." De Certeau suggests that religious discourse is always in danger of being shattered. "Faith speaks prophetically of a Presence who is both immediately felt and yet still to come, who cannot be refused without a betrayal of all language, and yet who cannot be immediately grasped and held in terms of any particular language."[46]

The intellectual assumptions of modernity place a powerful emphasis on intelligibility, not least that of God language. Because of this, de Certeau sees those people whose lives affirm the elusiveness and essential "otherness" of God as outsiders to the modern project.[47] Echoing the thoughts of de Certeau, David Tracy suggests that mystics, like the mad, represent a kind of "otherness" on the social margins. This "otherness" has an active quality. It has the capacity to challenge traditional centers of power and privilege.[48] Perhaps this is why de Certeau was fascinated throughout his life by the writings of Jean-Joseph Surin (whom he called "my guardian"). Surin was for many years also profoundly disturbed psychologically and consequently isolated and oppressed.[49] Because the way of "knowing" present in mystical texts is based on union with God rather than on the power of the human intellect to control reality, it bears some resemblance to what Michel Foucault called "subjugated knowledges." This way of knowing resists dominant structures of power and knowledge and opposes established forms of discourse rather than simply offering a pleasing alternative.[50]

Mysticism: Never-Ending Quest

It appears that at the end of Michel de Certeau's life his approach to "spirituality" in the broad sense eventually became detached from institutional religious faith and perhaps from conventional faith as it dispersed into the "practice of everyday life." Spirituality was not so much the "ecstasy" of a religious mystic but a more tentative self-transcendence experienced in a succession of fragmented encounters with everyday "others." Yet, the question remains: Is the enigmatic and poignant last page of the first volume of de Certeau's unfinished *The Mystic Fable* merely a nostalgic lament by a person who no longer has religious faith? Or was it, perhaps, that de Certeau was expressing, in his typically enigmatic way, the necessary pain of *theological* denial? Was his "agnosticism" that of a person who (like the mystics he studied) realizes that he cannot escape the never-ending journey of the human spirit beyond definable intellectual goals or spiritual desires that can definitively be named? For if, as seems more likely, deep desire and a kind of faith remained at the heart of de Certeau, the inner logic of his thinking surely demanded that "the Other" whom we continually seek is necessarily "absent" from the contingent world of the tangible and definable.

> He or she is a mystic who cannot stop walking and, with the certainty of what is lacking, knows of every place and object that it is *not that*; one cannot stay *there* nor be content with *that*. Desire creates an excess. Places are exceeded, passed, lost behind it. It makes one go further, elsewhere. It lives nowhere.[51]

7
THOMAS MERTON AND TWENTIETH-CENTURY SPIRITUALITY
Seeking an Authentic Self

Thomas Merton has been described as arguably the greatest Catholic spiritual writer of the twentieth century. He merited this description partly because he touched not only the hearts of Roman Catholics but also embraced a more open vision of catholicity beyond the limits of a single institution.[1] In the sense defined by David Tracy, Thomas Merton can be described as a "spiritual classic." We usually think of classics in terms of a written text. While all theological or spiritual texts are culturally and historically conditioned, some of them have the capacity to cross the boundaries of time or place and retain, or even increase, their popularity and importance in contexts very different from their origins. These are what we call "classics." "Classics" disclose something that remains compelling, continue to challenge us, and bring us into transforming contact with what is enduring and vital in the Christian tradition. In general, the strength of classics is that they do not merely offer us information but are capable of persuading and moving us to a response.[2]

Merton as Spiritual Classic

As noted earlier, David Tracy suggests the following about "classic texts."

> First, there exists a qualitative difference between a classic and a period piece; second, there exists an assumption that a

classic, by definition, will always be in need of further interpretation in view of its need for renewed application to a
particular situation; third, a classic, again by definition, is
assumed to be any text that always has the power to transform the horizon of the interpreter and thereby disclose new
meaning and experiential possibilities.[3]

How can Merton be a classic? Well, for Tracy, the category of a classic is not limited to written texts but is extended to include certain key
people who achieve across time some kind of paradigmatic status in reference to the Christian tradition. Thus, Thomas Merton may be thought
to be as much of a classic text as the *Showings* of Julian of Norwich.

Why do I consider Merton to be a twentieth-century classic? Precisely because there are so many Thomas Mertons; during and after his
lifetime people have been able to identify with a range of different aspects
of his personality, his insights, and his vision. Alister McGrath, the
English Protestant theologian at Oxford, can highlight Merton's contribution to the reintegration of spirituality and theology.[4] On the other
hand Sandra Schneiders, the American Catholic biblical scholar and
feminist theologian, takes the view that Merton's attempts to articulate
the contemplative life in the theological categories of his day (e.g., in *The
Ascent to Truth*, his study of John of the Cross) were a failure and that his
effectiveness arose from the fact that he subsequently preferred literature,
poetry, and autobiography as better fitting the subject matter.[5] Others,
such as David Tracy, already mentioned, or the Dutch theologian Kees
Waaijman, focus on Merton's openness to other world faiths and his special contribution (along with Raimundo Panikkar, Enomiya-Lasalle, and
Bede Griffiths) to bringing world spiritual traditions into dialogue with
each other and to showing how spirituality—especially the contemplative
way—possesses a special potential to create space for fruitful interreligious
encounter. Tracy refers to Merton as a prophetic figure of the "new ecumenism" where a closed Christian theological system is rethought and
rediscovered in the process of discovering "the other."[6]

Merton the Wanderer

I fully admit that what I wish to focus on is equally partial. For me, as for the great monastic scholar Dom Jean Leclercq, Merton's importance and continued popularity are linked to the fact that he both symbolized *and* addressed a time of critical transition in the West—religious, cultural, and political—that began with World War II. So, in Merton several worlds meet: a Western Church in process of renewal (reaching a particular peak in the Second Vatican Council), the rediscovery by the West of Eastern Christianity, the discovery by Christianity of other world religions—particularly Buddhism—plus a range of political and social movements of change and critique.[7]

This is not to say that Merton's continued impact has nothing to do with the quality of the man himself or of his spiritual wisdom. At least equally, however, it tells us a great deal about the spiritual climate in the English-speaking world in the last half of the twentieth century and today. Jean Leclercq focused on Merton's iconic role in a time of cultural and religious transition. In a real sense, Merton is a paradigm of the late twentieth-century spiritual quest. In particular, he stands for the movement outward from a spirituality of excessive interiority—ecclesiocentric and world-rejecting—to embrace the outer quotidian world and to encounter "otherness" in all its forms. There is a clear development from the traditional pre–Vatican II spirituality of *The Seven Storey Mountain* (1948) to the sympathetic and committed observations on the public world in *Conjectures of a Guilty Bystander* (1966).

As in the title of Anthony Padovano's book *The Human Journey: Thomas Merton, Symbol of a Century*,[8] it is the idea of the wanderer that most often comes to mind in reference to Merton. It is, I believe, the way in which Merton reflects the late-modern (or some would say, postmodern) spiritual and intellectual pilgrim that resonates with Western people seeking to make sense of a world in which they sit uneasily after Hiroshima and Auschwitz. In strange ways, Merton reminds me of the comparisons between mystics and postmodern wanderers in the later writings on mysticism by the maverick Jesuit and French intellectual Michel de Certeau, who, much more overtly than Merton, chose by the end of his life to stand on the margins of the Christian Church.

All mystics, according to de Certeau, are "drunk with desire"— drunk, that is, with what they do not possess. Because of this, they merit the name given to the seventeenth-century mystic Angelus Silesius, that is, *Wandersmann*, the wanderer.

> He or she is a mystic who cannot stop walking and, with the certainty of what is lacking, knows of every place and object that it is *not that;* one cannot stay *there* nor be content with *that.* Desire creates an excess. Places are exceeded, passed, lost behind it. It makes one go further, elsewhere. It lives nowhere. It is inhabited, Hadewijch also said, by a noble *je ne sais quoi*, neither this nor that, that leads us, introduces us to and absorbs us in our Origin.[9]

Seeking the Authentic Self

To a greater or lesser extent (explicit in *The Seven Storey Mountain, The Sign of Jonas*, and the diaries and implicit in many other works) auto-biography was Merton's chosen medium for writing—even when the focus was not really himself but monasticism or contemplation or a spirituality of social engagement. This means that the reader of Merton is always a companion on his inner or outer life journey. Even at his most "specific" or settled, when baptized as a Catholic in 1938, Merton invited as baptismal witnesses three Jewish friends. That gesture carried forward with him his past but was also an intimation of the way that, even at his most Roman Catholic, the inherent openness to other traditions of belief and values was never lost.

There are different views of Merton's autobiographical style. Mary Jo Weaver is uncomfortable with Merton's tendency to "ask read-ers to find themselves in his story," in contrast to Augustine or Teresa of Avila whose autobiographical classics invite the reader rather to see "the mysterious action of God in their lives."[10] Although she does in the end believe that Merton is a spiritual giant, this is almost despite, rather than because of, his preoccupation with "the self" and the jour-ney from inauthenticity to authenticity. In contrast, Lawrence Cunningham suggests that Merton's personal narrative style was an antirationalist (one might almost say postmodern) strategy.[11] That is, Merton was concerned to point out, through the use of narrative, that the Enlightenment, Cartesian, rationalist construction of the autonomous human ego was fatally flawed. In contrast he outlined the quest for a more authentic, healthy sense of the self. For this, the "fluidity" of personal narrative was an effective medium.

To my mind, it was actually Merton's preoccupation with the self that was in many respects his greatest attraction to the late-twentieth-century reader. He was the epitome of the contemporary preoccupation with a process of becoming, becoming our true selves. One of his most striking counterintuitive moves was to suggest, by his lifestyle as much as by his writing, that we need to step aside from the pressures and expectations of others, of society and of surrounding culture, in order to seek the mysterious depths of our heart within. Having said that, I think we need to be cautious. The self is not a prepackaged, predetermined "given" that merely has to be uncovered or discovered ready-made. Even if we believe, as the early monastic ascetics did, that our identity is the one given us by God, not by social convention or through self-creation, there is also a sense in which that God-given self is always in process of becoming—is, if you like, a self shaped from the very start by our outward relationships. God-given identity is not incarnated directly in some kind of self-contained private interiority but rather comes to be within the complexity of our relationships, both interpersonal and social.

If we follow the thoughts of Lawrence Cunningham, Merton can be seen as opposed to a false, empirical, exterior-superficial, solipsistic self which is the center of its own world. Like the Cartesian ego, such a self always fears uncertainty and the abyss. On the other hand, Merton positively sought another kind of self—the interior, hidden, real self—interior but at the same time a self capable of true dialogue and genuine encounter because it is not preoccupied with survival or self-importance.

This concern for the self and transformation actually illustrates very well the first of the two general points I now wish to make about Merton's contribution to spirituality, that is, his *countercultural stance*. What is countercultural about Merton's quest for "the self" is his growing conviction in the face of a prevailing individualistic culture that the self only truly exists *in communion*, in solidarity with others. One might say, too, that this self is also a *vulnerable* self, no longer protected behind walls of separation and spiritual superiority. That was one important aspect of his second "conversion experience" in downtown Louisville.

> This sense of liberation from an illusory difference [between monastic life and ordinary people] was such a relief and such a joy to me that I almost laughed out loud. And I suppose my happiness could have taken form in these words. "Thank God, thank God that I *am* like other men; that I am only a man among others." To think that for sixteen or seventeen years I have been taking seriously this pure illusion that is implicit in so much of our monastic thinking![12]

The Monk as Countercultural Icon

First of all, however, what do I mean by *countercultural?* When Merton published *The Seven Storey Mountain* in 1948, his presuppositions were in terms of dichotomies or polar opposites, especially monastery versus world. Although Merton acknowledged that humans are in the image of God, he believed that he (and implicitly, all of us) was a prisoner of sinfulness, self-centeredness, and violence. This viewpoint was symptomatic of a violent and fractured world in the violent and fractured age in which he grew up (recall, he was born in the midst of World War I and entered Gethsemani in the midst of World War II). So, at that point, "the world" was for Merton a human prison, framed by human egotism. In contrast, at the opposite pole, was "interiority," the mystical-contemplative life. This is what drew him to the Cistercians. The monastery was an "enclosed freedom" where people can learn how to be happy away from the flux and unreliability of the everyday world. For all that the book embarrassed the later Merton (and would be used by some traditionalist Catholics to try to imprison him in the image of the classic monk), there is no question that it laid the foundations for a commitment to an absolutely countercultural, counterintuitive relationship with God—what, in the more mature Merton, grew into a commitment to the renewal of the world in God.

By the time of *Life and Holiness*, published in 1964, he was writing in very different language:

The spiritual life is not a life of quiet withdrawal, a hot-house growth of artificial ascetic practices beyond the reach of people living ordinary lives. It is in the ordinary duties and labours of life that the Christian can and should develop his spiritual union with God....Christian holiness in our age means more than ever the awareness of our common responsibility to cooperate with the mysterious designs of God for the human race.[13]

As I have already mentioned, when Merton wrote *Conjectures of a Guilty Bystander* in 1966 he described in it a kind of second conversion experience during an earlier trip to Louisville (as he so precisely places it, "at the corner of Fourth and Walnut, in the center of the shopping district"). He was overwhelmed by a realization of his unity with and love for all the people on the sidewalks. This led him to a quite different, more vulnerable, sense of relationship to "the world." "It was like waking from a dream of separateness, of spurious self-isolation in a special world, the world of renunciation and supposed holiness. The whole illusion of a separate holy existence is a dream."[14]

Obviously, being countercultural could no longer stand for the simple polarizations of his original decision to enter Gethsemani and to embrace monastic life. Merton gradually came to understand the monk not as a person who withdrew from "the world" but as one whose contemplative solitude was to be understood as a radically "other" way of being *in* the world with a responsibility in and for that world. Part of his renewed countercultural, prophetic stance at this stage was actually to risk isolation and unpopularity not only from the great American public by his opposition to the Vietnam War and by his support for the civil rights movement but also from a section of the American Catholic Church (including some fellow monks) because of his rejection of his spiritual "pin-up" image.

The posthumously edited *The Asian Journal* offers some related insights into Merton's later understanding of the monk as a countercultural figure. First, in his final Bangkok paper[15] he suggests that "the monk is essentially someone who takes up a critical attitude towards the contemporary world and its structures." Then, in Appendix 4, the notes for a talk he gave in Calcutta, he offers three broad categories of the term *monastic*—which he intended to be inclusive enough to embrace world religions and people who, more generally, "lived in the spirit of monastic life." First, there is a certain distance or detachment from the secular concerns of a worldly life. Second, there is a preoccupation with the radical inner depths of one's religious or philosophical beliefs and their spiritual implications. Third, there is a special concern with inner transformation.

Fuga Mundi

This returns us to the very different kinds of countercultural stance. These particularly relate us to different understandings of what it means for a monk to adopt a "critical attitude towards the world and its structures." This in turn governs how we understand the notion of detachment and then approach the business of inner transformation. While Merton as he entered Gethsemani clearly saw withdrawal as a rejection of the world, conceived as evil and violent, he later came to realize that such an attitude completely undervalued the fundamental goodness of the created order—not to mention his own humanity. By 1966, Merton shared in the post–Vatican II debate about the public, worldly nature of faith. In an essay in *Commonweal* he suggested:

> To choose the world is not then merely a pious admission that the world is acceptable because it comes from the hand of God. It is first of all an acceptance of a task and a vocation in the world, in history and in time. To choose the world is to choose to do the work I am capable of doing, in collaboration with my brother, to make the world better, more free, more just, more liveable, more human.
>
> The world cannot be a problem to anyone who sees that ultimately Christ, the world, his brother and his own inmost ground are made one and the same in grace and redemptive love.[16]

To use the categories suggested by Richard Niebuhr in his book *Christ and Culture*, an analysis of different theological stances to the world and to history, Merton moved from the world-rejecting model of "Christ against culture" to the critical-conversion model of "Christ the transformer of culture."[17] A world-rejecting spirituality actually *undermines* an effective countercultural or counterintuitive witness. In the end, prophetic witness can arise only from the riskiness of a deep commitment rather than rejection, expressed in critical yet loving engagement with the everyday world.

The later Merton interpreted the classic monastic *fuga mundi* not as rejection of the everyday world or absolute withdrawal from it but rather as detachment from materialistic values and from whatever is world-centered. To be countercultural is, in this way of seeing things, to deny falsity and to affirm whatever is good and true in human living. If monasticism involves "changing places," both geographically and metaphorically, the move to the margins or monastic "distance" becomes a means of solidarity with social and political marginality. The monk is prepared to risk a loss of success, honor, and material acquisitions. Monastic "hiddenness" does not, however, mean a lack of visibility or a way of hiding away in self-protective isolation. Rather it implies an absence of self-promotion and disinterestedness in worldly accomplishment.

Fuga mundi, as a form of "standing on the edges," is not only a way of solidarity but also opens up the possibility of prophetic speech. Obviously this implies more than merely *saying* something—it is having something to say. In the title of his last self-prepared journal, the posthumously published diary for 1964–65, *A Vow of Conversation*,[18] Merton implies a play on the double meaning of the classic monastic vow (so difficult, so controversial to translate) *conversio*, or *conversatio morum*: a turning, a conversion, or a speech.[19] In the well-known 1981 edition of the Rule of St. Benedict it is noted that monastic copyists in earlier times preferred the simpler *conversio*.[20] That could imply that the vow stood simply for conversion of one's behavior. In Dom Cuthbert Butler's 1912 critical edition of the Rule, the text was changed back to what is now considered the original *conversatio*. In one sense, *conversatio* implies a way of life—or simply the monastic way. As the editors of the 1981 edition note,[21] however, it may be appropriate to link this, like the other vows, to certain things with which living under the Rule was intended to contrast. On this reading *conversatio* is what distinguishes the cenobitic monk from the unattached hermit. It implies living "in association with others" or even, as with Thomas Merton, living in "conversation."

In *The Sign of Jonas*, Merton records a discussion (1947) with the then abbot general of the Trappists, Dom Dominique Nogues, about the vow of *conversatio* where the abbot interpreted it as an ongoing quest to do always what is "more perfect."[22] Merton understood *conversatio* as central to the monastic way, implying as it did for him a commitment to progress in the contemplative-mystical life by "turning away" from the radically self-centered ego (a major preoccupation) and, also, as he progressed in monastic life, a "turning to" the world in order to engage in prophetic conversation with it.[23] The monk was one who listened first and only then spoke out. "Listening," "watching," "learning" lie at the heart of the Rule of St. Benedict. The very first word of the text is "Listen"! *Obsculta, o fili, praecepta magistri, et inclina aurem cordis tui*: "Listen carefully, my son, to the master's instructions and attend to them with the ear of your heart."[24]

The medieval historian and commentator on monastic spirituality Caroline Walker Bynum suggests that in medieval monasticism the notion that silence and solitude were preparations for meaningful speech is linked more to the Augustinian way of life (which had a pastoral emphasis summarized as *docere verbo et exemplo*, to teach by word and example) than to the Benedictine way. The evidence is slightly ambiguous, however, as there are some exceptions where Cistercian writers (and one Benedictine, Peter of Celle) appear to be attracted to the notions of concern for our neighbor and to the virtue of edification, *docere verbo et exemplo*.[25] Having said that, I think it fair to conclude that, historically speaking, "edification," "teaching," and "conversation" (at least, outside the monastic domain) were not generally understood as central monastic ideals in the tradition of the Rule of St. Benedict. In that sense, Merton's later writings represented a radically challenging (and to some people, questionable) reinterpretation of classic monastic spirituality. Merton came to see the hermit life attached to a cenobitic community as, at least for him, "what is more perfect" in the sense of Dom Dominique Nogues' interpretation of *conversatio*. This "more perfect" way was, however, a balance of solitude *and* communion, silence *and* speaking.

If the notion of being countercultural was my first theme, the connection between mysticism or contemplation and social transformation is my second and related theme. According to the Merton scholar William Shannon, the conflict between contemplation and action is "supposed" and a pseudo-problem.[26] The difficulty is that the contrast between the two has a long pedigree and has frequently been incarnated in certain versions of monastic spiritual writing. For David Tracy, Thomas Merton is one of the key figures who mark the transition within the Catholic spiritual tradition toward what Tracy calls "a new paradigm for Catholic spirituality: a mystico-prophetic model."[27] A major part of the (pseudo) problem has been a historical tendency to adopt an unbalanced rhetoric of interiority and to misunderstand what is implied by the "turn inward."

There has been a tendency to blame St. Augustine for initiating the prioritizing of interiority. Yet for St Augustine and other classic spiritual teachers the concept did not imply the same thing as its does in our modern era. The dangerous *rhetoric* of interiority, creating a dichotomy between inner and outer life, affected approaches to spirituality most acutely over the last two hundred years or so. This resulted from the influence of aspects of Enlightenment thinking (the priority of Descartes' autonomous thinking self, *Cogito, ergo sum)* and the impact of late nineteenth-century psychology that led to a fascination with personal subjective "religious experience." In writings on the pre-Conquest civilizations of Mexico, Merton eloquently expressed the state of this post-Enlightenment isolated "ego":

> For us, our 'self' tends to be 'realized' in a much more shadowy, abstract mental world [than 'archaic' people's sense of identity], or indeed in a very abstract and spiritualised world of 'soul'. We are disembodied minds seeking to bridge the gap between mind and body and return to ourselves through the mediation of things, commodities, products and implements.[28]

If we survey the Western spiritual tradition as a whole, "interiority" does not necessarily imply something inherently private, individualistic, and detached. Indeed, the heart of Christian spirituality may be expressed in terms of a tension between "interiority" and "exteriority"—between the mystical-contemplative and transformative practice (the prophetic).[29] It was a desire to reinstate this dialectic that so strongly influenced the later Merton.

Contemplation and Social Transformation

Although Merton's ways of expressing a reconnection of the contempla-
tive-monastic way with social transformation are uniquely his, and very
much of his time, he is far from isolated in the long tradition of Western
mysticism. Contemplative mysticism has often been interpreted as the
most radically interior form of Christian spirituality, yet the classic contemplative-mystical texts, properly understood, do not support this
viewpoint. Evelyn Underhill suggests in her classic book *Mysticism*[30] that
one defining characteristic of Christian mysticism is that union with
God impels a person toward an active, outward, rather than purely passive, inward life.[31] The most substantial representatives of Western mysticism were opposed to private experience. Underhill cites, among others,
the great Cistercian Bernard of Clairvaux. But Underhill's favorite, the
fourteenth-century Flemish writer John Ruusbroec, conceived the contemplative life as the life common to all. This common life joined created beings to one another in mutual service and thus harmonized the
initially distinct moments of action and contemplation. Thus the spiritually elevated person is also the common person:

> A person who has been sent down by God from these heights
> is full of truth and rich in all the virtues....He will therefore
> always flow forth to all who need him, for the living spring of
> the Holy Spirit is so rich that it can never be drained dry....
> He therefore leads a common life, for he is equally ready for
> contemplation or for action and is perfect in both.[32]

Ruusbroec was quite clear that people who practiced the attainment of peaceful inwardness as the goal of prayer and disregarded
charity or ethics were guilty of spiritual wickedness.[33] This chimes with
Merton's sentiments in, for example, *Conjectures of a Guilty Bystander*,
which so powerfully affirmed that solitude and solidarity are deeply
interconnected. In the language of Ruusbroec (incidentally, a monastic
founder as well as mystical theologian), a monastery is not an escape
from the "common life" (or, life common to all), but a way of sharing
in the life common to all.

As I have already suggested, Merton's later approach to the marginality of monasticism was a vulnerable act of solidarity with other

marginal people. The contemplative monk was a kind of social and political critic. Hardly surprisingly, given his literary bent, Merton also associated the marginality of monasticism with the kind of people who are a puzzle to a functional-materialistic culture, the artists and the poets. The later writings of Merton, while offering no clearly worked-out agenda for renewal, highlight a number of questions that can be asked about the future of monasticism. In the face of the possibility of simply absorbing or reflecting the prevailing cultural values, is monasticism able to maintain a spirit of resistance—to be creatively subversive—reflecting the disruptive presence of God in history? Will monasticism refuse to be bound by current convention and retain its prophetic freedom? Will monasticism be capable of standing for human solidarity against the privatization of life and the individualization of spirituality? Will monasticism be able to reinterpret its long tradition of "spiritual warfare" in terms of a struggle against the powers of darkness in the world? Finally, and vitally, will monasticism retain its visionary quality where the monk has a discerning, perceptive role? From "having a vision" the monk is called to learn how to "see truly" and by this to become an agent for the unmasking of illusion.

In one sense, such a view of the monk is deeply traditional. An important aspect of early monasticism was a desire to be freed from an identity provided by normal social-economic ties. Monastic disengagement from the start was a social and political statement as well as a theological one.[34] The lives of Anthony of Egypt and Simeon Stylites, representative figures respectively of Egyptian and Syrian-Palestinian asceticism, remind us that the holy men and women of the early Christian centuries did not leave social or public roles behind entirely. Especially in Syria, ascetics continued to live close to human habitation and remained visible challenges near where people lived. Their often wildly eccentric lifestyles (e.g., Simeon and others living on pillars) seemed deliberately to challenge convention.[35] In general, by standing both socially and geographically on the margins, the early ascetics were frequently accepted as spiritual guides and even at times took on the roles of local leadership or of social arbitrator.[36] In a sense, Merton seems to be offering a reinterpretation of this ancient role.

The contemplative, in other words, has a strange and paradoxical power to confront the world of false consciousness. For Merton the unmasking of illusion came to be the special mark of the monk or those who, more broadly, followed "the monastic way." Through solitude and inner struggle, the monk listens more deeply to the hidden voices of the world.[37] Merton was very struck by the meditations of Father Alfred Delp, the German Jesuit tortured and imprisoned by the Nazis. His comments on Delp show how he shared Delp's sense that solitude, silence, and contemplation were the contexts where the great issues facing humankind are worked through. Authentic contemplation confronts us with reality and Merton was clear that this bore no relation to the narcissism of a bogus interiority which is an evasion of conflict and struggle.[38]

The monastic way of speaking that arises from this contemplative listening bears a close resemblance to the sentiments expressed in the later writings of Merton's younger contemporary, Michel de Certeau. In his essay "The Weakness of Believing" (*La faiblesse de croire*) de Certeau suggests that in a world where the Church no longer dominates Western culture and where "strong" dogmatic statements are no longer heeded, the Christian is left to bear witness by faithfully following the way of Jesus as a prophetic "presence-in-the-world." Yet this weakness has a paradoxical power. The Christian (and, one might say, the monk) journeys with no security apart from the story of Christ which is enacted rather than dogmatically stated and yet, in its "performance," is profoundly disruptive.[39]

Finally, the intimate and necessary connection between contemplation and social engagement is perhaps most clearly and succinctly expressed in Thomas Merton's introduction to the Latin American edition of his writings (prematurely titled *Obras Completas!*) as early as 1958. Just three quotations will suffice.

Contemplation cannot construct a new world by itself....

But

Without contemplation we cannot understand the significance of the world in which we must act....

And finally

Without contemplation, without the intimate silent, secret pursuit of truth through love, our action loses itself in the world and becomes dangerous....

8

SPIRITUALITY AND RECONCILIATION
Catholicity and Hospitality

The origins of my commitment to reconciliation lie in personal experience and my subsequent reflection upon it.[1] First, I have been engaged with questions of religious reconciliation, particularly Roman Catholic–Anglican relations, for most of my life. This has not been merely a theological or professional involvement. Rather, it involves a strong personal commitment arising from childhood roots in a mixed Anglican–Roman Catholic family at a time when religious divisions in England were still sharply defined. This commitment to reconciliation broadened as I grew older. My first extended experience of interreligious encounter came during nearly a year studying in India in 1980–1981. In recent years this has also embraced some work in meetings of the three "Abrahamic faiths." Second, there was a growing realization that religious divisions inevitably mask some kind of social and cultural divisions, frequently solidified in political structures. Although this chapter largely derives from reflections on religious reconciliation, my experience is that it is impossible to be deeply concerned with this without a growing commitment to social reconciliation more broadly.

This chapter is essentially a manifesto for keeping faith with the vital importance of human reconciliation at a time when siren voices suggest that this is a hopeless task and that what is needed is protection from what threatens us by means of high walls or fences—whether metaphorical ones or the physical ones that divide Israeli from Palestinian, protect the United States from illegal immigration from Central America, or provide security-protected "gated communities" in cities worldwide. Against this, I hold strongly the unfashionable view that the complicated and challenging commitment to reconciliation is not only central to the inner life of the Christian Church but is also vital for an authentic Christian engagement with the wider world at the start of the twenty-first century.

Apart from my own mixed origins, why do I believe that reconciliation is so important humanly speaking as well as to what it means to be Christian? This is a theological question, for, as the South African theologian John de Gruchy suggests in his Cambridge Hulsean Lectures (in his case, strongly influenced by Karl Barth), the doctrine of reconciliation is "the inspiration and focus of all doctrines of the Christian faith."[2]

Over the years, I have become convinced of two things. First, consciously chosen separations and divisions within Christianity offer no real answer to the human problem of difference and disagreement. As a historian who originally specialized in the late Middle Ages and Reformation, I know full well that the separations at the Reformation did not produce some form of pure religion. For centuries it sadly encouraged in both Protestant and Catholic camps a dangerous mis-belief that what is contrary to the Spirit of God lies outside ourselves in a demonized or caricatured "other." St. Augustine's *City of God*, often cited as the manifesto of Christian separation from a sinful world, is no such thing. The tares and the wheat, as Augustine made clear, are destined to remain together until the end of time because we have no means of recognizing infallibly which is which.[3] Indeed, in our more honest moments we know that the tares and wheat actually coexist within each one of us.

Second, the world at large desperately needs to hear a new word about reconciliation. Christianity is called to speak such a word—precisely and unashamedly a theological-spiritual one. But a ruptured Church has little credibility in preaching reconciliation to a divided world. There is no point in *speaking* reconciliation unless we are manifestly committed to trying to live it ourselves in all its pain, ambiguity, and incompleteness. This is a counterintuitive message in a world so driven by the search for quick solutions, simple answers, and neat distinctions between good and bad, truth and falsehood.

The Words We Use

The words we use are important. So what does the word *reconciliation* imply? It is important to understand realistically the challenge, the knowledge we need, the actions to take, the likely process. A basic issue is whether reconciliation is the same as political models of conflict resolution. While I accept that conflict resolution is involved, reconciliation embraces more than strategies for changing systems. Several words are often treated as interchangeable: reconciliation, conciliation, and accommodation. Conciliation is associated with pacifying or placating. This lowers the temperature but does not necessarily promote deep change. For example, many peace negotiations aim to conciliate but fail to transform people at the deepest level. This leaves long-standing problems that will inevitably reemerge in other guises. Accommodation or tolerance enables the establishment of pragmatic arrangements, compromise, and a kind of parallelism. Reconciliation goes far deeper, however, as it suggests harmony and concord. Interestingly the *Oxford English Dictionary* defines reconciliation not merely as the restoration of harmony but also as "the reconsecration of desecrated places." If you like, all those people whose lives are marginalized by what we do or say in times of conflict are "desecrated places" because their unique value and identity as images of God are denied.

How far can we deal with reconciliation in a universal way? While the word has a general definition, its reality is always in terms of particularities and complexities. In South Africa, Northern Ireland, and the Holy Land religion played a formative role in the fracture of political life and a vital role in structures of injustice. In South Africa and Ireland, religion also played an effective role in the struggle for change. Yet, even though South Africa's Truth and Reconciliation Commission offers an inspiration to the Northern Ireland peace process (and Northern Ireland politicians are now in turn invited into other situations of conflict), everything nevertheless remained contextual. Simple translations from one context to another are impossible. Equally, conflicts are never reducible to one level of analysis. It is therefore unhelpful to juxtapose competing and reductionist explanations—for example, the Middle East is fundamentally a religious problem or fundamentally a political problem. In the Anglican–Roman Catholic ecumenical dialogue, for example, it is patently clear that even the theological and historical perceptions differ in different contexts (for example, in Rome and in England). Equally, even here the issues are not purely theological. A purely theological approach tends to interpret ecumenical problems as primarily a matter of changes in *understanding*. A fuller appreciation of history, however, soon reveals a complexity of social, political, economic, cultural, and even ethnic inequalities. Thus, in England, religion was used across several centuries to justify social discrimination and the political marginalization of Roman Catholics and other dissenters. Conversely, the established Church of England was accorded legal privilege, social advantage, and material rewards. It still remains a perversely contentious issue as to whether the Act of Succession, which prevents the monarch from either being a Roman Catholic or marrying one, should or indeed can be repealed. Any analysis or attempt to map strategies for reconciliation is bound to be complex.

Costly Reconciliation

Reconciliation, first of all, implies a complex balance between structural change and spiritual harmony.[4] No change of emotional climate can take place without structural change, yet structural change alone cannot guarantee reconciliation. In addition, the process of reconciliation is evolutionary.[5] A knowledge of history and of contemporary reconciliation processes suggests that long-term and deeply rooted reconciliation cannot be achieved without mutual repentance and the discovery of common ground. It is important to avoid quick or "cheap reconciliation" without truth-telling and justice. To appreciate the full complexity of reconciliation, a number of difficult questions need to be faced at the outset of a process to which protagonists are likely to have different instinctive responses. First, what exactly is to be reconciled? Are there two equally valid but opposing views, or are there issues of moral right and wrong? If the latter is the case, neutrality and consensus-building alone would be unethical and politically misplaced. Second, what is "justice" in this situation? All parties may agree that justice is important but see its reality very differently depending on their place in the prevailing power system. Third, is violence endemic in the current social and political system? Is readjustment sufficient or must a whole system be dismantled? Fourth, what is the true nature of the conflict? Is it religious, political, social, cultural, or a mixture of all of these? Conflict always involves issues of power, and so reconciliation implies a gradual redistribution of power in all sectors of life that cannot just be theoretical.

This leads me to the critical thought that reconciliation can only be *between equals.* A sharp question for protagonists on all sides of a conflict is whether they are capable of learning how to think of those with whom they disagree as their equals, morally, theologically, humanly, and before God. The uncomfortable reality is that reconciliation results from *making equal space for "the other."* This is different from tolerance, which can simply promote a series of parallel yet carefully protected spaces. This is a structural issue, but it is also a theological and spiritual issue. At the heart of reconciliation lies an initial belief that everyone is diminished by the situation we seek to change. So, the quest is for new ways of collaboration that will empower everyone. Historically, it is worth recalling that the changed relationship between Roman Catholics and Anglicans in England relied on two long-term factors. There was a gradual equalizing of perceptions whereby the opening of the universities to non-Anglicans led slowly to the creation of a common cultural discourse. Associated with this was a gradual equalization of status that was partly dependent on the first. The presence of Roman Catholics in higher education slowly eroded some of the most significant social distinctions between them and Anglicans.

Excluding Otherness

Reconciliation demands that everyone has to modify his or her view of the world and to risk the way he or she self-identifies, because people so often identify themselves "over against" something or another group. We tend to handle "otherness" by different strategies of exclusion. So, for example, we demonize others—we fear those who are different and seek to eliminate them. Our desire is that they surrender or die away.

Alternatively we colonize others—we think of them as inferior and to be pitied. They become objects of our charity or our attempts to control them. Frequently, we generalize about others by taking care not to see

142

them as individuals, but only as a type. Our desire is to keep control of the situation and not have to deal with the challenge of a personal encounter. A common strategy is to trivialize—we ignore disturbing differences and domesticate the strangeness by allowing some others to become honorary members of our club. Our desire is to be not challenged by their presence but affirmed as good people for allowing them to join us. Another version is to homogenize the situation—we say that there is no real difference at all. In a well-meaning way, we make premature pleas for tolerance and closure. Finally, we may ignore others—we simply make "the other" disappear by not acknowledging them at all.

Fear and Loathing

Underlying the various strategies for excluding "otherness" is some element of fear and loathing. This is manifestly the case in acute contexts of conflict and more subtly present in contexts where divisions have given way to tolerance but not reconciliation. Sadly, this has often been the case in varied forms of multiculturalism promoted in the Western world that have not addressed the deeper questions involved in renegotiating a sense of the "common good." Racism, often allied to religious-cultural suspicion, lurks just below the surface ready to re-emerge in situations of social or economic pressure or in response to isolated violence by extremists. Fear is one of the most powerful currents in our contemporary world. Ongoing religious or ethnic divisions, as well as the notorious, global "war on terror" since the events of 9/11, suggest how fear and its close associate anger shape our responses and cripple our ability to respond effectively to the deeper needs of fellow humans. The overwhelming imperative then becomes the satisfaction of emotional needs posed by fear and anger. We tend to rush toward emotionally satisfying but actually superficial actions—politically we create places to detain dissidents, expel illegals, or religiously marginalize certain voices without addressing the deeper challenges. Fear and anger are among the greatest spiritual blocks to effective corporate discernment and good choices.

Fear and unacknowledged anger tend to promote evasion, hiding, and paralysis, and work in three ways. First, both provide a narrative structure to answer the question of why we are in a mess. This needs a clear plot and a plausible cast of goodies and baddies. The story line must be big enough to provide a convincing description of our fear, which usually means that the threat is greatly inflated. Such narratives offer emotional reassurance on several levels. They affirm that it is understandable that we are afraid; that we are on the side of good versus evil; that good (meaning our perception of good) will prevail. Second, anger and fear respond to our desire for uncompromising clarity. When we are fearful, we want to know who is on our own side, and we want loyalty to be unconditional rather than complex. Everyone is assigned a label. "We stand for what is just and right. They need to change their ways (or repent). You need to be tougher and exercise proper authority." Nowadays, there is a growing tendency to escape into willful ignorance—people do not *want* to understand otherness if understanding is not straightforward. Third, fear and anger prompt a desire to bond with the apparently like-minded. There is much talk of forging alliances and of shared values. The quest for meaningful identity in such an oversimple sense is always at risk, however, of buckling under the weight of too many hidden contradictions.

Spaces

Reconciliation involves "making space" for the other, not least historically. As I have illustrated in an earlier chapter, our historical narratives are never neutral, value-free, or "true" in some simple way. All histories are partial in that they are built on what is included and excluded. A critical question for every human community, including the Church, is what kind of historical sense do we foster or live by? Humans tend to rehearse a particular version of history as the justification for maintaining barriers of separation.

Every conflict leaves scars. A process of reconciliation must make space for *memory*. The Latin word *memoria* has connotations of mindfulness. This relates both to attentiveness (to people, contexts, and my own reality) and to "embracing the whole" (the fundamental meaning of catholicity) as opposed to a comfortable and comforting forgetfulness. Reconciliation does not mean forgetting but re-membering in a new way, in a new context where we learn how to create a new, common history and how to remember *together* rather than continue to trade memories in the same way that we trade blows. Space for memory enables communities as a whole to begin to come to terms with the truth of the past. To have to speak and to have to listen are profoundly transforming. Reconciliation involves the healing of memories, particularly of belittlement, rejection, and denial. Part of a process of healing is to realize the incompleteness of any one story when isolated from the other stories. So a space for memory also implicitly celebrates diversity. I will come to the question of making space *theologically* in the next sections.

Both the space for history and the space for memory essentially involve a process of growing into a shared vocabulary that ultimately cannot be imposed but that arises from shared life and shared experience.

Christian Reconciliation

There are specifically Christian characteristics to reflections about reconciliation. It is not simply a political or psychological word with some incidental theological-spiritual gloss. Protestantism tends to emphasize reconciliation between God and humanity as a result of the cross (see Rom 5:6–11), and Catholicism tends to emphasize how the love of God poured out upon us as a result of the divine-human reconciliation creates a new humanity in which the walls of division between people are broken down (see 2 Cor 5:17–20; 6:1). In my own view, both dimensions need to be held in tension. Interhuman reconciliation is not simply a matter of giving each person his or her due but is really to give God *God's* due, by building a world and a Church that God's all-embracing forgiveness demands.

Catholicity and God

A key word in relation to reconciliation is "catholicity," which fundamentally relates to the nature of God.[6] Catholicity is not a denominational word but something all Christian traditions affirm about the nature of the Church. The way we describe the Christian community, however, is founded upon a particular understanding of God. We may suggest that only God is "catholic" in the fullest sense. That is, God alone embraces the "mystery of the whole." What do we learn about catholicity if we begin with God? This is a complex question that I can touch upon only briefly. God-as-Trinity speaks of a *koinonia* or com-

145

munion of mutually coinherent relationships in which the unique personhood of each is substantiated in mutuality.

Early Christian writers developed the theme that the *koinonia* between believers brought about by *koinonia* with Christ in the Spirit is a sharing in the very life of God. So, Paul (1 Cor 1:9) expresses gratitude for the Corinthians having been called by God into *koinonia* with Christ—often translated as "fellowship" but actually participation in the life of Christ. In 2 Corinthians 13:13 *koinonia* is a gift from the Spirit so that our life in common derives fully from our *koinonia* with Christ in the Spirit.

In other words, the implication of a trinitarian God for human existence is that God's presence-as-action is the source of, and goal of, the inner dynamism of every person. God may be said to ground every person in his or her particularity; however, the "catholicity" of God-as-Trinity not only grounds but also expands the inner dynamism of each person. If the Trinity expresses an understanding of God in which the particularity of the divine persons is shaped by mutual communion, the trinitarian presence within each of us underpins the uniqueness of particular identity yet at the same time subverts self-enclosure by orienting us to what is other. We might say that a trinitarian anthropology suggests an inherently transgressive rather than boundaried, individualized, and interiorized understanding of identity.[7] "Catholicity" implies giving space to everything and everyone that God gives space to.

Catholic People?

The notion of "catholicity" concerns how we "perform" Christianity. It implies "telling the whole truth," or "telling the whole story."[8] A vital part of that telling, beyond mere exposition or proclamation, consists in living what might be called catholic *lives*—that is, the way in which the fullness of God revealed in Jesus Christ is brought to realization in us. The catholicity of God-as-Trinity is expressed in time and space through the incarnation. Thus, the heart of the catholicity of the Church without which the concept remains insubstantial is the person of Jesus Christ. In Christ, "the whole fullness of deity dwells bodily, and you have come to fullness in him, who is the head of every ruler and authority" (Col 2:9–10). And "From his fullness we have all received, grace upon grace" (John 1:16). So the first element of catholicity is a *participation in God's catholicity in and through following Jesus Christ.*

We struggle with how "the whole story of Jesus Christ" is to be embodied in the particularities of our lives. I suggest that there are five key elements. First, becoming catholic is not at the most fundamental level a matter of affirming certain beliefs in an objective, intellectual sense, although belief is certainly part of the equation. It is a matter of people *living* Christ—in other words, a matter of how Jesus Christ's story of God-become-flesh, of the proclamation of God's kingdom, of the triumph of God-given life over suffering and death, is made present here and now in the lives of those who belong to the community of people bearing Christ's name. So a second fundamental element of catholicity is *being part of a people*, a universality of particularities, expressing unity in diversity by journeying with a family of faith that has integrity and yet is open to a God who cannot be confined within its boundaries. Third, this also implies *living in the stream of a tradition* in the sense of practicing a way of life shaped by the complex history of this community. The two foundational sacraments of baptism and Eucharist concern, among other things, incorporation into this people and this tradition. Becoming catholic concerns the process by which we enter into an Easter narrative of human existence.

Living within the "whole story" of Jesus Christ also implies coming to grips with the full story of our human existence, and so a fourth element of catholicity is that it is *all-embracing*. To "tell the whole story," however, is also a narrative of human incompleteness, failure, false aspirations—the ambiguity of lives that are both graced and sinful. The sacraments of baptism and Eucharist speak of this as well, and of the process of reordering the disordered, healing what is broken, reconciling what is alienated. Seeking catholicity implies the freedom to acknowledge a *whole* life in which our imperfections paradoxically become a foundation for receptive learning.

The notion of "becoming" is a crucial fifth element of catholicity. Becoming catholic is a process of hope, the hope of transformation that never ends within time and space. The whole truth of Jesus Christ is always *in process of being* realized in us. So, a fundamental quality of this vision of existence is expectancy. Expectancy implies knowing that there is always more and becoming ever more receptive to "the more" that we need. This receptivity is perhaps most sharply expressed in and through an engagement with people and communities that are unlike, other, strange, unnerving, and (if we recall some of the painful, even violent language used in inter-Anglican exchanges) even distasteful. By acknowledging that God, and the space God enables, is the fundamental reference point, catholicity is, in this sense, self-subverting in that it undermines its own tendency to become fixed and to proclaim its own self-sufficiency. This is perhaps counterintuitive.

The process of spiritual transformation that we name as holiness is precisely a movement of being drawn ever more deeply into the depths of God. This is inevitably, at the same time, a process of stepping into a way of unknowing or dispossession. Only by an engagement with the depths of God (who alone expresses "the mystery of the whole") may we ourselves be drawn into the mystery of catholicity. The Christian mystical tradition is a form of theological wisdom that reminds us of the limitations of our dogmatic certainties. As St. John of the Cross expressed it in his great text of mystical theology, *The Ascent of Mount Carmel*, to arrive at the mystery of the whole (God) or to possess "all" is not a matter of the accumulation of, or possession of, more and more particular things, even biblical, doctrinal, or moral truths. On the contrary, he emphasized a paradoxical theology of *dispossession* whereby the desire for more and more particular things (that by definition always remain less than the totality of all things—*todo* in John of the Cross's language) is stripped away in favor of union with the "all" that is God alone.

> To reach satisfaction in all
> desire its possession in nothing.
> To come to possess all
> desire the possession of nothing.
>
> To arrive at being all
> desire to be nothing.
> To come to the knowledge of all
> desire the knowledge of nothing.
> To come to the pleasure you have not
> you must go by a way in which you enjoy not.
> To come to the knowledge you have not

you must go by a way in which you know not.
To come to the possession you have not
you must go by a way in which you possess not.
To come to be what you are not
you must go by a way in which you are not....
(*The Ascent of Mount Carmel*, book 1, chap. 13, 11)[9]

Becoming Catholic: The Demands of Hospitality

In the context of all processes of reconciliation, it is important to realize that the quest for "the mystery of the whole" necessarily involves a sense that we continually need to receive. A receptive catholicity is not simply a matter of structures or doctrines but is at a deeper level an encounter of people—a conversation between different horizons that inevitably changes everyone in the process. The very process of engagement and conversation is revelatory in that we come to realize that God speaks not simply in *my* tradition (intratextuality) but in the very conversation and interaction that we share (intertextuality).

An important element of the ideal of catholicity is hospitality. Interestingly, the emphasis in both Hebrew and Christian scriptures is most strongly on hospitality to the stranger. In the Gospels, Jesus is frequently portrayed as the wanderer without a home (for example, Matt 8:20) or dependent on the hospitality of others (for example, Luke 9:58) or, in the Gospel of John, as the stranger in our midst (for example, John 8:14, 25 ff.). Hospitality to the stranger is presented as the vision of the Kingdom of God—and, indeed, has a bearing on our eternal destiny in Matthew 25. What is critical is that hospitality is not the same as assimilation of what is "other" into me. It is not a question of finding the last piece of the jigsaw that completes my lack or need—that ultimately gives me only what in a sense already belongs to me. Hospitality concerns the reception of what is strange and what *remains* strange or at least "other."

The Christian narrative of redemption describes the nature and destiny, alienation and glory, of humanity. It speaks of *alienation* (from God, from each other, and from creation) but also of how God overcomes alienation, redeeming humanity from the bondage of sin. The cross offers a new concept of reconciling love that risks everything, accepts death and rejection, and so enables the transformation of the unjust. The paradox is that it is out of weakness, rejection, and death that new life comes. Yet reconciliation is not yet experienced in its completeness—for the evil of human division remains a reality. For now there is an assurance, a confident hope that God will finally establish justice and peace. The Church, as prolongation of the mission of God, is called to embody proleptically the narrative of reconciliation.

In addition, reconciliation in Paul speaks of the one who is offended (God) as the one who takes the initiative in seeking an end to hostility. This contrasts with human assumptions that reconciliation should be initiated by "the offender" (whom every side is quick to identify) and that an admission of guilt and repentance are absolute *preconditions* of reconciliation. This naively presupposes a black-and-white world. A mutual commitment to enter a risky process of reconciliation as the first step may actually lead to the painful realization that the call to repentance is more complex and mutual than first anticipated. Christian reconciliation also challenges the notion that difference should be viewed purely as part of the human predicament. Trinitarian theology speaks powerfully of a God in whom difference is the foundation of existence. Ephesians also relates reconciliation to participation in the Church. A new covenant community becomes the carrier of the vision of a new humanity in which Jew and Gentile are reconciled as members of one body. What is it to "be in common"? Communion—existing in common—is more than a statement or definition, but equally it is also more than sentiment. It is, at its heart, an expression of the life of the Trinity. Precisely by struggling to *live this life* we share in God's work of reconciliation. Linking together Ephesians 2:11–22 with Galatians 3:23–29, Paul witnesses to a radical transformation of human status—the walls of enmity are broken down; those far off, even the enemy, are made near.

Spirituality of Reconciliation: The Rule of St. Benedict

In the final part of this chapter, I want to select two resources for what might be called a spirituality of reconciliation—first the Rule of St. Benedict (RSB) and second the Eucharist.

In my estimation, Benedictine spirituality has a great deal to offer in terms of the Christian vocation of reconciliation.[10] I simply want to

mention two words. First, the opening word of the Rule is "Listen!"—
Obsculta! This sets the tone for the whole Rule and its approach to the
Christian life. At the heart of reconciliation lies a commitment to listening. For this we need to learn silence, to cultivate attentiveness so
that we become capable of receiving what we are not and what we do
not have. Silence counteracts a rush to angry judgment and destructive
words. The Rule, of course, is full of scriptural quotations and resonances, and a broad analysis of the Bible shows that "listening" or
"hearing" takes precedence over activity. Listening, attentiveness, is
associated with true wisdom, and this, in turn, is connected not only
with our relationship to God but to the notion of obedience—obedience to the Rule but, by implication, to the community and its life
together. Listen contemplatively to your brethren, for here God speaks;
here is the "school of the Lord's service," a school of discernment and
wisdom. Listening implies giving oneself wholeheartedly rather than
conditionally to the common enterprise. And, finally, listening implies
being silent in order to learn or to be taught. Chapter 6, "On Silence"
(*De Taciturnitate*) reinforces this. The word used is *taciturnitas* not
silentium. That is, silence consists not merely in being quiet but being
sparing in what one asserts; being the opposite of domineering; keeping one's mouth firmly closed so that the evil thoughts or the lies in our
hearts may not issue forth. In this discipline, we may slowly be con-
verted to a gracious heart.

The spiritual quality of silence is closely related to reconciliation
because it implies a refusal to engage in polemic, which the Rule considers un-Christian. The Rule goes on to say that acceptable speech in
community should always be (i) modest, and (ii) reasonable. Other
monastic texts talk of silence as a necessary preparation for speech that
is meaningful rather than ill-thought-out.[11] Do not rush to speak, the
texts say, or to assert—above all, avoid speaking out of anger. But of
course there is a wrong kind of silence—refraining from speaking out.
By implication all *good* speech is informed by contemplation—of God
first but also, by extension, in a contemplative attentiveness to the
other. The point is that silence and listening are part of the process of
good communication.

Reconciliation is closely related to another key Christian virtue
taught by the Rule—hospitality. Rule Chapter 53: *Omnes supervenientes hospites tamquam Christus suscipiantur.* All are to be received as

Christ. But notice, the Rule goes on to say "for he himself will say, I was the stranger and you took me in." Christ is the stranger. This implies a deeper theology of hospitality than merely giving food and board to a passing visitor. Commentators have always noted the *omnes*—an inclusiveness linked particularly to *strangeness*, or we might say "otherness," in contrast to those who are "like us." *Supervenientes*, "those who arrive," underlines the point even more strongly. It literally means those who "turn up out of the blue." This is not, however, a question merely of those who did not warn us they were coming but those *who are a surprise to us* in a deeper and more disturbing sense. Close to the surface of the text is the understanding that Christian disciples are not to be choosy about whom they keep company with. And *hospites* is a nicely ambiguous word that can be translated as "strangers" as well as "guests." The former sense is reinforced by the reference to Matthew 25:35. Finally, *suscipiantur* literally means "to be received" but its deeper sense is to be *cherished*—the stranger turns into someone whom, while different, we learn to value as closely as if he or she were one of our own.

Spirituality of Reconciliation: The Eucharist

The heart of a Christian spirituality of reconciliation is the Eucharist. The catholicity of God is sacramentally expressed explicitly in the *koinonia* of believers filled with the Spirit of the Risen Jesus and shaped by the Eucharist. The Eucharist is not simply a practice of piety but the enactment of the special identity of Christian community. As such it is an *ethical* practice although not simply in the superficial sense that it provides an opportunity for a didactic form of moral formation.[12] It seems to me that the link between ethics and the Eucharist is intrinsic rather than extrinsic.[13] Ethics embodies a way of being in the world that is appropriated and sustained fundamentally in worship, especially the Eucharist. Conversely, the eucharistic enactment of catholicity necessarily opens the community to appropriate ways of living in the world.

A sacramental perspective on reality demands a reordering of the existential situation in which we exist. To live sacramentally involves setting aside a damaged condition in favor of something that is offered to us by grace, for "where we habitually are is not, after all, a neutral place but a place of loss and need" that needs to be transformed.[14] Part of this damaged reality consists of our flawed identities—whether these suggest that we are people of power or diminish us as people of no worth. The transforming dynamic of the Eucharist demands that the presumed identity of everyone be radically reconstructed. This necessitates honest recognition, painful dispossession, and fearless surrender as a precondition of reconciliation.

To enter the "space" of the Eucharist implies a radical transformation of human "location" such that it is no longer to be centered on the individual ego or on safe gatherings of the like-minded but discovered in being a-person-for-others. Every time the Eucharist is celebrated, all those who participate commit themselves to cross the boundaries of fear, of prejudice, and of injustice in a prophetic embrace of other people, without exception, in whom we are challenged to discover the real presence of an incarnate God.

> Reconciled in the Eucharist, the members of the body of Christ are called to be servants of reconciliation among men and women and witnesses of the joy of resurrection. As Jesus went out to publicans and sinners and had table-fellowship with them during his earthly ministry, so Christians are called in the Eucharist to be in solidarity with the outcast and to become signs of the love of Christ who lived and sacrificed himself for all and now gives himself in the Eucharist.[15]

The Eucharist is very much a landscape of memory—including ambiguous or conflicting memories. Beyond the immediate participants, there are wider and deeper narrative currents in all eucharistic celebrations. The central narrative, that is, the revelation of God's salvation in Jesus Christ, enables all human stories to have an equal place and yet at the same time reconfigures them. The eucharistic narrative makes space for a new history that tells a different human story beyond the selectivity of tribalism or sectarianism. It invites us to undertake the radical business of creating human solidarity and changing the status quo. Despite our various human attempts to regulate and control it, the Eucharist engages a power beyond the ritual enactments themselves to offer an entry point for the oppressed, the marginalized, and the excluded. The eucharistic action, according to its own inner logic, speaks radically of catholic "space" in the world of space and time. There is, therefore, a perpetual and uncomfortable tension between the sacramental practice of God's reconciliation and the many efforts of Christians to resist the logic of reconciliation. At the heart of the Eucharist is the continual reaffirmation and consolidation of personal and collective human identities initially brought about in baptism. Christian disciples are bound into solidarity with those they have not chosen or whose presence they have not negotiated and indeed would not choose of their own free will. Consequently, the new community, the new world, spoken of in baptism and the Eucharist is deeply subversive of humanly constructed social order.[16]

The Eucharist does not simply bind individuals to God in a vertical relationship or bind people to each other in another kind of purely social construction. We are bound to one another *en Christo*. And Christ, the head of the body, is to be found persistently on the margins among those who are the least in the kingdom of the world. The margins include those who are other, foreign, strange, dangerous, subversive—even socially, morally, or religiously distasteful in our eyes. Yet the Eucharist insists that humans find solidarity where they least expect it and, indeed, least want to find it. As discussed in chapter 2, we recall the story in his final *Testament* of Francis of Assisi's encounter with the despised and distasteful leper by means of which he passed from a romantic understanding of God's presence in the world to embrace God incarnate in the excluded "other."

The most challenging dimension of the Eucharist is the question of *recognition*. Whom do we recognize as our co-heirs with Christ, and whom are we able to respond to in the real presence of Jesus Christ? The core of the eucharistic notion of real presence, however one understands this, is *God's* critical recognition of us, God's affirming and life-giving gaze. All are incorporated solely because of God's recognition. The demands on those who practice the Eucharist are consequently more powerful than any notion of solidarity based solely on a social theory, however inclusive or just it seeks to be.[17]

An affirmation of "real presence" also stands in judgment on all our exclusions and negative judgments. A most challenging question is, Whom and what do we receive with Jesus? In receiving Jesus Christ the disciple receives at the same time all that makes up his Body. We find ourselves in communion not merely in some romantic way with the whole court of heaven, a communion of saints that safely visits us from elsewhere and represents merely the past and the future. We also find ourselves, if we dare to name it, in communion with the truly catholic "mystery of the whole" in present time and space as well. We know from the gospel narratives of the Last Supper that the catholicity of Jesus' act of incorporation included not only disciples like Peter who denied him but Judas who betrayed him. In Christ, the revelation of the transcendent God, those we prefer to exclude from communion with us in the public world are already uncomfortable ghosts at our eucharistic feasts.

Conclusion

My fundamental belief is that the Christian vocation of reconciliation lies at the heart of discipleship rather than being incidental to it. Being "in communion" with anyone at all is paradoxically both less than and more than complete harmony. It is a risky commitment to others within the economy of God's unconditional commitment to humankind, expressed by the struggle to stay together in difference, even in disputes, within a single "common house."

Any attempt at reconciliation demands sound discernment as much as institutional negotiation, but a climate of anger and despair inhibits the spiritual freedom needed for this. The long Christian tradition of discernment (*diakrisis* or *discretio*) teaches a process of prayerful and critical reflection on human experience as the basis for right choice and action. To be capable of discernment, we must have enough freedom to recognize the varied forces and emotions that influence us for what they are and to leave aside our prior judgments in order to defer to the movements of grace. This demands considerable Christian maturity.

> Spiritual discernment has arisen naturally and most necessarily for such a common life, because it reflects the pressure of a living truth—refusing partiality and bias, pushing beyond individual understanding, opening the discerning community to the creative, self-sharing life from which all truth springs.[18]

For St. Paul, discernment is a gift of the Spirit (1 Cor 12:10) and, like all genuine spiritual gifts, should be tested in terms of whether it builds up unity and a desire for the common good in the Christian community (1 Cor 12:7, 12 f.). Ignatius Loyola (1491–1556), a key figure in the discernment tradition and the author of the *Spiritual Exercises*, builds on ancient wisdom and helpfully identifies two kinds of spiritual influence that he calls "consolation" (which inclines us to the good) and "desolation" (which is ultimately destructive).[19] Discernment involves recognizing the energies that drive us, collectively as well as individually. "Collective desolation" is a phenomenon with a potentially destructive impact on a communal and social level that demands more attention than it sometimes receives. Sadly, it is all too easy to mistake strength of feelings for an indication of what should direct decisions. Paradoxically, "desolation" can initially feel attractive—even expressive of righteousness—yet in fact be evil appearing under the guise of the true and good.

> ...the evil angel, who takes on the appearance of an angel of light...brings good and holy thoughts attractive to...an upright soul and then strives little by little to get his own way, by enticing the soul over to his own hidden deceits and evil intentions.[20]

Behind this dated language lies the perception that even our best motives and commitments can be channeled in ways that are ultimately destructive, just as our capacity for love can be perverted. Loyola's wisdom was that no major choices should be made as a result of an experience of desolation as they could prove dangerously misguided.

Thus, a challenging question to all parties in a reconciliation process is what kind of energy has been released in the divisions of the past, what energies are released in both resistance to and commitment to a quest for reconciliation. Whatever one's views on the presenting political, theological, or ethical issues in situations of conflict, some responses to these are mixed with darker energies characteristic of Ignatian "desolation." These tend to undermine the Christian vocation of reconciliation, not least by suggesting that this is impossible, a lesser value or even positively dangerous.

Part Three

SPACE AND
THE SACRED

9
SPIRITUALITY AND THE CITY
Urban Visions, Civic Virtues

The future of cities is one of the most critical spiritual as well as economic and social issues of our time. The city is where, for an increasing proportion of humanity, the practice of everyday life takes place, either constructively or destructively. Cities represent and create a climate of values that defines how we understand ourselves and gather together. The growth rate of cities offers a critical challenge. The figures over the last fifty years or so are illuminating. In 1950, 29 percent of the world's population lived in urban environments. By 1990 this had risen to 50 percent and is likely to reach between 66 percent and 75 percent by 2025.[1] At the dawn of the twenty-first century humanity for the first time faces an urbanized world. Not only do most humans live in cities but we are dealing increasingly with mega-cities. Most of these are in the so-called developing world—Mexico City has 18 plus million; Mumbai, 18 million; São Paulo, 17 plus million; Shanghai, 14 plus million; and Seoul, 13 million. The mega-urbanization of the world is often simultaneously a growth of slums and shantytowns. Roughly one in six city dwellers worldwide is currently a slum dweller and, at the present rate of increase, by 2050 one in three people on the planet—three billion—will be.

In Western cultures, over the last fifty years or so, cities have undermined place identity in pursuit of values driven largely by economic considerations. In an increasingly placeless culture we become "standardised, removable, replaceable, easily transported and transferred from one location to another."[2] The French anthropologist Marc Augé, a student of Michel de Certeau, distinguishes between place, full of historical monuments and creative of social life, and non-place ("curious places which are both everywhere and nowhere"), where no organic social life is possible. By this he means such contexts as supermarkets, airports, hotels, freeways, in front of the television, working at a computer. These experiences bring about a fragmentation of awareness that leads to incoherence in relation to "the world." Unlike nonplace, true "place" has three essential characteristics—it engages with our identity, with our relationships, and with our history.[3]

Again, as the French philosopher Henri Lefebvre reminds us, systems of spatialization are historically conditioned—not merely physical arrangements of things but also patterns of social action, as well as historical conceptions of the world. The metanarratives of the people who hold power take over the public places they control. However altruistic or benign their agendas, the history of these places often becomes a story of dominance and repression.[4]

If cities are to be places that reinforce a sense that human life is sacred rather than merely an organic phenomenon, they must embrace all dimensions of human existence—functional, ethical, and spiritual. First, we need somewhere to pass effectively through the stages of life and reach our full potential. Second, we need places where we belong to a community. Third, we need cities that continue to facilitate a fruitful relationship with the natural elements. Finally, we need environments that offer access to the sacred (however we understand it)—or, better, relate us to *life itself as sacred*.[5]

We need to build into cities what is precious to us. In particular, cities have always been powerful symbols of how we understand and construct community. Yet, the monumental modernist planning and architecture that still dominate many Western cities evoke neither the value of individual people nor focused community. Rather, they speak the language of size, money, and power. Commercial complexes like Canary Wharf tower in London's Docklands too often exist in brooding isolation rather than in relationship to anywhere else. Cities built since World War II frequently lack proper centers that express holistically the life of a multifaceted community. A major part of the problem was modernist "design rationalism," which divided cities into separate zones for living, working, leisure, and shopping. This fragmented human living emptied parts of cities at night, especially the centers, and separated areas by distance and clear boundaries, substantially increasing the need for travel and pollution. This differentiation into discrete areas may also be said to reflect a growing secularization of Western culture. There is no longer a centered, let alone spiritually centered, meaning for the city. It becomes a commodity, fragmented into multiple activities and multiple ways of organizing time and space.[6]

Cities represent and create a climate of values that implicitly define how we understand ourselves and gather together. There are four aspects of cities that urban planning must take seriously. First, the two Latin concepts of the city as *urbs* (a physical place, the buildings) and as *civitas* (people and their life together) are interdependent. Second, urban issues are never purely practical. For example, transportation obviously involves management, investment, and strategy. The balance of private and public transport, however, also highlights how we relate individual choice to the "common good." Third, cities have always been complex realities. We cannot separate planning technology from people, the local from the global, or a sense of place from increasingly mobile lives. Finally, although there is no way back to the relatively compact city of premodern Europe, cities and their development must nevertheless critically embrace their past if human desires for the future are to be effectively grounded.

The City and Christian Thought

Western thinking about cities has been deeply influenced over the last thousand years by Christian theology. Christianity has sometimes been accused of antiurban bias. Certainly the scriptures get off to a difficult start. The Book of Genesis seems deeply gloomy about cities. Cain, symbol of human pride and violence, is portrayed as the founder of Enoch, the first city (Gen 4:16–17). Later the people of Babel and their tower seek to replace the authority of God (Gen 11:1–9). The cities of Sodom and Gomorrah are classic symbols of corruption (Gen 19). For the French Protestant thinker Jacques Ellul, the Bible offers no law for the city because the city, far from being sacred, embodies humanity's refusal of God's gift and desire to shape its destiny autonomously. "God has cursed, has condemned the city instead of giving us a law for it."[7]

Yet, this is one-sided. There are other positive biblical images of the city in the Hebrew scriptures, for example in the Book of Psalms. God is enthroned in the sanctuary of Zion (Ps 9), the city becomes a living reminder of God's power and faithfulness (Ps 48) and is described as the house of God (Ps 122). The city is intended to express the peace of God. Those who live in the city are required to share God's peace with one another (Ps 122:6–9). Turning to the New Testament, Jerusalem is the focal point and climax of Jesus' mission. The cities of the Roman Empire become the center of Christian mission in the Book of Acts, particularly in the strategy of the Apostle Paul. Christianity rapidly became an urban religion.[8] Most striking of all, on the very last page of the New Testament (Rev 21), the new Jerusalem, perfectly harmonious and peaceful, is made the image of the final establishment of God's kingdom.

The apparent ambivalence of the Judeo-Christian tradition toward the city, however, provides ammunition for Richard Sennett when he blames Christian theology, in part, for the soulless nature of cities. Sennett argues that Western culture suffers from a "divide between subjective experience and worldly experience, self and city."[9] This is based on an unacknowledged fear of self-exposure, viewed as a threat rather than life-enhancing. City design has concentrated on creating safe divisions between different groups of people.[10] For the city to recover, Sennett suggests, we need to reaffirm the inherent value of the outer embodied life.

For Sennett, St. Augustine's classic *City of God* is the foundational expression of the triumph of an inner spiritual "world" restlessly searching for eternal fulfillment over the physical, everyday city.[11] Human social places are to be viewed with suspicion. Sennett equates the Christian "sacred" with *sanctuary*, which implies an image of protection and refuge from a wider world. Sennett also makes connections between the sterility of modern urbanism and what he calls "a Protestant ethic of space."[12] This had a long-term impact on what he terms "the compulsive neutralising of the environment." This reflected a puritanical suspicion of pleasure and color.

Augustine's Human City

True, Augustine states at the start of his *City of God* (book 1, preface) that the earthly city is marked by a "lust for domination." This is, however, a critique of Imperial Rome, his urban paradigm and a prophetic warning to those who wish to canonize any political system. Yet, the majority of Augustine scholars are clear that he does not deny the status of "the secular" or of the human city. We need to distinguish between the "profane," which took on the negative connotation of whatever is contrary to the "sacred," and the "secular," which is simply the world of "this age," the here and now. We also need to distinguish carefully between Augustine's "earthly city" (the *civitas terrena*, realm of sin) and the political realities of the state and human city. The secular realm is a neutral space where the spiritual reality of the city of God and the counterspiritual reality of the earthly city coexist and contend, like the wheat and tares, until the end of time. While far from indifferent to the moral foundations of the city, Augustine defended a legitimate place for the secular realm within a Christian interpretation of the world.[13] Indeed, some commentators suggest that the vocation of the human city was to strive to become a trace of the *civitas Dei*.[14] Further, in Augustine's commentary on the Book of Genesis, the root of all evil is self-enclosure or privacy since humanity *as a whole* is created in God's image. Moral virtue involves defending what is public or held in common. The Heavenly City will be a community in which the fullness of sharing is experienced.[15]

Urbs and *Civitas*—Isidore of Seville

Western Christianity gradually embraced theoretically and architecturally a positive vision of the city. At a relatively early period, the seventh-century Christian thinker Isidore of Seville had a positive view of the city. By his time, the remaining Roman cities were vital survival capsules in a turbulent world of barbarian invasion. Cities were the medium for the transmission of culture and civilization, and the Church actively promoted urban structures. As Peter Brown put it, "Walls and bishops went together."[16]

For Isidore, there was no absolute separation between "the city of stones" (*urbs*) and "cities of people" (*civitas*).[17] Yet, what makes a city a city are people not walls. "A city [*civitas*] is a number of men joined by a social bond. It takes its name from the citizens [*cives*] who dwell in it. As an *urbs* it is only a walled structure, but inhabitants, not building stones, are referred to as a city."[18]

Cathedrals and Urban Vision

In the hundred years between 1150 and 1250 western and central Europe underwent a major cultural shift caused by a revival of cities, which increased roughly eightfold. This resulted in the creation of new classes of merchants and skilled artisans and had a serious impact on social and religious perspectives. There was an increased optimism about material existence and a renewed sense that the sacred could be vividly represented by the physical world of buildings. The notion of "heaven" lost some of its philosophical abstraction and became associated with a wider worldview. In religious writing heaven shifted increasingly from the re-creation of the Garden of Eden of the Book of Genesis to the New Jerusalem of the Book of Revelation, from nature to culture.[19]

One of the most evident consequences of the new urbanism was the development of the great Gothic cathedrals. The spirituality of religious buildings will be addressed more fully in the next chapter. The architecture of the cathedrals acted as a microcosm of the cosmos and sought to evoke a harmony between Creator and creation. Yet, the social symbolism of cathedrals was ambiguous. While they portrayed divine-human unity they also manifested this-worldly social hierarchies in their demarcated interior spaces and subdivisions that reflected ranks and distinctions.[20]

Cathedrals were repositories for the cumulative memory of the city community. Such an urban "center" offered communion with something deeper than the need for ordered public life. Cathedrals deliberately spoke of "the condition of the world." They expressed human history and yet transcended an easy understanding of it.

The City as Sacred Landscape

Medieval notions of "the sacred" in the city were not restricted to cathedrals and churches. There was a clear sense that the whole city embraced a wider "sacred landscape of the streets." Streets in predominantly Catholic countries frequently retain examples of medieval religious shrines. For example, the rich collection of street shrines in the *città vecchia* of the Italian city of Bari, ranging from the twelfth century to the present, has been the subject of scholarly writing.[21]

The sense that the city as a whole was a sacred landscape was reinforced by processions and blessings. In medieval cities the Christian Eucharist was a *public drama*, not only in the many churches but also in the feast-day pageants, mystery plays, and street processions. Processions before Lent and on Rogation Days, or ceremonies to mark out the boundaries of each parish (known as "beating the bounds"), together symbolized a purification of the city from the spirit of evil.[22] Medieval citizens sometimes made the heavenly Jerusalem of the Book of Revelation, chapter 21, a model for urban planning. Thus the Statutes of Florence of 1339 emphasized the existence of the sacred number of twelve gates even though, in fact, the city had by then extended the number to fifteen gates.[23]

Conversely, the heavenly city was often imaged in terms of actual human cities. New religious images for paradise were inspired by the recently flourishing cities of walls, towers, cathedrals, busy marketplaces, public squares, workshops, and wealthy merchants' houses. For example, the thirteenth-century Franciscan friar and poet Giacomo de Verona, in his "On Heavenly Jerusalem," describes heaven in terms of the avenues and piazzas of a beautiful city. This clearly reflects his significant knowledge of urban architecture and especially his own city of Verona.[24]

Later in the Middle Ages, the development of the great Italian piazzas owed much to the new religious orders and their preaching churches. These opened onto great spaces where crowds gathered to listen to sermons (for example, Santa Croce or Santissima Annunziata in Florence). The colonnaded piazza offered a vision of the city, metaphorically (it engendered a concept of public space for intermingling) and practically (it opened up new urban vistas).

Italy also defended the ideal that city life, with its organized citizenry living in concord, could be just as much a way to God as monastic life. A literary genre of poems, the *laudes civitatis*, articulated a utopian ideal of civic life. The *laudes* depict the human city as a place where, like the Heavenly City, diverse people are able to live together in peace. The *laudes* further portrayed cities as renowned for the quality of communal life in which every citizen found a particular place contributing to building up the whole.[25] The faith of the citizenry underpinned a city's claim to holiness. Thus a Milanese hymn of c. 740

praised the inhabitants because they fulfilled all the requirements of Matthew 25 that the hungry would be fed, strangers welcomed, the sick cared for, and so on.

Aquinas and the Good Life

On a more intellectual level, the writings of Thomas Aquinas articulated the idea of a city as the most complete of human communities. The study of cities is "politics," whose aim, according to Aquinas, is to be a practical philosophy for procuring goodness in human affairs through the use of reason.[26] For Aquinas, cities and politics were important because he understood community as vital to human flourishing. Aquinas even borrowed from his hero Aristotle plans for constructing cities aimed at making the good life realizable. Based on Aristotle's notion of cities as creative of the virtues, Aquinas noted that they originate by small units initially uniting for pragmatic reasons but continuing for the sake of "the good life"—that is, the properly human goals of courage, temperance, liberality, greatness of soul, companionable modesty. These only arise in cities because virtue is learned by interaction in community. Based on this Aristotelian vision, Aquinas also believed that it was unnatural for humans to live outside community.[27]

A Protestant Ethic of Space?

Despite the fact that the sixteenth-century Reformation was largely an urban phenomenon, the "high" medieval view of cities largely dissolved in Protestant Europe. Protestantism affirmed the unbridgeable gulf between the holiness of God and the world of sinful creatures. It also relocated "the holy" to the *sacred community* of believers and downgraded physical mediations of God's presence. Rudolph Bultmann describes the Protestant ambivalence toward the physical world: "Luther has taught us that there are no holy places in the world, that the world as a whole is indeed a profane place. This is true in spite of Luther's 'the earth everywhere is the Lord's' (*terra ubique Domini*), for this, too, can be believed only in spite of all the evidence."[28] Whether this is an adequate interpretation of Luther or not, Protestantism provoked a shift in sensibilities that saw the end of religious street shrines and processions that had previously revealed the city as sacred landscape. "The sacred" retreated from public places and life into the spaces of religious gatherings and into the private realm.

Yet, despite these changed sensibilities, the second great European and North American urban expansion during the Industrial Revolution evoked the city as a religious symbol in a new guise. There was a renewal of paradise imagery in some Protestant circles, particularly in North America. A number of portrayals of heaven in religious literature drew on urban imagery in a way that was different from that of the Middle Ages. They no longer focused on visual imagery. Rather, heaven was now described as an *active* place, modeled on the productivity of the new industrial cities. So, the morally righteous would not find in heaven a place of eternal *rest*, for that would be lazy and frivolous, but would lead industrious and busy lives of decent work and public service. This is especially striking in the book *Physical Theory of Another Life* by the American Scott Isaac Taylor in the 1830s. William Clark Wyatt, a late-nineteenth-century New York pastor, also suggested that "Heaven will be a busy hive, a center of industry."[29]

Michel de Certeau, Le Corbusier, and the Modern City

In reflecting on more recent urban realities, the writings of Michel de Certeau are especially provocative.[30] In English-speaking circles, it is largely his nonreligious work that receives attention, yet de Certeau remained preoccupied with religious belief until his death.[31]

In his famous essay for architects, "Ghosts in the City," it seems probable that one of de Certeau's targets was Le Corbusier, who had a powerful influence on European urban regeneration during the mid-twentieth century.[32] Le Corbusier stood for two aspects of modernist planning that de Certeau sought to counter: a tendency to erase the past and to subordinate the realities of people's lives to abstract concepts of space. Le Corbusier was influenced by aspects of Christian symbolism and by the writings of the Jesuit Pierre Teilhard de Chardin but fundamentally believed in a kind of mystical utopianism based on

Platonism and a version of Gnostic matter-spirit dualism rather than Christianity.[33]

For Le Corbusier, true knowledge and value were found in the inner, individual life. The outer, public world was of dubious worth. Consequently, Le Corbusier's city schemes made it difficult for people to congregate casually because uncontrolled socializing was a distraction. His city theory sought to eliminate anything that reinforced public life as a determining factor in human identity. Not surprisingly, Le Corbusier disliked participatory politics. The motivation for his support of right-wing groups is complex but in part is *anti*-political in that totalitarian systems offered efficient bureaucracy without the need for political debate. Although Le Corbusier's politics were quasi-fascist, he was nevertheless highly influential in modernist city planning, especially its emphasis on rationality and efficiency and its tendency to create sterile public spaces.[34]

Le Corbusier's emphasis on the "radiant city" with glass towers reaching to the sky appealed to a transcendent horizon where the *city itself* becomes the Temple. Le Corbusier's city had no churches because all human desires could be met and realized in this environment. In this spirit, Le Corbusier called the skyscrapers of Manhattan "new white cathedrals." They engineered a kind of euphoria and not only embodied transcendence in their sublime height but offered a "total vision" symbolized by panoramic vistas.

In contrast, de Certeau was concerned that modernist "restoration," which generated upmarket apartments and shopping malls, displaced existing communities and forced them to disperse to outer areas where, for example, low-cost housing projects in the 1960s created new instruments of isolation. "Restoration" or regeneration in this sense implied for de Certeau a separation of buildings from human lives. He was a prophet of the "ineffable something" that a poetics of everyday life brings to a city. De Certeau may be said to have a person-centered rather than design-centered view of planning. For de Certeau, a city is a richly textured fabric woven by its "users" (the inhabitants)—their ways of proceeding, their walking, their chance encounters, the stories they tell, the dreams they nurture.

This viewpoint was not purely political. There was an essentially spiritual underpinning for de Certeau's pleading with architects and planners.[35] His defense of provisionality and objection to utopian

168

visions accords with his implicitly Augustinian view, inherited from his mentor Henri de Lubac, that a harmonious arrangement of human environments implies more than order. Part of the aesthetics of a healthy city, in contrast to an efficient "mechanics," is the way it facilitates the transcendence of static order. The kinds of space theories that planners can impose on cities in order to "make sense" of them are frequently totalitarian.

In his essay "Walking in the City," de Certeau expressed one of his favorite themes, that of "resistance" to systems that leave no room for otherness and transgression.[36] The "weak," in this case those who actually live in the city rather than stand to one side and plan it, find ways to make space for themselves and to express their self-determination. De Certeau offers a striking contrast. Standing on top of the World Trade Center, he writes of the almost erotic pleasure and temptation of "seeing the whole," of looking down upon the city and of thereby totalizing it. There we are (or were) lifted out of Manhattan's grasp—becoming *voyeurs* not walkers. We then "read" the city as a simple text. But this is really an illusion. As de Certeau puts it, "The fiction of this kind of knowledge is related to a lust to be a viewpoint and nothing more."[37] De Certeau compares this way of seeing to the aloofness of the urban planner. Meanwhile the ordinary practitioners of the city live "down below." For de Certeau, what he called "the Concept-city" of modernist abstraction was decaying. What outlives this decay are "the microbe-like, singular and plural practices which an urbanistic system was supposed to control or suppress."[38] These everyday practices by ordinary people are what make the city *lived* space as opposed to mere concept-space. Such urban practices are plural and defy differentiation, classification, and the imposition of social divisions and hierarchies.

Those who "practice" the city are the people who actually walk its streets. This dimension of the city is what de Certeau called the "noise"—the "difference" that is a city's lifeblood, without which it becomes an empty shell. That is why he believed the role of indeterminacy or casual time was so important. "Thus to eliminate the unforeseen or expel it from calculations as an illegitimate accident and an obstacle to rationality is to interdict the possibility of a living and 'mythical' practice of the city."[39]

De Certeau's attacks on modernist planning for destroying history were not mere nostalgia. On the contrary, he strongly emphasized the power of narrative to shape environments and to transform them. Indeed, in terms of everyday life, it is story as much as architecture or planning that enables people to *use* the city as a means of creative living.[40] Stories take ownership of spaces, define boundaries, and create bridges between individuals. As Paul Ricoeur notes, *narrative is power* and without it we risk two things. First, we undermine a key element of human solidarity (we bond together by sharing stories), and second, we reduce or remove a key incentive for changing the status quo as well as an important means of bringing this about. "We tell stories because in the last analysis human lives need and merit being narrated. The whole history of suffering cries out for vengeance and calls for narrative."[41] Similarly, for de Certeau, making space for narrative is a vital factor in creating the city as community rather than as an agglomeration of buildings and spaces.[42] His understanding of narrative embraced the *history* of "place" because without respecting the past a city would become dysfunctional and dangerous.

De Certeau rejected the urban utopias of people such as Le Corbusier partly because they reduced "transcendence" to abstractions about "space" and "light" but most of all because they overestimated the possibility of ultimate fulfillment engineered purely by design. The problem with believing in utopias rather than being provoked by them is that this misrepresents the utopian genre. The point of Thomas More's *Utopia* of 1515 was not only that such a place did not exist but that it was *never meant to exist*. Utopia is an imaginary place whose rhetorical purpose is to question the values of "real" places.[43]

De Certeau's rejection of definitive urban utopias and his espousal of a fluid, mobile city forever "on the way" in the life and practices of its citizens parallel in some ways Augustine's City *on pilgrimage* toward the Kingdom of God until the end times. It is not unreasonable to see in de Certeau a mixture of an Augustinian theological horizon, suspicious of any notion of the ultimate fulfillment of human desire within contingent time and space, and a sociopolitical concern to transgress all "programmed and regulated operations in the city."[44] De Certeau's statement that "the Concept-city is decaying" embraces a spiritual and political antipathy to idolizing abstract notions of the city. For de Certeau, like Augustine, the human city is a virtual reality that, at best, anticipated a visionary future. Hence his opposition to all forms of secularized salvation especially when realized through the social engineering of highly regulated city planning.

The Spiritual and Spatial Structures

Many of us may not be used to thinking about spirituality in relation to spatial structures. So, first, I want to note several ways that buildings and spaces may shape a spiritual vision. The spiritual or sacred encapsulates a vision of ultimate value in human existence—an "interpreted world," if you like. This moves city design and building beyond a purely utilitarian understanding of human needs. We need city buildings and spaces that, like the great city churches of previous centuries, speak to us of "the condition of the world."

One design question concerns *awe*. This may refer to a sense of God or a more diffuse sense of transcendence. It is important to reflect on what makes buildings or spaces "awesome" in a constructive sense. This surely implies more than sheer amazement at design innovation or the unavoidable presence of a building that materially dominates my local skyline. It also reflects *motive and purpose*. I suggest that genuine reverence and awe are more likely in relation to built spaces that consciously reinforce the value of people at large and shared public life rather than merely project the profiles of economic or social elites. In this context it is interesting to reflect on contemporary debates about what is implied by the contemporary genre of "iconic buildings." These have replaced the symbolic monuments of yesteryear, landmarks that had a power to persuade, or that enshrined permanent reminders of the fundamental values of a society.[45] People's reactions to iconic buildings are ambivalent. On the positive side, thoughtful architects suggest that, apart from being impressively designed and highly visible, iconic structures should once again act as collective symbols that animate and articulate the very nature of a city. Two prominent architectural thinkers have interesting comments to make. Laurie Peake suggests that the authentic iconic structure has a kind of material spirituality in that it embodies a kind of ascetic self-denial. "This may be seen as their principal role, a selfless denial of their own significance for the betterment of their context."[46] They are a "symbol of aspiration, rising above the dreary mediocrity of buildings measured by profit margins and

171

speed of construction," and they function as a landmark, "giving us security on the horizon in a fast moving world."[47] Charles Jencks even suggests that an iconic building, like religious icons, always has "a trace of sanctity about it, the aura of a saint. By definition it is an object to be worshipped, however fitfully."[48]

Serious questions remain, however. Is the purpose of iconic buildings, particularly if they are not public spaces, merely to shock and awe people in ways that suggest a fundamentally contemptuous culture? In the midst of our current financial crisis this has a particularly sharp edge when what are described as modern icons are often commercial buildings or investment banks (for example, Norman Foster's prize-winning Swiss Re building for Credit Suisse in the City London). As Jencks sharply asks, if religion or other metanarratives are no longer central to the life of a commercial city, are we left simply with money, size, and power as the new "universals" to be worshipped?

A second spatial element in shaping a spiritual city is the question of how we design urban centers and public spaces. A number of European cities infected by the modernist sterility of public space constructed in the 1960s and 1970s are regenerating their centers precisely as spaces that more effectively symbolize a city's consciousness and aspirations. The eminent British architect and influential advisor to a number of governments, Richard Rogers, has been a notable proponent of humane urban designs. This is especially evident in his promotion of what he calls "open-minded space."[49] This has spiritual resonances. Fundamentally such space (for example, the plaza or public square) is person-centered. Its function is left open rather than predetermined by architects, planners, or politicians. It does not prioritize efficiency but human participation. Consequently, it is accessible physically, intellectually, and spiritually. Its very design should evoke inclusivity and encourage diversity. Such space enables creativity, celebration, and play versus constraint. Rogers believes in indeterminacy, an ability to transcend static order. Rogers grew up in Florence and values the purposeful Italian custom of *passeggiata*—casual "wandering about in public" that leaves room for surprise and celebrates people's social persona. Open-minded space reinforces public existence against a tendency to segregate different groups in protected enclaves and gated communities. The public square offers a physical center, a spiritual *centering*, to a city and its inhabitants.

As we confront urban futures in the twenty-first century, one key question is, What are cities *for?* They no longer have strictly practical roles as defense against attack or as the necessary focus for economic systems. If cities are to have *meaning* rather than merely an irreversible existence, this will increasingly be to fulfill the wider requirements of human life. There needs to be greater reflection on the civilizing possibilities of cities and the opportunity they offer for social humanization. Cities have a unique capacity to focus a range of physical, intellectual, and creative energies. They create new sets of relationships simply because they have an unparalleled ability to combine differences of age, ethnicity, culture, gender, and religion. Their large size and diversity of spaces can also balance encounter and anonymity.

This highlights another question: What is a good city? Published in 1985, *Faith in the City* was the controversial and influential report on the state of Britain's cities produced by a Church of England commission. Now a new Commission on Urban Life and Faith (containing representatives of several Churches including Roman Catholics and other faiths) has just published a further report, *Faithful Cities*.[50] A question throughout the report is: What makes a "good city"? Interestingly, the words used are not overtly religious. They include "active," "diverse" and "inclusive," "safe," "well-led," "environmentally sensitive," with an "active civil society," "values the inhabitants" and with "opportunities for all," "attracts wealth creators" but also "shares its wealth," big enough to be viable but small enough to be on a human scale. In a sentence, it is where people do not merely exist but truly *belong*.

The report then moves to suggest that a critical *spiritual* issue in the modern city is the need to push beyond that catchword of liberal societies, "tolerance," which we have already criticized in the last chapter—a passive notion that also suggests the magnanimity of the powerful toward those less favored. The report promotes the more challenging biblical theme of "hospitality." Hospitality implies a *real* relationship with those who are different and the risk that we may be moved out of our comfort zone to be changed in the encounter. In this context, the report refers briefly to hospitality in the Rule of St. Benedict (chapter 53). I would suggest that, in our contemporary Western cities, the notion of "hospitality" should be supplemented by an even sharper concept, "solidarity." Theologically, this notion derives implicitly from much of Catholic social teaching and appears explicitly in liberation theology, for example in the writings of Gustavo Gutiérrez. Solidarity implies a great deal more than a purely political slogan.[51] It is a moral imperative based on a belief in the fundamental unity of humanity rooted in the doctrines of the Trinity and the Communion of Saints and demanding a profound conversion of heart and conscious commitment to a quest for "the common good" as an essential ethical virtue.[52]

As a balance of *urbs* and *civitas*, a "good city" is essentially person-centered. It is not dependent simply on physical shaping but on improving people's lived experience. A classic case is what is understood by "regeneration." Too often this implies seeing a place merely as a wasteland waiting to be developed after the slate has been wiped clean rather than seeing it as the home of local people who want a personal stake in its future. Planning needs to escape seeing matters in mainly physical terms, "disregarding the more subtle psychological effects on people."[53]

The influential British architect Richard Rogers has been a notable proponent of person-centered architecture and planning. In his vision for future cities, Rogers highlights principles that are spiritual as much as functional. He argues that a city needs to be *just* (accessible to all and participative), *beautiful* (an aesthetic that uplifts the spirit), *creative* (stimulating the full potential of all citizens and able to respond easily to change), *ecological* (where landscape and human action are integrated), *of easy contact* (where communication is facilitated and public spaces are communitarian), *polycentric* (integrating neighborhoods and maximizing proximity), and finally *diverse*, expressing the pluralism and multiculturalism of the contemporary city.[54]

Urban Virtues and the Common Good

Clearly, an urban spirituality most importantly expresses the interaction of people. Spirituality is not merely concerned with devotional practices but involves our overall "conduct of life." This includes the notion of virtue. So, my question is: What are urban virtues for the early-twenty-first-century city? Eduardo Mendieta, whom I mentioned earlier, has written about frugality.[55] Charles Leadbeater of the British social think tank Demos promotes renunciation and restraint related to the need for a renewed sense of mutuality in response to the dominant reality of diversity in contemporary cities.[56] Mutuality demands that we give up the absolute claims of individual choice in favor of civic cohesion. As Leadbeater admits, in a consumer culture this is a counterintuitive view. Other ethical-spiritual values, such as memory, desire, aspiration, and a sense of the sacred, find a place in the writings of the international planning guru, Leonie Sandercock.[57]

Finally, the American Jesuit social ethicist David Hollenbach offers a challenging exposition of the continued validity of seeking to negotiate "the common good" in contexts of urban and global diversity. Such negotiation is not a quick fix. What matters most is commitment to a never completed process of making meaning, creating values, and negotiating a common vocabulary rather than the immediate prospect of a successful conclusion.

> This common pursuit of a shared vision of the good life can be called intellectual solidarity…for it calls for serious thinking by citizens about what their distinctive understandings of the good imply for a society made up of people with many different traditions. It is a form of solidarity, because it can only occur in an active dialogue of mutual listening and speaking across the boundaries of religion and culture. Indeed, dialogue that seeks to understand those with different visions of the good life is already a form of solidarity even when disagreement continues to exist.[58]

Conclusion

Overall our spiritual visions for the city need to be robust enough to confront the dark side of life. Spirituality needs to offer us a language to confront structural evils such as power dominance, violence, injustice, and social exclusion. Spirituality involves a vision about how our human existence is intended to be and in what ways it needs to be transformed. To put it in more theological language, spirituality must include a narrative of "redemption"—the hope we are called to affirm and the process of change. In this sense, a robust Christian spirituality "interrupts" or disrupts the everyday city—effectively acting as a civic critique built on spiritual values.

As Christians we classically enact our theology and spirituality of community in celebrations of the Eucharist. The report *Faithful Cities* touches on this in a brief but pregnant paragraph. The trouble is that some versions of a theology and spirituality of the Eucharist concentrate on building up the community of the Church in and for itself. In this case, the Eucharist ends up as the celebration of the spiritual equivalent of the well secured "gated communities" we increasingly find in upscale areas of large mixed cities such as London and Paris or nowadays New Delhi. This is what the Bolivian Jesuit Victor Codina in his reflections on the Eucharist refers to as "drawing room communitarianism."[59]

However, this dilutes the spirituality implied by the risk of celebrating Eucharist. To live eucharistically beyond the church doors commits us to cross the boundaries of fear and prejudice in an embrace of strangers in the public square in whom we are challenged to recognize the Real Presence of God. I cannot help but recall the courage of a Church of Scotland minister in a housing estate near Glasgow, later joined by a Catholic priest, who confronted local hatreds by throwing open his church day and night even during services as a safe space for Muslim refugees after one of them had been assaulted and murdered. "Reconciled in the Eucharist, the members of the body of Christ are called to be servants of reconciliation among men and women and witnesses of the joy of resurrection."[60]

The redemptive narrative of the Eucharist tells a different story from the one shaped by human divisions. There is therefore an uncomfortable tension between this sacrament of reconciliation and efforts by Christians to resist human solidarity in the city. At the heart of a spirituality shaped by the Eucharist is the belief that human identities are determined by God rather than by our presuppositions. A prayerfully driven and ethically principled practice of everyday life in the public sphere, in the diversity of a bustling modern city, is a form of spiritual practice. A sacramental view of spirituality also implies that through spiritual practices, whether that is the Eucharist or the practice of everyday life, we also open ourselves to hope. We also access power, the power of God, which promises and enables infinitely more in and for the city than our human actions alone can achieve.

10
MATERIALIZING THE SACRED
Churches as Spiritual Texts

The Sacred

In thinking about what sacred space means and its role in plural Western cultures, much depends on how we understand "the sacred." The conventional understanding of "sacred" as expressed by the great historian of religion Mircea Eliade is something that is "wholly other" than the ordinary even if experienced in and through the mundane. Classically, sacred also means "the holy"—something which, whether we understand it in supernatural terms or not, implies what is understood to be "the whole."[1] In this sense, the sacred means what is complete rather than partial or flawed. By extension, it suggests ultimate rather than passing values and what matters most deeply to people in a given society. Thus, the impact and purpose of sacred *spaces* may be to provoke a sense of what we are lacking and equally to evoke possibility and hope. Such spaces also enable us to engage fruitfully with the meaning of life and with human destiny.

Another insight of Mircea Eliade's is helpful: "the sacred" and its opposite pole, "the profane" are actually two contrasting ways of viewing the world and living in it.[2] For example, the Christian way of viewing the world as sacred understands it, despite some ambivalence toward existential realities, as the gift of God's creation and as a revelation of divine presence. As a result, the sacred is not removed from the world or history onto some other spiritual plane. No part of the world is *inherently* opposed to the sacred, although it may be profaned by human sinfulness. A collection of essays by prominent agnostics and even atheists defends the notion of the sacred, which stands for what is inviolable or of intrinsic rather than instrumental worth and remains a viable and important concept even in a secular post-religious culture.[3] "The sacred" is articulated in a variety of ways, of which material and spatial structures make up one example. In multicultural plural Western cities, however, these articulations are likely to involve more than traditional religious buildings.

Why Is Sacred Space Important?

Why does sacred space remain important in today's plural and increasingly nonreligious cities? Equally, what difference does an idea of "the sacred" make to city life? The answer, I believe, is that it encapsulates a vision of ultimate value in human existence—an "interpreted cosmos," if you like. By introducing a critical note of otherness (whether the human other or the divine Other), "the sacred" grounds what is centrally important about existence in something more than mere self-enhancement. We need symbolic spaces and structures in the modern city that, like the great churches of a previous age, speak to us of "the condition of the world" and consequently free us from a sense of fundamental estrangement.

It is vital to recover a sense that a city can somehow be sacred to its inhabitants. A church or other religious building is a kind of paradigm. It points to the fact that, at its best, our sense of place is equally a sense of sacredness—what is sacred to oneself, to the community, and in relation to a transcendent order, however that is understood. If a city is to be more than merely an efficient machine, it needs to embrace some sacred qualities—above all, it must affirm and underline the sacredness of people and promote the human capacity for transcendence. This is precisely the function of the great churches in an earlier age—to be at the same time an image of God and a symbol of the ideals of the citizens set physically in the heart of the city.

In this way, city landscapes were given a focus by the "sacred spaces" in their midst. Apart from being spaces for ritual and the worship of God, these buildings operated spiritually on several other levels. They countered a purely functional reading of city life by evoking a kind of metaphysical environment, offering a treasury of spiritual meaning, and acting as symbols in stone of the ideals of a city community. Church architecture was originally designed to be a microcosm in stone of the cosmos, intended in part to evoke oneness between the Creator and human creatures. Church buildings were a kind of utopian space where the heavenly harmony we were to hope for in the future, as well as idealized images of creation, were materialized in the here and now through a variety of artistic and complex architectural codes.

While the majority of people today who enter churches in the great cities of the Western world may have little sense of the original meaning of the buildings, this does not necessarily imply a total abandonment of such spaces as spiritual foci by a nonreligious majority. Indeed, there is plenty of evidence throughout Europe that historic churches attract far more interest than museums. A residual sense of the sacred or spiritual even in apparently secular cultures not only draws large numbers of visitors to such buildings but also makes them uncomfortable with entry charges. They perceive that churches are not the same as museums or other buildings simply associated with historical heritage. As a noted expert on the subject has revealed, the fact is that in the minds of a surprising number of people "sacred space is in some way public space, even if it is not used by most people on a regular basis."[4]

It is worth noting in passing that in modern Western society "the sacred" has not so much disappeared as become dispersed into many cultural forms and structures. What kinds of places qualify? This elicits a range of responses. Although for some people a protected domestic life and thus "the home" is particularly sacred, it is interesting that many responses to the question point to various forms of *public* space. Two that are regularly mentioned are natural features, such as parks, lakes, or rivers, and art galleries and museums. In the case of the first, I have often found that when I ask the question in workshops what sums up their town or city, without which it would lose its heart, the overwhelming response is not the local football stadium but a river or some other natural feature. "The River Thames is London's soul," as one person said. More broadly, the open spaces of urban parks and gardens evoke deep feelings of connection to nature or a sense of the numinous and equally enhance the human spirit. For other people, galleries and museums, especially national ones attached to evocative public spaces (such as the National Gallery on Trafalgar Square in London), have a particular capacity to be "sacred." Whatever form it takes, a sacred space is likely to embody powerful symbols of a community's creativity, aspirations, and quest for self-transcendence. It will also tend to be a kind of sanctuary from the pace of city life—a space for silence, thinking, even for a kind of healing.

Churches as Spiritual Texts

Turning to the broader question of how we approach Christian spirituality, I combine a long-standing interest in architecture with a concern to extend the notion of what we mean by classic spiritual "texts." As I have already noted, understandings of Christian spirituality have frequently been limited by giving disproportionate attention to *written texts*. My contention in this chapter is that religious buildings, whether parish churches, cathedrals, or monastic complexes, have been a vital source of theological and spiritual meaning for centuries and continue to be so today.

When I worked in Cambridge, a display that introduced visitors to the world-famous King's College Chapel began, "We exist not only in the world but in an image or picture of the world." In other words, consciously or not, we all have a worldview in terms of which we exist, identify ourselves, and act. Specifically, the great historic churches and cathedrals express in their very architecture and decoration a quite specific image of reality. Unfortunately, the meaning of such places is not self-evident. They are "texts" in the broad sense implied by semiotics. We need a key in order to read their sign systems and thus interpret their meaning. Because Christian churches were originally intended to be material acts of worship in themselves, as well as spaces for ritual, it is not unreasonable to say that they were constructed with certain levels of meaning built into the stonework. Their architecture and artwork are directly at the service of theology and of spirituality. Religious architecture is a bearer of specific ideas and symbols—not least images of God and understandings of human existence.

Yet, Christianity did not begin as a religion of buildings. It originated with a wandering Jewish teacher. Even after Christianity parted company with Judaism toward the end of the first century CE, for a long time it remained essentially a network of small cells of initiates who did not need permanent buildings. The *ekklesia* was the gathering of believers called out of the world long before the word ever came to mean a religious building. In the latter context, the crucial period was during the fourth century when official cultic approval was given to Christian communities. The achievement of public presence by the Church brought with it the need for public architecture. This initially took on a functional character for congregational worship. At first, churches were really no more than meeting houses. With the legalization of Christianity under the Emperor Constantine, and then its establishment as the religion of the Empire, came the building of basilicas, the creation of complex public liturgies, and the growth of schools of artistic decoration. The sites of the major churches, especially in Rome itself, were usually associated with the tombs of holy people. The primacy of the Roman Church was built upon the tombs of the apostles both literally and metaphorically. It is also worth recalling that churches were built first and foremost for rituals, such as baptism and the Eucharist. These symbolized the incorporation of the believer into the death and resurrection of Jesus Christ. Thus the origins of the sacredness of church buildings cannot be separated from their role in facilitating the union between the Christian believer and Jesus Christ as savior.

A major feature of Christian theories about the sacredness of place is therefore from the early period associated with buildings as physical containers for the living Body of Christ, the community of Christians gathered together as Church. A Christian church building is not meant to be primarily a theater or a classroom, that is, a place *essentially* concerned with ritual or with teaching. Churches have been traditionally oriented architecturally toward the east—that is, toward the rising sun that in turn symbolizes the divine Son of God. Placing the main altar at the east end was not an end in itself; for the high altar's sole purpose was, in its decorations and associated rituals, to lift the eyes of the believers toward Christ who sat at the right hand of God. The sanctuary of the church thus pushed the believer onward on the journey of following Christ in discipleship.

Aesthetics and Theology

It is now widely recognized that during the great age of Gothic architecture, and the development of a sophisticated theology of architecture, there was a diversity of aesthetic theories and therefore of theological symbolism. This has been emphasized by such important studies as those of Umberto Eco.[5] Gothic space has been characterized as, among other things, dematerialized and spiritualized. It thereby expressed the limitless quality of an infinite God through the soaring verticality of arches and vaults. These were a deliberate antithesis to human scale. The medieval fascination with the symbolism of numbers cannot be ignored either. Thus the basic three-story elevation of Gothic church architecture (main arcade, triforium, and clerestory) cannot be explained purely by developments in engineering. Important writers such as Rupert of Deutz and Abbot Suger in the twelfth century drew explicit attention to the trinitarian symbolism of the three-story elevation. Later Gothic buildings, however, such as King's College Chapel in Cambridge, are also notable for another typical characteristic. The stone walls that support the chapel have been reduced to a minimum and replaced by vast expanses of glass. The biblical stories portrayed in the stained glass of the fifteenth-century windows could teach the worshipper much about the doctrine of God and of salvation. But there was also a sense in which Gothic stained glass, and its patterned effect on the stonework of the interior of the building, expressed what might be termed a "metaphysics of light." God was increasingly proclaimed as the one who dwelt in inaccessible light yet whose salvific light illuminated the world.[6]

Until recently there has been an unbalanced concentration on the aesthetics implicit in the theology of the sixth-century mystical theologian known as Pseudo-Dionysius. In fact it is now considered that Augustine's aesthetics played at least as important a part in the monastic theology of someone like Abbot Suger as the theology of Pseudo-Dionysius. And even the Dionysian elements are often affected by Augustine's thought.[7] Hence *harmonia* or a fitting order established by God is a central theme. This fitting order refers both to the building and to the worshipping community that it contains. Abbot Suger, the great twelfth-century theorist associated with the birth of Gothic architecture at the Abbey of Saint-Denis in Paris, referred to "perspicacious order" as the key to his vision for the building—and *ordo* is the characteristic word in Augustine for the harmonious beauty of the cosmos.[8] There may be various ways of understanding the integration of architectural style and buildings. An Augustinian approach would certainly begin with the fundamental understanding of the Church as a community of people, of the faithful who make up the Body of Christ. This, rather than the building in isolation, is the *tabernaculum admirabile*, the "wonderful tabernacle" of Augustine's sermon on Psalm 41 (in the Vulgate) within which we attain to God.

"I will go," [David] says, "into the place of the wonderful tabernacle, even unto the house of God! For there are already many things that I admire in 'the tabernacle'. See the great wonders I admire in the tabernacle! For God's tabernacle on earth is the faithful."[9]

This *tabernaculum admirabile* has, however, a physical place where it is both shown forth and continually reinforced. This "place" is, first, the liturgy, particularly the Eucharist, and then the building that contains this action. Thus the building in the mind of someone like Suger should evoke wonder, be adequate to its purpose of worship, and point beyond itself to the ultimate "house of God" in heaven. The building is a doorway or access point to the heavenly places, and its harmony is represented not simply by geometry or architectural coherence but by the degree to which it fulfills this key function. That is its real beauty, its true *harmonia*.

This mixture of Augustinian and Dionysian elements seems to have been characteristic of Abbot Suger. This has led to a rereading of the theology Suger employed in reconstructing the Abbey of Saint-Denis, a building considered central to the development of all subsequent Gothic cathedrals. In fact Suger is replete with Augustine's sense of *harmonia*. For Suger, the inner meaning of an Augustinian theory of signs always pointed beyond the external material order to what was "more," "greater," or "higher." It was not so much a question of an aesthetic grounded in the physical beauty of the building as a higher sense of beauty that *necessitated* a transition from the material to the spiritual. Thus Suger actually quoted Augustine in the inscription on his great west doors:

> Portarum quisquis attollere queris honorem
> Aurum nec sumptus operis mirare laborem
> Nobile claret opus sed opus quod nobile claret
> Clarificet mentes ut eant per lumina vera
>
> Ad verum lumen ubi Christus ianua vera
> Quale sit intus in his determinat aurea porta
> Mens hebes ad verum per materialia surgit
> Et demersa prius hac visa luce resurgit.

Whoever you are, if you seek to extol the glory of these doors
Do not marvel at the gold and the expense but at the
    craftsmanship of the work.
Bright is the noble work; but, being nobly bright, the work
Should brighten the minds so that they may travel through
    the true lights...

To the true light where Christ is the true door.
The gold door defines the manner in which it is inherent.
The dull mind rises to truth through what is material
And, in seeing this light, is resurrected from its former
    submersion.[10]

The implication was that our higher understanding would "see" the physical door of the building as really the "door of Paradise." Here, Suger summarized both his theologies of light and his understanding of the great church as a symbol of paradise.

There is a passage in chapter 5 of Suger's *Libellus Alter de Consecratione Ecclesiae Sancti Dionysii* that explicitly links the "admirable tabernacle" of the faithful in the Body of Christ to the church building. The latter sets forth and makes concrete this family of believers and leads them on to Paradise.

The whole building—whether spiritual or material—grows into one holy temple in the Lord. In whom we, too, are taught to be builded together for an habitation of God through the Holy Spirit by ourselves in a spiritual way, the more loftily and fitly we strive to build in a material way.[11]

Part of the intellectual formation of Suger that lay behind his reading of a church building was sacramental theology. What integrated and gave harmony to the building was Christian *practice*. As physical places, churches were locations of liturgical assembly. This is not merely a mechanical or practical issue—for example, associated with the development of passageways for processions or the placing of windows so as to provide light for critical liturgical focuses such as the high altar.[12] One of the key features of the theology of Suger and of the cathedrals, and even the Dionysian theology propounded by Richard of St. Victor, is that what is material is *necessary* in order to draw humanity upward to the heavenly realms. To speak of cathedrals as microcosms of the macrocosm, the cosmic order, is more than simply a question of representation but is a vision of Christian practice that acts as a medium of transition and transformation.

It is also important to add that medieval people had an integrated worldview rather than a differentiated one. They conceived of an ultimate unity in the universe. The conception of the Gothic cathedral is a good example. Every detail in the building recapitulates a grand architectonic design of the structure as a whole. This reflects in stone a conceptual approach to life in which the whole is somehow reflected in each part. This would apply to each separate chapter of a theological treatise such as the *Summa Theologiae* of Aquinas. Or it might involve a perception that every event in human history exemplifies something in sacred history. For the medieval person, a microcosm is simply a replica of the macrocosm. In antiquity people were not able to break out of the sphere of natural existence or stand up for themselves against the natural environment. There was a dependence on nature and an inability to see it as an object on which one could act from the outside. This experience finds a cultural reflection in the idea of an inner analogy between humanity as microcosm and world as macrocosm—both having the same construction and elements.

Abbot Suger was clear that material realities were necessary rather than accidental to an apprehension of the divine. Every element of the building could be interpreted in reference to a higher meaning. "Those who criticise us claim that the sacred function needs only a holy soul and a pure mind. We certainly agree that these are what principally matter, but we believe also that we should worship through the outward ornaments of sacred vessels…and this with all inner purity and with all outward splendour."

Suger and the Abbey of Saint-Denis were undoubtedly influenced, even if not exclusively, by the works of Pseudo-Dionysius. For one thing, the "saint" was supposedly buried there (hence the monastery's dedication) and the monastery preserved the Greek text of his *Theologia Mystica*. An important element of Dionysian theology is the concept of light. God can be spoken of especially as light.

Light comes from the Good, and light is an image of this archetypal Good. Thus the Good is also praised by the name 'Light', just as an archetype is revealed in its image. The goodness of the transcendent God reaches from the highest and most perfect forms of being to the very lowest. And yet it remains above and beyond them all, superior to the highest and yet stretching out to the lowliest. It gives light to everything capable of receiving it, it creates them, keeps them alive, preserves and perfects them.[13]

Everything created stems from that initial uncreated light. Each receives that light as appropriate to its place—a place according to the ordered hierarchy of beings established by God. The cosmos was a kind of explosion of light, and the divine light united everything, linking all things by love and with Love. There was, therefore, an overarching coherence. A gradual ascent or movement back toward the source of all things and all light complemented this outward movement of the divine into the cosmos. Everything returned by means of the visible, from the created to the uncreated.[14] The principal theme was the oneness of the universe. Having said this, we need to be careful. An overemphasis on this theology of light is, it seems to me, to misunderstand Dionysius. We may describe God as Light, yet, according to Dionysius' own principles (especially as taught in the *Theologia Mystica*), we must also deny that God *is* anything. God is not this, not that—not even Supreme Light. In Augustinian terms, light is the sign that may especially draw us to higher realities. But that reality is ultimately beyond all concepts.

Trinity! Higher than any being,
Any divinity, any goodness!
Guide of Christians
In the wisdom of heaven!
Lead us up beyond unknowing and light,
Up to the farthest, highest peak
Of mystic scripture,
Where the mysteries of God's Word
Lie simple, absolute and unchangeable
In the brilliant darkness of a hidden silence.
Amid the deepest shadow

They pour overwhelming light
On what is most manifest.
Amid the wholly unsensed and unseen
They completely fill our sightless minds
With treasures beyond all beauty.[15]

The theology of both Dionysius and Augustine was focused on the Trinity. This doctrine affirmed God's creative outpouring into the cosmos and yet, at the same time, is an affirmation of the impossibility of defining the ultimate nature of God. After the time of Suger, Gothic portrayals of God also focused on the union of God with human nature. As a result, one of the greatest symbols of the doctrine of the incarnation and of the humanity of Jesus, the Virgin Mother, came to be situated at the heart of the iconography of cathedral glass. Scenes of the Annunciation, the Visitation, and the Nativity were also found on the decoration of high altars. The Christianity embodied in Gothic was built on a theology of God as almighty and unknowable yet incarnate and revealed. Gothic architecture portrayed humanity as graced with divine illumination.

It has been suggested of the medieval visitors to cathedrals that "they were the enraptured witnesses of a new way of seeing."[16] So what is this new way of seeing? Cathedrals in a sense contained all the information in the world and about the world for those who knew the codes. The way of seeing involved visual and other aids that drew the participant forward from self-awareness toward God as the "object" of higher vision. Richard of St. Victor in the twelfth century described the modes of vision in his commentary on the Book of Revelation. There were four modes of vision divided between bodily and spiritual. In the first, we open our eyes to what is straightforwardly there—the color, the shapes, the harmony—a simple visualization of matter. In the second mode, we view the outward appearances but also see their mystical significance. The movement is from immediate perception to a deeper knowledge. In the third mode, we move to the first part of spiritual seeing. Here there is a discovery of the truth of hidden things—such as the writer of the Book of Revelation experienced, according to Richard of St. Victor. Finally, in the fourth mode, we reach the deepest level of spiritual seeing—the mystical. Here one has been drawn through the other modes to a pure and naked seeing of divine reality.

The "real" lay beyond the apparent realm of the senses. Abbot Suger understood the architecture of churches as a harmonizing of opposites—the act of divine creation reflected in the church.

> The awesome power of one sole and supreme Reason reconciles the disparity between all things of Heaven and Earth by due proportion: this same sweet concord, itself alone, unites what seem to oppose each other, because of their base origins and contrary natures, into a single exalted and well-tuned Harmony.[17]

In fact the Christian theology of physical "sacred places," such as great churches or places of pilgrimage, is also essentially associated with people, living or dead, as the *loci* of the sacred. Pilgrimages were to the shrines of saints, and the great church was simply a space within which the living story of God's dealings with the human community could be told through architecture, glass, stone, and the liturgical assembly. If the architectural order of the great church was a microcosm of the cosmic order, that order consisted of a hierarchy of beings rather than simply an impersonal geometrical pattern.

Churches and Cities

In social terms, the development of the great cathedrals was most obviously an urban phenomenon that, as we have seen, took place after about 1150 during the first major urban renewal since the demise of the Western Roman Empire.

In the great urban church, heaven was not only invoked symbolically but also, as it were, brought down from heaven in the spirit of the Book of Revelation, chapter 21. To enter the cathedral was to be elevated spiritually into a heaven on earth. In the thirteenth century William Durandus in his *Rationale divinorum officiorum* suggested, in reference to solemn liturgical processions through the church and up into the sanctuary, "When entering the church while we sing we arrive with great joy in our [heavenly] fatherland.…The chanters or clerics in their white robes are the rejoicing angels."[18] For Suger the church building had to be more impressive than other buildings of the city.

The treasures should evoke the splendor of heaven and the liturgical officiants, like the blessed in heaven, would dress in silks and gold.

The art of the cathedrals celebrated an incarnate God and attempted to portray, evoke, and invoke a peaceable oneness between Creator and creation. This was a utopian space in which an idealized harmony, to be realized only in heaven, was anticipated in the here and now. But it was *idealized*. As Georges Duby, one of the most distinguished French medievalists, reminds us, "Yet it would be a mistake to assume that the thirteenth century wore the beaming face of the crowned Virgin or the smiling angels. The times were hard, tense, and very wild, and it is important that we recognise all that was tumultuous and rending about them."[19] The social symbolism of cathedrals was thus also ambiguous. We cannot ignore the fact that while cathedrals symbolized a Christian vision of human-divine unity they also solidified the divisions of the social order. *Harmonia*, or order, tended to be conservative in its results. The perfect, harmonious community of course reflected current social hierarchies and values. So, for example, it has been noted that representations of heaven idealized in the art of cathedrals tended to reproduce rather than subvert the separation of laity from clergy and the peasantry from the aristocracy and the monarchy. Thus, on the west front of Chartres above the great door,

> ...elongated figures of 'saints' thinned out of the world to reach a God above, and stout, stocky figures of this-worldly artisans and peasants supporting with the sweat of their brows that other 'leisure class' who have all the time and energy for liturgies and mystical contemplation, point to a conception of spirituality indelibly sculptured in the cathedrals of our collective unconscious.[20]

In a sense, the cathedral offered a focus not simply for a two-dimensional pattern of the city—its static "map" or "grid"; there was also a third dimension, that of movement through space that was not generated merely on the horizontal plane but also upward. Indeed, the cathedral even spoke of a fourth dimension—that of time and especially of transformation through time. In his attempt to describe an urban aesthetic, the American philosopher Arnold Berleant suggests that the role of the cathedral was to be a guide to an "urban ecology" that contrasts with the monotony of the modern city, "thus helping transform it from a place where one's humanity is constantly threatened into a place where it is continually achieved and enlarged."[21] Such an urban "center" offers communion with something that lies much deeper than simply the need for regularity and order in shared public life. This kind of center is not purely functional but evocative. If we leave behind for the moment the kind of specialist theological language that we must inevitably use of such an explicitly Christian religious symbol, it is possible to speak in more general terms of what something like a cathedral achieves in its role as a heart for the city. So, for example, it deliberately speaks of "the condition of the world." It both expresses the history of human experience and yet transcends an easy or superficial understanding of it. Perhaps most important of all, the cathedral is a repository for the memory and the aspirations of the community that have been constantly renewed and changed through time. To enter such a building is to enter into communion with centuries of human pains, achievements, and ideals. Indeed, the moment a building such as a cathedral becomes fixed rather than continually mobile and changing, it is a museum rather than a living symbol of the city.

Interpreting the Text

Churches may be thought of as spiritual texts and as such demand careful interpretation. A notable collection of essays on Gothic architecture clearly showed just how complex the question of interpretation is. Historians will adopt one perspective that is often cultural and contextual; art historians take yet another. Then again, the very notion of a Gothic cathedral as "a work of art," to be preserved in essentially constant form, raises all kinds of difficulties for those people (liturgists and theologians) who would suggest that the "meaning" of churches can only be arrived at in terms of interpretation-through-use.[22]

A concrete example is provided by the argument some years ago at Sherborne Abbey in England, a medieval church of the first rank, over the replacement of deteriorating nineteenth-century glass by a new window of quality. On the one side there were the parishioners of the abbey and on the other the national committee responsible for the preservation of historic churches. Those who *used* the building on a regular basis wished to replace the window by a modern design worthy of the setting. The distant experts wished to retain the old window purely on the grounds that it had historical value rather than artistic merit or spiritual quality. In the end the parishioners and clergy won the battle. The words of one art historian sympathetic to the parishioners speak of the abbey buildings as a text and are particularly apposite. "Works of art...have life when they resonate with our own lives and the lives of many within (and beyond) the community to which they belong....Sherborne Abbey...can...be likened to a palimpsest with many generations of erasures and rewritings revivifying the story being told."[23]

Such a model of interpretation raises the problematic question as to whether each and every architectural revision over time can be justified as an appropriate "rewriting" of the text for its own historical period. In the case of medieval English cathedrals, with a long and turbulent post-Reformation history, this is no easy question. What precisely is the integrity of such a building? Clearly this is a spiritual and theological issue as much as an architectural one. If we take the example of the famous Salisbury Cathedral, it went through the Reformation of the sixteenth century and also a period of fierce iconoclasm during the seventeenth-century Civil War and Commonwealth (republic). There are particularly painful issues associated with various periods of major deconstruction. With the substantial dilution of the medieval sacramental system and the replacement of a great deal of ritual movement by the proclamation of the Bible, hearing and speech rather than sight were given primary importance. Clearly a new national Church of England with a new liturgy needed a different kind of building. So, following the principle that buildings need to resonate with the lives of the community that uses them, there was undoubtedly some integrity in the reforms to the building as there also was in the sometimes heavy-handed ritualist recovery of idealized medievalism in late-Victorian restoration. Neither change was purely aesthetic but expressed shifts in liturgical practice as well as theological-spiritual principles.

In the case of Salisbury Cathedral, in many respects the worst destruction of medieval art took place not at the Reformation but toward the end of the eighteenth century. This "restoration" was thoroughly inimical to anything medieval, as it was inspired by an Enlightenment aesthetic that suggested that buildings should be freed from clutter and also be light and bright. The result was that all medieval glass was removed and largely replaced by plain windows. Remaining traces of medieval color on vaulting and walls were whitewashed with lime. Tombs were repositioned in the nave in tidy lines; a number of medieval screens and other divisions between chapels were pulled down. In many respects, therefore, the request in 1785 to the architect James Wyatt to "restore and beautify" the cathedral served the integrity of the building less well than the Reformation. This was not merely because the changes were so disrespectful of the building's fundamental logic but also because they happened during a low ebb liturgically and could not really be said to express important spiritual values in the lives of the worshippers.[24]

Who Are the Valid Interpreters?

There is a final question about churches as texts. Most people do not approach churches out of purely antiquarian interest but as a kind of spiritual classic. We then face the question that must be addressed to all spiritual texts. Who constitutes the appropriate community of interpretation?

In the case of spiritual texts that exist to be *performed*, such as historic church buildings, the "community of capable readers" changes over time. One aspect of recent scholarship on medieval cathedrals seeks to integrate art history and medieval studies with theology and spirituality. The result is a move away from the idea that buildings are simply monuments of pure architecture. The spirituality implicit in cathedrals is not based on an abstract notion of "sacred place." It is critical to their theological interpretation that cathedrals are places of social connection and of community definition. To put it another way, a building without performance is merely an item of abstract styling, and, whatever else is true, that never was the meaning of religious space.

Ancient religious buildings today stand in a completely different time frame and are experienced by a completely different audience from their original one. There is no way back to "real" cathedrals or "real" medieval audiences. Interestingly, there has developed a desire to overcome the sterile separation of mechanical details in interpreting cathedrals in order to recover the "integrated" cathedral. Shortly after World War II this approach was represented by the art historian Otto von

Simson's attempt to describe a new integrated spirituality after the appalling experiences of the Nazi era.[25] Was this attempt to capture a holistic vision for humanity, embedded in cathedrals, a genuine *historical* insight or an expression of late-twentieth-century spiritual hunger? Even if it was the latter, a hermeneutical "conversation" leaves open the possibility that today's visitor to a medieval cathedral, whether a Christian worshipper or not, may be part of an expanded community of "readers" of this spiritual text. This view is problematic for those who believe that cathedrals exist only to serve Christian worshippers. Today's visitor may be just as easily a tourist as a worshipper and may have little sense of what the cathedral originally expressed or how cathedrals are used liturgically.

Both editors in a collection of essays on the role of cathedrals in contemporary English society refer sympathetically to the "odd," "unusual," or "disadvantaged" people who regularly enter cathedrals from the city streets in order to find physical warmth or mental solace.[26] There is still a tendency, however, to speak in terms of "visitors," whether the "odd" or merely tourists, being responded to in ways that suggest that the integrity of the building is merely as a place of liturgy. Here, there is a danger of a purified notion of integrity, as if this might not embrace spiritually or socially different people. Another contributor to the same collection of essays notes how difficult it is for great church buildings such as cathedrals to become genuinely countercultural signs.[27] Yet, the marginal, however they are conceived, may actually offer a "reading" of church buildings that is a vital part of the integrity of the buildings rather than a problem for it.

My point is that while the majority of people who enter historic churches these days may be unclear about the original meaning of the buildings, this does not necessarily suggest an inevitable abandonment of churches as (broadly speaking) "spiritual texts" by a non-Church majority. Indeed, there is plenty of evidence that cathedrals attract far more interest than any associated museum, treasury, or visitors' center.[28]

It is true that tourism can be superficial, and it is also true that the "heritage industry" has a tendency to reduce history to what is pleasurable or diverting. This suggests to me, however, that the modern visitor to cathedrals should be neither patronized nor pandered to. A "conversation" model of interpretation offers the potential for both the "text" of the building and the "audience," and their respective integrities, to be taken equally seriously. In the flow of "conversation," building and visitor are both challenged. Contemporary horizons as well as the spiritual wisdom potentially enshrined in the "spiritual classic" of a cathedral may then find their proper expression.

Conclusion

For all the contemporary fascination with sacred places, there are alternative voices that speak compellingly of the movement of the sacred beyond the boundaries of religious buildings—the dispersal rather than simply the protection of the sacred. These views need to be held in creative tension alongside the notion of religious buildings as sacred spaces.

The first voice is Albert Rouet, bishop of Poitiers, who, in a striking essay on architecture and liturgy, comments, "Sacred space is that of God's nomads. This itinerancy is an important characteristic of those who seek God, of those who are members of the People of God."[29] Without ignoring the sacramental symbolism of church buildings or denying their rare power to shape communities of contemplation, Rouet notes that, beginning with an empty tomb, Christ's "place" is now his Body. "The Body of Christ is the place where charity becomes visible." For this reason, church buildings make sense ultimately in relation to the human community that they enable.

> Ecclesial space also denies itself in a way. The hope which Christ gave to the Church cannot be contained in any limited geographical spot. The Good News drives us beyond. The holiness of the person of Christ is shared, exteriorised, and communicated....Christianity is a religion without spatial limits.[30]

Another voice is that of Michel de Certeau. In his later years he sought to speak in a Western culture where institutional Christianity was no longer treated as the context of definitive meaning. Like Rouet, de Certeau suggested that the primary symbol of discipleship is the empty tomb.[31] Jesus is not finally here; he is always going ahead of us. Drawing on his background in Ignatian spirituality, with its emphasis on mobility and the quest for the magis (what is always "more"), de Certeau suggested that Christian spirituality must avoid the temptation to settle for a definitive place but instead pursue the age-old call to discipleship and conversion. Believers are asked to follow faithfully in the direction of Jesus' perpetual movement onward.[32] Christians are to journey with no security apart from the story of Christ that is to be "practiced" rather than merely stated.

> The temptation of the "spiritual" is to…transform…conversion into an establishment, to replace the 'poem' [of Christ] which states the hyperbole with the strength to make history or to be the truth which takes history's place, or, lastly, as in evangelical transfiguration…to take the 'vision' as a 'tent' and the word as a new land. In its countless writings along many different trajectories, Christian spirituality…ceaselessly criticises this trap.…[33]

These voices do not undermine the understanding of sacred spaces as sacramental, but they remind us that such buildings, like all sacramental symbols, are boundary places and points of departure. As de Certeau commented, "Boundaries are the place of the Christian work, and their displacements are the result of this work."[34]

This brings us full circle. I commented earlier that placing the main altar at the east end was intended to lift the eyes of the worshipping community to Christ and consequently to push believers outward from the building to follow Christ in discipleship. A sacramental theology demands material symbols, including church buildings that materialize the sacred. These spaces do not, however, protect the sacred against an inherently profane "out there." Church buildings are truly themselves if they facilitate a risky "movement beyond" to seek again the sacred in the ambiguities of the city streets.

NOTES

Introduction

1. Evelyn Underhill, *Mysticism: The Nature and Development of Spiritual Consciousness* (1911; Oxford: Oneworld Publications, 1993), 16–17.

2. See Phyllis Tickle, *Rediscovering the Sacred: Spirituality in America* (New York: Crossroad, 1995).

3. See for example, Jeremy Carrette and Richard King, *Selling Spirituality: The Silent Takeover of Religion* (London: Routledge, 2004).

4. For more details of the history of the term *spirituality* and of its equivalents in the Christian tradition see Philip Sheldrake, *Spirituality and History: Questions of Interpretation and Method.* (London: SPCK/Maryknoll, NY: Orbis Books, 1995), chap. 2.

5. In Michel de Certeau, "How Is Christianity Thinkable Today?" *The Postmodern God*, ed. Graham Ward (Oxford: Blackwell, 1997), 142.

6. Rowan Williams, *The Wound of Knowledge: Christian Spirituality from the New Testament to St. John of the Cross* (London: Darton Longman and Todd/Boston: Cowley Publications, 1990), 2.

7. See especially, Mircea Eliade, *The Sacred and the Profane: The Nature of Religion* (New York: Harcourt Brace Jovanovich, 1987), Introduction.

8. Ibid., 11.

9. For an explanation of this important distinction between "secular" and "profane" and an analysis of the positive view of "the secular" in Augustine's theology, see Robert A. Markus, *Christianity and the Secular* (Notre Dame: University of Notre Dame Press, 2006).

10. See the fascinating book by Deborah Cohen, *Household Gods: The British and Their Possessions* (New Haven: Yale University Press, 2006).

11. See Michel de Certeau, *The Practice of Everyday Life* (Berkeley: University of California Press, 1988); also, with Luce Giard and Pierre Mayol, *The Practice of Everyday Life*, vol. 2 (Minneapolis: University of Minnesota Press, 1998).

12. See Philip Sheldrake, ed., *The New Westminster Dictionary of Christian Spirituality*, outside North America, *The New SCM Dictionary* (Louisville: Westminster-John Knox Press/London: SCM Press, 2005).

13. For a summary of this debate, see Sheldrake, *Spirituality and History*, 196–98.

14. On this point, see Sandra Schneiders, "The Study of Christian Spirituality: Contours and Dynamics of a Discipline," in *Minding the Spirit: The Study of Christian Spirituality*, ed. Elizabeth A. Dreyer and Mark S. Burrows (Baltimore: Johns Hopkins University Press, 2005), 5–24.

15. For a study of the impact of critical theory on theology, see Graham Ward, *Theology and Contemporary Critical Theory* (New York: St. Martin's Press, 2000).

16. See Schneiders, "The Study of Christian Spirituality," 7–8.

17. For explorations of the connection between ethics and spirituality, see the collection of essays, *Spirituality and Ethics*, ed. Michael Barnes, *The Way Supplement* 88 (Spring 1997). See also Anne E. Patrick, "Ethics and Spirituality: The Social Justice Connection," *The Way Supplement* 63 (1988): 103–16. For a Protestant perspective that reengages spirituality with ethics, see James M. Gustafson, "The Idea of Christian Ethics," in *Companion Encyclopedia of Theology*, ed. Peter Byrne and Leslie Houlden (London: Routledge, 1995), 691–715. A recent approach within the Roman Catholic tradition is William Spohn, *Go and Do Likewise: Jesus and Ethics* (New York: Continuum, 2000).

Chapter One

1. Rowan Williams, *The Wound of Knowledge: Christian Spirituality from the New Testament to St. John of the Cross*, rev. ed. (London: Darton Longman and Todd/Boston: Cowley Publications, 1990), 1.

2. A. J. Gurevich, *Categories of Medieval Culture* (London/Boston: Routledge and Kegan Paul, 1985), 94.

3. Williams, *The Wound of Knowledge*, 1–2.

4. Felipe Fernández-Armesto, "Time and History," in Kristen Lippincott, with Umberto Eco, E. H. Gombrich, et al., *The Story of Time* (London: Merrill Holberton, 1999), 246–49.

5. See Hugh Rayment-Pickard, *The Myths of Time: From St. Augustine to "American Beauty"* (London: Darton Longman and Todd, 2004).

6. Pat Barker, *Another World* (London: Penguin Books, 1999), 85 and 87.

7. Paul Ricoeur, *Time and Narrative*, vol. 1 (Chicago: University of Chicago Press, 1984), 3.

8. Ibid., vol. 3, 103.

9. Ibid., 3:202.

10. Ibid., 1:75.

11. Mark Wallace, Introduction to Paul Ricoeur, *Figuring the Sacred: Religions, Narrative and Imagination* (Minneapolis: Fortress Press, 1995), 11.

12. See the three volumes of Ricoeur, *Time and Narrative* but especially vol. 1, part 2, "History and Narrative."

13. See Augustine, *City of God*, in *Nicene and Post-Nicene Fathers of the Christian Church*, vol. 2 (Edinburgh: T and T Clark/Grand Rapids, MI: Eerdmans, 1993, or the translation in Penguin Books, London, 1984).

14. H. Richard Niebuhr, *Christ and Culture* (London: Faber and Faber, 1952).

15. See, for example, remarks in John McManners, Introduction to *The Oxford History of Christianity* ed. John McManners (Oxford/New York: Oxford University Press, 1993), 1–18

16. See John O'Meara, Introduction to *St. Augustine: City of God*, trans. Henry Bettenson (London: Penguin Books, 1984), vii.

17. See the classic work on Augustine's theory of history, R. A. Markus, *Saeculum: History and Society in the Theology of St. Augustine* (Cambridge: Cambridge University Press, 1970), especially chap. 1, "History: Sacred and Secular."

18. See Philip Sheldrake, *Spirituality and History: Questions of Interpretation and Method*, rev. ed. (London: SPCK, 1995/Maryknoll, NY: Orbis Books, 1998), especially chap. 4.

19. David Ford, *Self and Salvation* (Cambridge: Cambridge University Press, 1999), 163. Although Ford's precise phrase concerns baptism, his wider context is the theology of the Eucharist.

20. G. Ruggieri, "Faith and History," in *The Reception of Vatican II*, ed. G. Alberigo, J.-P. Jossua, and J. A. Komonchak (Washington, DC: Catholic University of America Press, 1987), 92–95.

21. Jacques Le Goff, "Francis of Assisi between the Renewals and Restraints of Feudal Society," *Concilium* 149 (1981).

22. Charles Geertz, *The Interpretation of Cultures* (New York: Basic Books, 1973), 89.

23. Sheldrake, *Spirituality and History*, 84–86, 167–68; also Michel de Certeau, "Culture and Spiritual Experience," *Concilium* 19 (1966): 3–31.

24. Karl Rahner, *The Dynamic Element of the Church* (London: Burns and Oates, 1964), 85–87.

25. H. O. Evennett, *The Spirit of the Counter-Reformation* (Cambridge: Cambridge University Press, 1968), 55–56 and 126–32.

26. See Pierre Pourrat, *La Spiritualité Chrétienne*, 4 vols. (Paris: Desclée, 1918); Louis Bouyer, *A History of Christian Spirituality*, 3 vols. (London:

Burns and Oates, 1968); Bernard McGinn, John Meyendorff, and Jean Leclercq, eds., *Christian Spirituality I: Origins to the Twelfth Century* (New York: Crossroad, 1986); J. Raitt, ed., *Christian Spirituality II: High Middle Ages and Reformation* (New York: Crossroad, 1987); Louis Dupré and Don Saliers, eds., *Christian Spirituality III: Post-Reformation and Modern* (New York: Crossroad, 1989).

27. Caroline Walker Bynum, *Jesus as Mother: Studies in the Spirituality of the High Middle Ages* (Berkeley: University of California Press, 1982), 3–6.

28. See Columba Stewart, "Asceticism and Spirituality in Late Antiquity: New Vision, Impasse or Hiatus?" *Christian Spirituality Bulletin* 4, no.1 (Summer 1996): 11–15.

29. Sheldrake, *Spirituality and History*, chaps. 3, 4, and 7.

30. Raitt, *Christian Spirituality II*, Introduction.

Chapter Two

1. J. Scott and P. Simpson-Housley, eds., *Sacred Places and Profane Spaces: Essays in the Geographics of Judaism, Christianity and Islam* (Westport, CT: Greenwood, 1991), 178.

2. Philip Sheldrake, *Spirituality and Theology: Christian Living and the Doctrine of God* (London: Darton Longman and Todd/Maryknoll, NY: Orbis Books, 1998), 88–93.

3. Sandra Schneiders, *The Revelatory Text: Interpreting the New Testament as Sacred Scripture* (Collegeville, MN: Liturgical Press, 1999), 11–25.

4. See K. Flanagan, *The Enchantment of Sociology: A Study of Theology and Culture* (London: Macmillan/New York: St. Martin's Press, 1999); also Michael P. Gallagher, *Clashing Symbols: An Introduction to Faith and Culture* (London: Darton Longman and Todd, 1999).

5. Philip Sheldrake, *Spirituality and History: Questions of Interpretation and Method*, rev. ed. (London: SPCK/Maryknoll, NY: Orbis Books, 1995), 58, 84–86, 167–68; also Michel de Certeau, "Culture and Spiritual Experience," *Concilium* 19 (1966): 3–31.

6. See Michael Downey, *Understanding Christian Spirituality* (New York: Paulist Press, 1997), 126–31. See also Sandra Schneiders, *Written That You May Believe: Encountering Jesus in the Fourth Gospel* (New York: Crossroad, 1999), passim; Rowan Williams, *On Christian Theology* (Oxford: Blackwell, 2000), chap. 4.

7. S. Fowl, ed., *The Theological Interpretation of Scripture* (Oxford: Blackwell, 1997), xii–xvii.

8. Ibid., xiii.

9. David Tracy, *The Analogical Imagination: Christian Theology and the Culture of Pluralism* (New York: Crossroad, 1991), 77–78; R. Williams, *Teresa of Avila* (London: Geoffrey Chapman, 1991), chap. 5.

10. Tracy, *Analogical Imagination*, chap. 3.

11. Sheldrake, *Spirituality and History*, 172–73.

12. David Tracy, *On Naming the Present: God, Hermeneutics and Church* (Maryknoll, NY: Orbis Books, 1994), 115.

13. Ibid., 118.

14. Hans-Georg Gadamer, *Truth and Method* (London: Sheed and Ward, 1988), passim.

15. Sheldrake, *Spirituality and History*, chap. 1.

16. Schneiders, *Written That You May Believe*, 10.

17. Williams, *On Christian Theology*, 147.

18. Ibid., 124.

19. Nicholas Lash, *Theology on the Way to Emmaus* (London: SCM Press, 1986), chap. 3.

20. Gadamer, *Truth and Method*, 324–25.

21. Ibid., 274–75.

22. Paul Ricoeur, *Interpretation Theory: Discourse and the Surplus of Meaning* (Fort Worth: Texas Christian University Press, 1976), passim.

23. Williams, *On Christian Theology*, 6.

24. Ibid., 163.

25. See, e.g., Gadamer, *Truth and Method*, 325–41.

26. See, e.g., Elisabeth Schüssler Fiorenza, *In Memory of Her: A Feminist Theological Reconstruction of Christian Origins* (New York: Crossroad, 1983), passim; O. John, "The Tradition of the Oppressed as the Main Topic of Theological Hermeneutics," *Concilium* 200 (1988): 143–55.

27. Downey, *Understanding Christian Spirituality*, 129.

28. Tracy, *On Naming the Present*, 64.

29. Ibid., 65.

30. See G. Ganss, trans. and ed., *The Constitutions of the Society of Jesus* (St. Louis: Institute of Jesuit Sources, 1970).

31. H. Gray, "What Kind of Document?" 21–34, and J. Veale, "How the Constitutions Work," 3–20, both in *The Way Supplement* 61 (1988).

32. Translation in Frances-Teresa Downing, *Living the Incarnation: Praying with Francis and Clare of Assisi* (London: Darton Longman and Todd, 1993), 129.

33. *Francis and Clare: The Complete Works*, ed. R. Armstrong and I. Brady, Classics of Western Spirituality (New York: Paulist Press, 1982), 154.

34. See B. Geremek, "The Marginal Man," in *The Medieval World*, ed. J. Le Goff (London: Collins and Brown, 1990), 367–69, also R. I. Moore, *The Formation of a Persecuting Society* (Oxford: Blackwell, 1994), 45–63.

35. *The Cloud of Unknowing*, trans. James Walsh, Classics of Western Spirituality (New York: Paulist Press, 1981), chap. 36.

36. Sheldrake, *Spirituality and History*, 184–92.

37. *Ignatius of Loyola: Spiritual Exercises and Selected Works*, trans. and ed. George E. Ganss, Classics of Western Spirituality (New York: Paulist Press, 1991), 126–28.

38. David Tracy, *Blessed Rage for Order* (New York: Seabury Press, 1975), 72–79.

39. David Lonsdale, *Eyes to See, Ears to Hear: An Introduction to Ignatian Spirituality*, rev. ed. (London: Darton Longman and Todd/Maryknoll, NY: Orbis Books, 2000), Introduction and chap. 10.

40. Philip Sheldrake, ed., *Ignatian Spirituality in Ecumenical Context*, *The Way Supplement* 68 (Summer 1990).

41. See a discussion of the issues in Paul Ricoeur, "Hermeneutics and the Critique of Ideology," in *Hermeneutics and the Human Sciences*, ed. J. B. Thompson (Cambridge: Cambridge University Press, 1981), 63–100.

Chapter Three

1. See for example, Ann Astell, "Postmodern Christian Spirituality: A *coincidentia oppositorum?*" and Philip Sheldrake, "The Crisis of Postmodernity," both in *Christian Spirituality Bulletin* 4, no. 1 (Summer 1996).

2. Among some theorists, "Auschwitz" has become a paradigm of the postmodern experience. See, for example, Jean-François Lyotard, *The Postmodern Explained* (Minneapolis: University of Minnesota Press, 1993), 18–19. This has also been adopted in Ann W. Astell, ed., *Divine Representations: Postmodernism and Spirituality* (New York: Paulist Press, 1994), 2–3.

3. For example: Bradley Hanson, ed., *Modern Christian Spirituality: Methodological and Historical Essays* (Atlanta: Scholars Press, 1990), part 1; Bernard McGinn, "The Letter and the Spirit: Spirituality as an Academic Discipline," *Christian Spirituality Bulletin* (Fall 1993): 1–10; Walter Principe, "Towards Defining Spirituality," *Sciences Religieuses*, 12, no. 2 (1983): 127–41; Sandra Schneiders, "Theology and Spirituality: Strangers, Rivals or Partners?" *Horizons*, 13, no. 2 (1986): 253–74; idem, "Spirituality in the Academy," *Theological Studies* 50 (1989): 676–97; idem, "A Hermeneutical Approach to the Study of Christian Spirituality," *Christian Spirituality Bulletin* (Spring 1994): 9–14; idem, "Spirituality as an Academic Discipline: Reflections from Experience," *Christian Spirituality Bulletin* (Fall 1993): 10–15; Philip Sheldrake, *Spirituality and History: Questions of Interpretation and Method*, rev. ed. (London: SCM, 1995/Maryknoll, NY: Orbis Books, 1998); idem,

Spirituality and Theology: Christian Living and the Doctrine of God (London: Darton Longman and Todd, 1998).

4. There are few overall historical surveys of the relationship between theology and spirituality. For a slightly more extended account, see Sheldrake, *Spirituality and Theology*, chap. 2. For an earlier account, see Eugene Megyer, "Spiritual Theology Today," *The Way* 21, no. 1 (January 1981): 55–67.

5. For an excellent summary of patristic and medieval exegesis, see the essay by Sandra Schneiders, "Scripture and Spirituality," in *Christian Spirituality I: Origins to the Twelfth Century*, ed. Bernard McGinn, John Meyendorff, and Jean Leclercq (New York: Crossroad/London: Routledge, 1986), 1–20. On monastic exegesis, the classic study remains the four volumes of Henri de Lubac, *Exégèse Médiévale: Les Quatres Sens de L'écriture* (Paris: Aubier, 1959–63).

6. See Louis Bouyer, "Mysticism: An Essay on the History of the Word," in *Understanding Mysticism*, ed. R. Woods (London: Athlone, 1980). Also Paul Rorem, "The Uplifting Spirituality of Pseudo-Dionysius" in *Christian Spirituality, I: Origins to the Twelfth Century*, ed. Bernard McGinn, John Meyendorff, and Jean Leclercq (New York: Crossroad, 1986).

7. See the classic study of monastic theology, Jean Leclercq, *The Love of Learning and Desire for God* (London: SPCK, 1978), especially chap. 9.

8. See Vladimir Lossky, *The Mystical Theology of the Eastern Church* (London: SPCK, 1973).

9. For a critical study of the relationship in the twelfth century between traditional monastic theology and the new "theology of the schools" see Jean Leclercq, "The Renewal of Theology" in *Renaissance and Renewal in the Twelfth Century*, ed. Robert Benson, Giles Constable, and Carol Lanham (Toronto: University of Toronto Press, 1991), 68–87. For a pioneering study of the creation of the universities and the origin of "the intellectual," see Jacques Le Goff, *Intellectuals in the Middle Ages* (Oxford: Blackwell, 1993).

10. See, for example, Wolfhart Pannenberg, *Christian Spirituality and Sacramental Community* (London: Darton Longman and Todd, 1984), chap. 1.

11. See Andrew Louth, *Discerning the Mystery: An Essay on the Nature of Theology* (Oxford: Oxford University Press, 1983), chaps. 1 and 6.

12. On Protestant spirituality, see, for example, Frank C. Senn, ed., *Protestant Spiritual Traditions* (New York: Paulist Press, 1986); various essays in *Christian Spirituality III: Post-Reformation and Modern*, ed. Louis Dupré and Don Saliers (New York: Crossroad, 1989/London: SCM Press, 1990).

13. See Sheldrake, *Spirituality and History*, 52–55. For the manuals, see A. A.Tanquerey, *The Spiritual Life* (Tournai: Desclée, 1930); also R. Garrigou-Lagrange, *Christian Perfection and Contemplation* (St. Louis: B. Herder, 1937). For an Anglican work see F. P. Harton, *The Elements of the Spiritual Life* (London: SPCK, 1932).

14. Pierre Pourrat, *Christian Spirituality*, vol. 1 (London: Burns, Oates and Washbourne, 1922), preface, v.

15. See Louis Bouyer, *An Introduction to Spirituality* (New York: Desclée, 1961). For Bouyer's vision of the relation of spirituality to other theological disciplines, see his *A History of Christian Spirituality*, vol. 1 (London: Burns and Oates, 1968), preface, vii–ix.

16. Schneiders, "Theology and Spirituality," 253–74; idem, "Spirituality in the Academy," 687–97. See also Peter Van Ness, "Spirituality and Secularity," *The Way Supplement* 73 (1992): 68–79.

17. Rowan Williams, *The Wound of Knowledge: Christian Spirituality from the New Testament to St. John of the Cross*, rev. ed. (London: Darton Longman and Todd, 1990), 2.

18. On the relationship between postwar Roman Catholic theology and spirituality, see, for example, David Tracy, "Recent Catholic Spirituality: Unity and Diversity," in *Christian Spirituality II: Post-Reformation and Modern*, ed. Louis Dupré and Don Saliers (New York: Crossroad, 1989/London: SCM Press, 1990), 152–53.

19. Bernard Lonergan, *Method in Theology* (London: Darton Longman and Todd, 1972), 6–20, 101–24, 235–66.

20. Karl Rahner, *Theological Investigations*, vol. 5 (London: Darton Longman and Todd, 1966), 3–22. See also *The Practice of Faith: A Handbook of Contemporary Spirituality*, ed. K. Lehmann and A. Raffelt (New York: Crossroad, 1984).

21. See Hans Urs von Balthasar's multi-volume systematic theology, *The Glory of the Lord* (San Francisco: Ignatius Press/Edinburgh: T and T Clark, 1982–92).

22. See *Concilium* 9, no. 1 (1965): 5–13.

23. See Jürgen Moltmann, "The Theology of Mystical Experience," in *Experiences of God* (London: SCM Press/Philadelphia: Fortress Press, 1980), 55–80. See also idem, "Teresa of Avila and Martin Luther: The Turn to the Mysticism of the Cross," *Studies in Religion/Sciences Religieuses* 13 (1984): 265–78.

24. Wolfhart Pannenberg, *Christian Spirituality and Sacramental Community* (London: Darton Longman and Todd, 1984), 13–17. See also idem, "Baptism as Remembered 'Ecstatic' Identity," in *Christ: The Sacramental Word*, ed. David Brown and Ann Loades (London: SPCK, 1996).

25. See Williams, *The Wound of Knowledge*. See also *Teresa of Avila* (London: Chapman/Wilson, CT: Moorhouse, 1991), 54–55 and chap. 5, "Mysticism and Incarnation."

26. See Gustavo Gutiérrez, *We Drink from Our Own Wells: The Spiritual Journey of a People* (Maryknoll, NY: Orbis Books/London: SCM Press, 2003),

and *On Job: God-Talk and the Suffering of the Innocent* (Maryknoll, NY: Orbis Books, 1998).

27. Anne E. Carr, *Transforming Grace: Christian Tradition and Women's Experience* (San Francisco: Harper, 1990), 202.

28. Ibid., 117–33.

29. Ibid., 204–14.

30. See Sandra Schneiders, *The Revelatory Text: Interpreting the New Testament as Sacred Scripture* (Collegeville, MN: Liturgical Press, 1999).

31. See Elizabeth Johnson, *She Who Is: The Mystery of God in Feminist Theological Discourse* (New York: Crossroad, 1996). See also Catherine Mowry LaCugna, *God for Us: The Trinity and Christian Life* (San Francisco: HarperCollins, 1993).

32. See Grace Jantzen, *Power, Gender and Christian Mysticism* (Cambridge: Cambridge University Press, 1995). Also Dorothee Sölle, *The Silent Cry: Mysticism and Resistance* (Minneapolis: Augsburg Fortress Press, 2001).

33. Sandra Schneiders, "Theology and Spirituality: Strangers, Rivals or Partners?" *Horizons* 13, no. 2 (1986): 253–74; idem, "Spirituality in the Academy," *Theological Studies* 50 (1989): 676–97; idem, "Spirituality as an Academic Discipline: Reflections from Experience," *Christian Spirituality Bulletin* 1, no. 2 (Fall 1993): 10–15; idem, "A Hermeneutical Approach to the Study of Christian Spirituality," *Christian Spirituality Bulletin* 2, no. 1 (Spring 1994): 9–14.

34. Bernard McGinn, "The Letter and the Spirit: Spirituality as an Academic Discipline," *Christian Spirituality Bulletin* 1, no. 2 (Fall 1993): 1–10.

35. See the articles in *Christian Spirituality Bulletin* 3, no. 2 (Fall 1995): Philip Endean, "Theology out of Spirituality: The Approach of Karl Rahner," 6–8; Mark McIntosh, "Lover without a Name: Spirituality and Constructive Christology Today," 9–12; J. Matthew Ashley, "The Turn to Spirituality? The Relationship between Theology and Spirituality," 13–18; Anne M. Clifford, "Re-membering the Spiritual Core of Theology: A Response," 19–21.

36. David Tracy, *Blessed Rage for Order* (New York: Seabury Press, 1975), 64–71.

37. Ibid., 72–79. See also Dermot Lane, *The Experience of God* (Dublin: Veritas, 1985), 26, and Walter Principe, "Pluralism in Christian Spirituality," *The Way* (January 1992): 58–60.

38. See Catherine LaCugna, "Trinitarian Spirituality," in *New Dictionary of Catholic Spirituality*, ed. Michael Downey (Collegeville, MN: Liturgical Press, 1993), 968–71.

39. Andrew Louth, *Theology and Spirituality*, Fairacres Publications 55 (Oxford: SLG Press, 1978), 4.

40. See Williams, *Teresa of Avila*. See also Moltmann, "Teresa of Avila and Martin Luther."

41. See John Meyendorff, *Byzantine Theology* (New York: Fordham University Press, 1974), Introduction. See also Lossky, *Mystical Theology*, chap. 1.

42. David Tracy, *The Analogical Imagination: Christian Theology and the Culture of Pluralism* (New York: Crossroad, 1991), 77–78.

43. On the broader context of patristic theology, see Jaroslav Pelikan, *Christianity and Classical Culture* (New Haven: Yale University Press, 1993), chap. 4. See *Pseudo-Dionysius: The Complete Works*, ed. Colm Luibhéid and Paul Rorem, Classics of Western Spirituality (New York: Paulist Press, 1987). For useful studies of Dionysius see Andrew Louth, *The Origins of the Christian Mystical Tradition* (Oxford: Oxford University Press, 1981), chap. 8 and his *Denys the Areopagite* (London: Chapman, 1989); also Denys Turner, *The Darkness of God: Negativity in Christian Mysticism* (Cambridge: Cambridge University Press, 1995), chap. 2.

44. See Rowan Williams, "The Via Negativa and the Foundations of Theology: An Introduction to the Thought of V. N. Lossky," in *New Studies in Theology, 1*, ed. Stephen Sykes and Derek Holmes (London: SPCK, 1980), 96. Italics are in the original.

45. Tracy, *Analogical Imagination*, 360.

46. Ibid., 385.

Chapter Four

1. See Rowan Williams, *On Christian Theology* (Oxford/Malden, MA: Blackwell, 2000): chap. 16, "Interiority and Epiphany: A Reading in New Testament Ethics."

2. Ibid., 259.

3. Augustine, *Confessions and Enchiridion*, ed. Albert Outler, The Library of Christian Classics (London: SCM Press, 1955), book 10, chap. 3, sec. 4.

4. Augustine, *Tractates on the Gospel of John*, section 18.10.

5. Catherine Mowry LaCugna, *God for Us: The Trinity and Christian Life* (San Francisco: HarperCollins, 1993), 1.

6. Karl Rahner, *The Trinity* (London: Burns and Oates, 1970), 22.

7. For example, Colin Gunton, "The Trinity in Modern Theology," in *Companion Encyclopedia of Theology*, ed. Peter Byrne and Leslie Houlden (London: Routledge, 1995), 948.

8. *The Spiritual Exercises of St. Ignatius*, trans. Louis Puhl (Chicago: Loyola University Press, 1951), paragraphs 101–9.

9. There are a number of useful surveys of contemporary trinitarian writing. See, for example, David S. Cunningham, "Trinitarian Theology since 1990," *Reviews in Religion and Theology* (1995): 8–16; Christoph Schwöbel,

Notes

"Introduction: The Renaissance of Trinitarian Theology: Reasons, Problems and Tasks" in *Trinitarian Theology Today*, ed. Schwöbel (Edinburgh: T and T Clark, 1995); also Gunton, "The Trinity in Modern Theology," in *Companion Encyclopedia of Theology*, ed. Byrne and Houlden, 937–57.

10. See especially Jürgen Moltmann, *History and the Triune God: Contributions to Trinitarian Theology* (London: SCM Press/New York: Crossroad, 1992).

11. See, for example, LaCugna, *God for Us*, chap. 8, "Persons in Communion," and Elizabeth A. Johnson, *She Who Is: The Mystery of God in Feminist Theological Discourse* (New York: Crossroad, 1996), chap. 10, "Triune God: Mystery of Relation."

12. Leonardo Boff, *Trinity and Society* (Maryknoll, NY: Orbis Books/Tunbridge Wells, UK: Burns and Oates, 1982).

13. For example, Colin Gunton, *The Promise of Trinitarian Theology* (Edinburgh: T and T Clark, 1990), and LaCugna, *God for Us*.

14. John Zizioulas, *Being as Communion* (Crestwood, NY: St. Vladimir's Seminary Press, 1985). See also his "The Doctrine of the Holy Trinity: The Significance of the Cappadocian Contribution," in *Trinitarian Theology Today*, ed. Schwöbel. But the medieval mystical theologian Richard of St. Victor in the twelfth century also argued for the *necessity* of a community within God if God is truly to be conceived of as "Love." See *De Trinitate*, book 3, chap. 19 in *Richard of St. Victor*, ed. Grover Zinn, Classics of Western Spirituality (New York: Paulist Press, 1979).

15. See Jean-Luc Marion, *God without Being* (Chicago: University of Chicago Press, 1995), especially 46–49.

16. For example, LaCugna, *God for Us*, chap. 9; Rowan Williams, "Trinity and Revelation," *Modern Theology* (1986): 197–212; and Daniel Hardy and David Ford, *Jubilate: Theology in Praise* (London: Darton Longman and Todd, 1984).

17. *Julian of Norwich: Showings*, ed. E. Colledge and J. Walsh, Classics of Western Spirituality (New York: Paulist Press, 1978), Long Text (LT), 73.

18. Ibid.

19. Ibid., 8.

20. Ibid., 2–9.

21. Ibid., 4.

22. Ibid.

23. Ibid., 31.

24. Ibid., 75.

25. Ibid., 23

26. Although the Middle English "poynte" is translated by Colledge and Walsh as "an instant of time" (197), the chapter overall is more suggestive of a spatial image. "By which vision I saw that he is present in all things." "For he is at the centre of everything."

27. *Julian of Norwich: Showings*, ed. Colledge and Walsh, Long Text (LT, 11).

28. Ibid., 58.

29. Ibid., 4.

30. Ibid., 51.

31. Ibid., 54.

32. Ibid., 45–49.

33. *Julian of Norwich: Showings*, ed. Colledge and Walsh, Short Text (ST, viii).

34. *Julian of Norwich: Showings*, ed. Colledge and Walsh (LT, 11).

35. Ibid.

36. Ibid., 27.

37. Ibid., 45.

38. Ibid., 46.

39. Ibid., 51.

40. Ibid.

41. Ibid., 11.

42. Ibid., 54.

43. Ibid., esp. 54–59.

44. They certainly do not mean "spirit"/soul and "matter"/body. They bear some, but not total, resemblance to the Augustinian concept of higher and lower parts of the soul. See, for example, Grace Jantzen, *Julian of Norwich* (London: SPCK, 1987), 137–49, and Joan Nuth, *Wisdom's Daughter: The Theology of Julian of Norwich* (New York: Crossroad, 1991), 104–16.

45. *Julian of Norwich: Showings*, ed. Colledge and Walsh (LT, 4).

46. Ibid., 51.

Chapter Five

1 Karl Rahner, "Prayer," in *Encyclopedia of Theology* (London: Burns and Oates, 1975), 1275.

2. Lawrence S. Cunningham and Keith J. Egan, *Christian Spirituality: Themes from the Tradition* (New York: Paulist Press, 1996), especially their chapter on prayer, 66–83.

3. Ibid., 67.

4. Ibid., 73.

5. Ibid., 78.

6. José Casanova, *Public Religion in the Modern World* (Chicago: University of Chicago Press, 1994), 42.

7. See, for example, the work of the Orthodox theologian John Zizioulas, *Being as Communion* (Crestwood, NY: St. Vladimir's Seminary Press, 1985), and a more detailed discussion of the relationship between God-as-Trinity and human identity in Philip Sheldrake, *Spirituality and Theology: Christian Living and the Doctrine of God* (London: Darton Longman and Todd/Maryknoll, NY: Orbis Books, 1998), especially 75–83.

8. Augustine, *City of God*, in *Nicene and Post-Nicene Fathers of the Christian Church*, vol. 2 (Edinburgh: T and T Clark/Grand Rapids, MI: Eerdmans, 1993).

9. Martin Luther, "Secular Authority: To What Extent It Should Be Obeyed" in Martin Luther, *Selections from His Writings*, ed. John Dillenberger (Garden City, NY: Anchor Books, 1961), 371.

10. Stanley Hauerwas, *In Good Company: The Church as Polis* (Notre Dame: University of Notre Dame Press, 1995).

11. John Milbank, *Theology and Social Theory: Beyond Secular Reason* (Oxford: Blackwell, 1990).

12. Wolfhart Pannenberg, *Christian Spirituality and Sacramental Community* (London: Darton Longman and Todd, 1984), 56.

13. See, for example, remarks in John McManners, Introduction to *The Oxford History of Christianity*, ed. John McManners (Oxford/New York: Oxford University Press, 1993), 1–8.

14. See John O'Meara, Introduction to *St. Augustine: City of God*, trans. Henry Bettenson (London: Penguin Books, 1984), vii.

15. See the classic work on Augustine's theory of history, R. A. Markus, *Saeculum: History and Society in the Theology of St. Augustine* (Cambridge: Cambridge University Press, 1970), esp. chap. 1, "History: Sacred and Secular."

16. See Peter Brown, "Late Antiquity," in *A History of Private Life*, vol. 1: *From Pagan Rome to Byzantium*, ed. Paul Vayne (Cambridge MA: Harvard University Press, 1996).

17. Augustine, *De Gen ad litt* XI.15. 19–20.

18. Ibid., 20.

19. On this point see R. A. Markus, *The End of Ancient Christianity* (Cambridge: Cambridge University Press, 1998), 78.

20. Thomas Martin, *Our Restless Heart: The Augustinian Tradition* (London: Darton Longman and Todd, 2003), 43.

21. Gaspar Martinez, *Confronting the Mystery of God: Political, Liberation and Public Theologies* (New York: Continuum, 2001).

22. Segundo Galilea, "The Spirituality of Liberation," *The Way* (July 1985): 186–94.

23. Segundo Galilea, "Liberation as an Encounter with Politics and Contemplation" in *Understanding Mysticism*, ed. R. Woods (London: Athlone Press, 1980), 535, 536.

24. Leonardo Boff, "The Need for Political Saints: From a Spirituality of Liberation to the Practice of Liberation," *Cross Currents* 30, no. 4 (Winter 1980/81): 371.

25. Ibid., 373.

26. Ibid., 372.

27. Ibid., 374.

28. Martinez, *Confronting the Mystery of God*, 148. See Gustavo Gutiérrez, *On Job: God-Talk and the Suffering of the Innocent* (Maryknoll, NY: Orbis Books, 1998).

29. See the illuminating comments and citations in Martinez, *Confronting the Mystery of God*, chap. 2, but especially this paraphrase on 87.

30. Ibid., 148.

31. Rowan Williams, "Sacraments of the New Society," in his *On Christian Theology* (Oxford: Blackwell, 2000), 213.

32. Jürgen Moltmann, "The Theology of Mystical Experience," in his *Experiences of God* (Philadelphia: Fortress Press, 1980), 73.

33. Ibid., 72.

34. See Dorothee Sölle, "To Be Amazed, to Let Go, to Resist: Outline for a Mystical Journey Today," in *Mysticism and Social Transformation*, ed. Janet Ruffing (Syracuse, NY: Syracuse University Press, 2001), 45–51.

35. Ibid., 46.

36. Ibid., 47.

37. Ibid., 48.

38. Rowan Williams, "Theological Integrity," in *On Christian Theology*, 5.

39. Ibid., 10–11.

40. Ibid., 11.

41. Ibid., 12.

Chapter Six

1. For a general overview of questions of definition, see Harvey Egan, *What Are They Saying about Mysticism?* (New York: Paulist Press, 1982).

2. For a philosophical approach, see Stephen Katz, ed., *Mysticism and Religious Traditions* (New York: Oxford University Press, 1983).

3. William James, *The Varieties of Religious Experience*, originally 1902, but available in various modern editions.

4. For a wide selection of examples of the variety of Christian mysticism, see Louis Dupré and James Wiseman, eds., *Light from Light: An Anthology of Christian Mysticism* (New York: Paulist Press, 2001).

5. Augustine, *Christian Doctrine*, 1.6. For Meister Eckhart, see, for example, Sermon 9, German Sermons, in *Meister Eckhart: Teacher and Preacher*, ed B. McGinn, Classics of Western Spirituality (New York: Paulist Press, 1986), 255–61.

6. On this understanding of Christian mysticism and for an overall critique of the experientialist approach, see Denys Turner, *The Darkness of God: Negativity in Christian Mysticism* (Cambridge: Cambridge University Press, 1995).

7. See Louis Bouyer, "Mysticism: An Essay on the History of the Word," in *Understanding Mysticism*, ed. R. Woods (London: Athlone Press, 1980).

8. See *Origen: An Exhortation to Martyrdom, Prayer and Selected Works*, ed. R. Greer, Classics of Western Spirituality (New York: Paulist Press, 1979).

9. See *Pseudo-Dionysisus: The Complete Works*, ed. Colm Luibhéid and Paul Rorem, Classics of Western Spirituality (New York: Paulist Press, 1987). For a classic study of the early mystical theologians, see Andrew Louth, *The Origins of the Christian Mystical Tradition* (Oxford: Clarendon Press, 1992).

10. Bernard McGinn is in the process of writing a comprehensive multivolume history of Western Christian mysticism, entitled *The Presence of God*. Four of the six volumes have so far been published by Crossroad, New York.

11. See, for example, Grace Jantzen, *Power, Gender and Christian Mysticism* (Cambridge: Cambridge University Press, 1995).

12. *Julian of Norwich: Showings*, ed. E. Colledge and J. Walsh, Classics of Western Spirituality (New York: Paulist Press, 1978).

13. See *Meister Eckhart: The Essential Sermons, Commentaries, Treatises and Defense*, ed. B. McGinn and E. Colledge, Classics of Western Spirituality (New York: Paulist Press, 1985), and McGinn, ed., *Meister Eckhart: Teacher and Preacher*.

14. See the excellent collection of essays in Janet Ruffing, ed., *Mysticism and Social Transformation* (Syracuse, NY: Syracuse University Press, 2001).

15. For Ruusbroec's mystical writings, see *John Ruusbroec: The Spiritual Espousals and Other Works*, ed. J. Wiseman (New York: Paulist Press, 1985). All subsequent quotations are from this edition and translation.

16. John Ruusbroec, *The Sparkling Stone*, Conclusion, in ibid.

17. John Ruusbroec, *The Spiritual Espousals*, book 1, pt. 2, chap. 65, in ibid.

18. Ibid., book 2, "The Interior Life."

19. Evelyn Underhill, *Mysticism* (1911; Oxford: Oneworld Publications, 1993).

20. See Segundo Galilea, "Liberation as an Encounter with Politics and Contemplation" in *Understanding Mysticism*, ed. Woods, and Galilea, "The Spirituality of Liberation," *The Way* (July 1985): 186–94.

21. See Bernard McGinn, *The Foundations of Mysticism: Origins to the Fifth Century* (New York: Crossroad, 1992), General Introduction, xi–xx.

22. Michel de Certeau, *The Mystic Fable*, Eng. trans. (Chicago: University of Chicago Press, 1992), 299.

23. Michel de Certeau, "'Mystique' au XVIIe siècle: Le problème du language 'mystique'" in *L'Homme Devant Dieu: Mélanges Offerts au Père Henri du Lubac* (Paris: Aubier, 1964), 2:267–91.

24. The essay "Mystic Speech," in Michel de Certeau, *Heterologies: Discourse on the Other*, trans. Brian Massimi (Minneapolis: University of Minnesota Press, 1995), 83.

25. Ibid, 80.

26. Ibid., 81.

27. A point noted by Luce Giard, one of de Certeau's closest collaborators and coauthors, in Michel de Certeau, Luce Giard, and Pierre Mayol, *The Practice of Everyday Life*, vol. 2 (Minneapolis: University of Minnesota Press, 1998), xxii–xxiii.

28. See comments by John O'Malley in *The First Jesuits* (Cambridge, MA: Harvard University Press, 1993), 8.

29. De Certeau, "Mystic Speech," 81.

30. De Certeau, *Mystic Fable*, 77.

31. Ibid., 5, but see the complete Introduction, 1–26.

32. Ibid., 13.

33. Ibid.

34. Ibid., 14

35. Ibid.

36. Ibid., 20.

37. Ibid., "Introduction," 1–26.

38. De Certeau, "Mystic Speech," in Graham Ward, *The Certeau Reader* (Oxford: Blackwell, 2000), 191.

39. Ibid., 191–92.

40. See ibid., 85–86.

41. Michel de Certeau, "The Weakness of Believing: From the Body to Writing, a Christian Transit," in *The Certeau Reader*, ed. Graham Ward, 226.

42. See ibid., passim.

43. Ibid., 236.

44. Ibid., 234.

45. In Michel de Certeau, "How Is Christianity Thinkable Today?" in *The Postmodern God*, ed. Graham Ward (Oxford: Blackwell, 1997), 151.

46. Michel de Certeau, "Culture and Spiritual Experience," *Concilium* 19 (1966): 3–16.

47. De Certeau, *Mystic Fable*, esp. Introduction, 1–26.

48. David Tracy, *On Naming the Present: God, Hermeneutics and Church* (Maryknoll, NY: Orbis Books, 1994), 3–6.

49. See de Certeau, *Mystic Fable*, esp. chap. 7, "The Enlightened Illiterate." De Certeau also edited the work of Surin: *Jean-Joseph Surin: Correspondence* (Paris: Desclée, 1963) and *Jean-Joseph Surin: Guide Spirituel pour La Perfection* (Paris: Desclée, 1963).

50. Michel Foucault, *Power/Knowledge: Selected Interviews and Other Writings 1972–77* (London: Pantheon Books, 1980), 81.

51. De Certeau, *Mystic Fable*, 299.

Chapter Seven

1. See Gordon Mursell, ed., *The Story of Christian Spirituality: Two Thousand Years from East to West* (Oxford: Lion Publishing, 2001), 340.

2. On the nature of "classics" see David Tracy, *The Analogical Imagination: Christian Theology and the Culture of Pluralism* (New York: Crossroad, 1991), esp. chap. 3.

3. David Tracy, *On Naming the Present: God, Hermeneutics and Church* (Maryknoll, NY: Orbis Books, 1994), 115.

4. Alister McGrath, *Christian Spirituality* (Oxford: Blackwell, 1999), 32–33, citing Thomas Merton, *Seeds of Contemplation*.

5. Sandra Schneiders, "A Hermeneutical Approach to the Study of Christian Spirituality," *Christian Spirituality Bulletin* 2, no. 1 (Spring 1994): 11.

6. See Tracy, *On Naming the Present*, 136–39, and Kees Waaijman, *Spirituality* (Leuven: Peeters, 2002), 404.

7. See Jean Leclercq, Preface, in Thomas Merton, *Contemplation in a World of Action* (New York: Doubleday Image, 1973), 12.

8. Anthony Padovano, *The Human Journey: Thomas Merton, Symbol of a Century* (Garden City, NY: Doubleday, 1982).

9. Michel de Certeau, *The Mystic Fable* (Chicago: University of Chicago Press, 1992), 299. The citation is from the thirteenth-century Beguine mystic Hadewijch in her collected mystical writings.

10. Mary Jo Weaver, "Conjectures of a Disenchanted Reader," *Horizons* 30, no. 2 (2003): 285–96.

11. Lawrence S. Cunningham, *Thomas Merton and the Monastic Vision* (Grand Rapids, MI: Eerdmans, 1999), esp. chap. 7, "Summing Up a Life."

12. Thomas Merton, *Conjectures of a Guilty Bystander* (New York: Doubleday, 1966), 141.

13. Thomas Merton, *Life and Holiness* (New York: Doubleday, 1964), 9–10.

14. Merton, *Conjectures of a Guilty Bystander*, 140-41.

15. Thomas Merton, *The Asian Journal* (London: Sheldon, 1974), 329.

16. Thomas Merton, "Is the World a Problem?" *Commonweal* 84 (June 3, 1966): 307, 309.

17. H. Richard Niebuhr, *Christ and Culture* (New York: Harper and Row, 1975).

18. Thomas Merton, *A Vow of Conversation. Journals 1964–65*, ed. Naomi Burton Stone (New York: Farrar, Straus, 1988).

19. This play on words is affirmed by Merton's editor, Naomi Burton Stone, in her Preface, x–xi, to *A Vow of Conversation*. The notion that Merton sought to link the vow to speaking to the world is also noted in Cunningham, *Thomas Merton and the Monastic Vision*, 206.

20. Timothy Fry, OSB, ed., *The Rule of St. Benedict. In Latin and English with Notes* (Collegeville, MN: Liturgical Press, 1981).

21. Ibid., 461.

22. Thomas Merton, *The Sign of Jonas* (New York: Harcourt Brace, 1981), 36.

23. On Merton's preoccupation with "the self" and the transformation of the self away from radical self-obsession, see Anne E. Carr, *A Search for Wisdom and Spirit: Thomas Merton's Theology of the Self* (Notre Dame: University of Notre Dame Press, 1988).

24. Fry, *Rule of St. Benedict*, prologue, 1.

25. See Caroline Walker Bynum, *Jesus as Mother: Studies in the Spirituality of the High Middle Ages* (Berkeley: University of California Press, 1982), chaps. 1 and 2.

26. See William Shannon's entry on "Contemplation, Contemplative Prayer" in *The New Dictionary of Catholic Spirituality*, ed. Michael Downey (Collegeville, MN: Liturgical Press, 1993).

27. David Tracy, "Recent Catholic Spirituality: Unity amid Diversity" in *Christian Spirituality III: Post-Reformation and Modern*, ed. Louis Dupré and Don Saliers (New York: Crossroad, 1989), 164.

28. Thomas Merton, *Ishi Means Man* (Greensboro, NC: Unicorn Press, 1976), 65.

29. On the dialectic of interiority and exteriority in Christian spirituality, see Philip Sheldrake, "Christian Spirituality as a Way of Living Publicly:

A Dialectic of the Mystical and the Prophetic," *Spiritus: A Journal of Christian Spirituality* 3, no. 1 (Spring 2003): 19–37.

30. Evelyn Underhill, *Mysticism: The Nature and Development of Spiritual Consciousness* (Oxford: One World Publications, 1993).

31. Ibid., 172. On this point see 172–74.

32. John Ruusbroec, *The Sparkling Stone*, Conclusion, in *John Ruusbroec: The Spiritual Espousals and Other Works*, ed. James Wiseman, Classics of Western Spirituality (New York: Paulist Press, 1985), 184.

33. Ruusbroec, *The Spiritual Espousals*, 136–43.

34. See Peter Brown, *The Making of Late Antiquity* (Cambridge MA: Harvard University Press, 1994), chap. 4.

35. See Peter Brown, *Society and the Holy in Late Antiquity* (Berkeley: University of California Press, 1989), 110–14.

36. Ibid., "The Rise and Function of the Holy Man in Late Antiquity."

37. See Thomas Merton, *Contemplative Prayer* (London: Darton Longman and Todd, 1973), 25.

38. See Merton's commentary on Delp in his *Faith and Violence* (Notre Dame: University of Notre Dame Press, 1968), e.g., 52. On bogus interiority, see Merton, *Contemplative Prayer*, 135.

39. See Michel de Certeau,"The Weakness of Believing: From the Body to Writing, a Christian Transit" in *The Certeau Reader*, ed. Graham Ward (Oxford: Blackwell, 2000).

Chapter Eight

1. Some of the material for this chapter originates in an article "A Spirituality of Reconciliation: Encouragement for Anglicans from a Roman Catholic Perspective," published in the *Journal of Anglican Studies* 6, no. 1 (June 2008). In turn this was a reworking of keynote addresses to the Society for the Study of Anglicanism in November 2006 and to the House of Bishops of The Episcopal Church (formerly ECUSA) in September 2005.

2. John de Gruchy, *Reconciliation: Restoring Justice* (London: SCM Press, 2002), 44.

3. See Henry Bettenson, trans., *St. Augustine: City of God* (London: Penguin Books, 1984).

4. On the process of reconciliation, see especially Robert J. Schreiter, *The Ministry of Reconciliation: Spirituality and Strategies* (Maryknoll, NY: Orbis Books, 1998), and *Reconciliation: Mission and Ministry in a Changing Social Order* (Cambridge, MA: Boston Theological Institute Series, 2000).

5. On process, I am grateful for the insights of Schreiter, *Ministry of Reconciliation*.

6. For a fuller development of what follows, see Philip Sheldrake, "Practising Catholic 'Place'—The Eucharist," *Horizons: The Journal of the College Theology Society* 28, no. 2 (Fall 2001): 163–82.

7. See Colin Gunton, *The Promise of Trinitarian Theology* (Edinburgh: T and T Clark, 1997), 112 ff., and also his *The One, the Three and the Many* (Cambridge: Cambridge University Press, 1995), 164.

8. For an expanded treatment of "Catholic Persons" see Philip Sheldrake, "On Becoming Catholic People: Hopes and Challenges," in *Catholic Learning: Explorations in Receptive Ecumenism*, ed. Paul Murray (Oxford: Oxford University Press, 2008).

9. Translation from the Spanish in *John of the Cross: Selected Writings*, ed. K. Kavanaugh, Classics of Western Spirituality (New York: Paulist Press, 1987).

10. There are several good editions of the Rule of St. Benedict with translations and scholarly commentaries. One of the best is Terrence C. Kardong, OSB, ed., *Benedict's Rule: A Translation and Commentary* (Collegeville, MN: Liturgical Press, 1996).

11. On the different interpretations of silence in monastic writers and among those leading the canonical life, see Caroline Walker Bynum, *Jesus as Mother: Studies in the Spirituality of the High Middle Ages* (Berkeley: University of California Press, 1982), chap. 1.

12. The link between the enactment of identity and the ethical nature of the Eucharist is discussed by the Catholic moral theologian William Spohn, *Go and Do Likewise: Jesus and Ethics* (New York: Continuum, 1999), 175–84.

13. On this point, see Donald E. Saliers, "Liturgy and Ethics: Some New Beginnings" in *Introduction to Christian Ethics: A Reader*, ed. Ronald Hamel and Kenneth Himes (New York: Paulist Press, 1989), 175–86.

14. Rowan Williams, *On Christian Theology* (Oxford: Blackwell, 2000), 209–10.

15. *Baptism, Eucharist and Ministry*, Faith and Order Paper 111 (Geneva: World Council of Churches, 1982), para. 24.

16. See Williams, *On Christian Theology*, chap. 14, "Sacraments of the New Society."

17. Ibid., 212–14.

18. See Mark McIntosh, *Discernment and Truth: The Spirituality and Theology of Knowledge* (New York: Crossroad, 2004), 255.

19. Philip Endean and Joseph Munitiz, eds., *St. Ignatius Loyola: Personal Writings* (London/New York: Penguin Books, 1996); see *Spiritual Exercises*, para. 313–36.

20. Ignatius, *Spiritual Exercises*, para. 332.

Chapter Nine

1. Figures from the United Nations, cited by Crispin Tickell in his introduction to Richard Rogers, *Cities for a Small Planet* (London: Faber and Faber, 1997), vii.

2. Arnold Berleant, *The Aesthetics of Environment* (Philadelphia: Temple University Press, 1992), 86–87. For sustained reflection on place, see Philip Sheldrake, *Spaces for the Sacred: Place, Memory and Identity* (Baltimore: Johns Hopkins University Press, 2001). See also Gaston Bachelard, *The Poetics of Space* (Boston: Beacon Press, 1994); Edward S. Casey, "How to Get from Space to Place in a Fairly Short Stretch of Time: Phenomenological Prolegomena" in *Senses of Place*, ed. Steven Feld and Keith H. Basso (Santa Fe: School of American Research Press, 1996); J. E. Malpas, *Place and Experience: A Philosophical Topography* (Cambridge: Cambridge University Press, 1999).

3. Marc Augé, *Non-Places: Introduction to an Anthropology of Super-modernity* (London/New York: Verso, 1997), esp. 51–52, 77.

4. See Henri Lefebvre, *The Production of Space* (Oxford: Blackwell, 1991).

5. See the comments by the architect Robert Mugerauer, *Interpretations on Behalf of Place: Environmental Displacements and Alternative Responses* (Albany: State University of New York Press, 1994), esp. chap. 10.

6. See J. Matthew Ashley, *Interruptions: Mysticism, Politics and Theology in the Work of Johann Baptist Metz* (Notre Dame: University of Notre Dame Press, 1998), 10–12.

7. Jacques Ellul, *The Meaning of the City* (Grand Rapids, MI: Eerdmans, 1970), 16.

8. See, for example, Wayne Meeks, "St. Paul of the Cities" in *Religious Interpretations of the City*, ed. Peter S. Hawkins (Atlanta: Scholars Press, 1986), 15–23.

9. Richard Sennett, *The Conscience of the Eye: The Design and Social Life of Cities* (London: Faber and Faber, 1993), xii.

10. Ibid., xii–xiii.

11. Ibid., 6–10.

12. Ibid., 42.

13. For an updated defense of a positive view of "the secular realm" in Augustine, see Robert A. Markus, *Christianity and the Secular* (Notre Dame: University of Notre Dame Press, 2006).

14. D. Mayernik, *Timeless Cities: An Architect's Reflections on Renaissance Italy* (Boulder, CO: Westview Press, 2003), 5–13.

15. Augustine's commentary on Genesis is cited in Robert Markus, *The End of Ancient Christianity* (Cambridge: Cambridge University Press, 1990), 78.

16. Peter Brown, *The Rise of Western Christendom* (Oxford: Blackwell, 1996), 61.

17. Isidore of Seville, *Etymologiarum Libri*, ed. W. Lindsay (Oxford: Clarendon Press, 1911), 15.2.1.

18. Ibid.

19. See Colleen McDannell and Bernhard Lang, *Heaven, A History* (New Haven: Yale University Press, 1988), 70–80.

20. Brigitte Bedos-Rezak, "Form as Social Process" in *Artistic Integration in Gothic Buildings*, ed. Virginia Chieffo Raguin, Kathryn Brush, and Peter Draper (Toronto: University of Toronto Press, 1995), 243–44.

21. See Nicola Cortone and Nino Lavermicocca, *Santi di Strada: Le Edicole Religiose della Città Vecchia di Bari*, 5 vol. (Bari: Edizione BA Graphis, 2001–2003).

22. See Peter Ackroyd, *The Life of Thomas More* (London: Random House, 1999), 111.

23. See Chiara Frugoni, *A Distant City: Images of Urban Experience in the Medieval World* (Princeton: Princeton University Press, 1991), 27.

24. See McDannell and Lang, *Heaven*, 69–80.

25. See Peter Raedts, "The Medieval City as a Holy Place" in *Omnes Circumadstantes: Contributions towards a History of the Role of the People in the Liturgy*, ed. Charles Caspers and Marc Schneiders (Kampen: Uitgeversmaatschappij J. H. Kok, 1990), 144–54.

26. Thomas Aquinas, *Sententia Libri Politicorum. Opera Omnia*, VIII (Paris, 1891), Prologue A 69–70.

27. E.g., Thomas Aquinas, *De Regimine Principum*, chap. 2 in *Aquinas: Political Writings*, ed. R.W. Dyson (Cambridge: Cambridge University Press, 2002), 8–10.

28. Rudolph Bultmann, *Jesus Christ and Mythology* (New York: Scribner, 1958), 84–85.

29. See McDannell and Lang, *Heaven*, 280 ff.

30. Michel de Certeau's thinking about cities is to be found especially in "Walking in the City" and "Spatial Stories" in *The Practice of Everyday Life* (Berkeley: University of California Press, 1988); part 1: "Living," esp. "Ghosts in the City," in de Certeau, Giard, and Mayol, *The Practice of Everyday Life*, vol. 2 (Minneapolis: University of Minnesota Press, 1998); "The Imaginary of the City," and other isolated comments in *Culture in the Plural* (Minneapolis: University of Minnesota Press, 2001).

31. See Ian Buchanan, *Michel de Certeau: Cultural Theorist* (London: Sage Publications, 2000).

32. See comments in ibid., chap. 1, esp. 20.

33. For sharp criticisms of the kind of Cartesian "rhetoric of interiority" that imbued Le Corbusier, see, e.g., Walter A. Davis, *Inwardness and Existence* (Madison: University of Wisconsin Press, 1989), and also Fergus Kerr, *Theology after Wittgenstein* (London: SPCK, 1997), chap. 1, "The Modern Philosophy of the Self."

34. For a detailed study of Le Corbusier's theories of self and society see Simon Richards, *Le Corbusier and the Concept of the Self* (New Haven: Yale University Press, 2003).

35. De Certeau, "Ghosts in the City," in de Certeau, Giard, and Mayol, *The Practice of Everday Life*, vol. 2.

36. De Certeau, "Walking in the City," in de Corteau, *The Practice of Everyday Life*, 91–110.

37. Ibid., 92.

38. Ibid., 96.

39. "Indeterminate" in *The Practice of Everyday Life*, 203.

40. De Certeau, *The Practice of Everyday Life*, 115.

41. Paul Ricoeur, *Time and Narrative*, vol. 1 (Chicago: University of Chicago Press, 1984), 75.

42. De Certeau, *The Practice of Everyday Life*, 122–30.

43. For more detailed comments on the meaning of More's *Utopia* see Sheldrake, *Spaces for the Sacred*, 94–97.

44. De Certeau, "Walking in the City," in de Certeau, *The Practice of Everyday Life*, 95.

45. See, for example, Laurie Peake, "Smashing Icons" in *Will Alsop's SuperCity* (Manchester: Urbis, 2005), 39–49, and Charles Jencks, "The Iconic Building Is Here to Stay," *City* 10, no. 1 (April 2006): 3–20.

46. Peake, "Smashing Icons," 41.

47. Ibid., 49.

48. Jencks, "The Iconic Building Is Here to Stay," 4.

49. Rogers, *Cities for a Small Planet*, 9–10.

50. *Faithful Cities: A Call to Celebration, Vision and Justice* (London: Church House Publishing, 2006).

51. See Gustavo Gutiérrez, *We Drink from Our Own Wells*, 2nd ed. (Maryknoll, NY: Orbis Books, 2003), esp. chap. 6.

52. See Michael Himes and Kenneth Himes, *Fullness of Faith: The Public Significance of Theology* (New York: Paulist Press, 1993), chap. 7.

53. Charles Landry and Franco Bianchini, *The Creative City* (London: Demos, 1998), 13.

54. Rogers, *Cities for a Small Planet*, esp. 167–68.

55. Eduardo Mendieta, "Invisible Cities: A Phenomenology of Globalisation from Below," *City* 5, no.1 (2001): 1–25.

56. Charles Leadbeater, *Civic Spirit: The Big Idea for a New Political Era* (London: Demos, 1997), Demos Arguments 14, 30.

57. See, for example, Leonie Sandercock, *Cosmopolis II: Mongrel Cities in the 21st Century* (London/New York: Continuum, 2003).

58. David Hollenbach, *The Common Good and Christian Ethics* (Cambridge: Cambridge University Press, 2002), 137–38.

59. Victor Codina, "Sacraments," in *Systematic Theology: Perspectives from Liberation Theology*, ed. Jon Sobrino and Ignacio Ellacuría (London: SCM Press, 1996), 218–19.

60. World Council of Churches, *Eucharist*, 24.

Chapter Ten

1. On the sacred as "wholly other," see Mircea Eliade, *The Sacred and the Profane: The Nature of Religion* (New York/London: Harcourt Brace Jovanovich, 1987), Introduction.

2. Ibid., 14.

3. See Ben Rogers, ed., *Is Nothing Sacred?* (London: Routledge, 2004).

4. See G. Davie, *Religion in Modern Europe: A Memory Mutates* (Oxford: Oxford University Press, 2000), 164.

5. Umberto Eco, *Art and Beauty in the Middle Ages* (New Haven: Yale University Press, 1986).

6. For some reflections on what might be called the theology of Gothic, see Christopher Wilson, *The Gothic Cathedral* (London: Thames and Hudson, 1990), esp. the Introduction, 64–66, 219–20, 262–63.

7. On this mixture of theological aesthetics see the essay by Bernard McGinn, "From Admirable Tabernacle to the House of God: Some Theological Reflections on Medieval Architectural Integration" in *Artistic Integration in Gothic Buildings*, ed. Virginia Chieffo Raguin, Kathryn Brush, and Peter Draper (Toronto: University of Toronto Press, 1995).

8. *Libellus Alter De Consecratione Ecclesiae Sancti Dionysii*, IV translated in Erwin Panofsky, *Abbot Suger on the Abbey Church of St. Denis and Its Art Treasures* (Princeton: Princeton University Press, 1979), 100–101.

9. Augustine, *Expositions on the Book of Psalms*, Psalm 42, sec. 8, 134, translation in *A Select Library of the Nicene and Post-Nicene Fathers of the Christian Church*, ed. Philip Schaff (Grand Rapids, MI: Eerdmans/Edinburgh: T and T Clark, 1996), vol. 8.

10. The original Latin text is to be found in "The Book of Suger, Abbot of St. Denis," 27, in Panofsky, *Abbot Suger*, 46–48. The English translation is mine.

11. Translation by Bernard McGinn in his essay, "From Admirable Tabernacle to the House of God," 49, from the Latin text in Panofsky, *Abbot Suger*, 104.

12. On such practicalities and their impact on architectural developments, see Richard Morris, *Churches in the Landscape* (London: J. M. Dent, 1989), 96–98, 289–95.

13. Pseudo-Dionysius, *The Divine Names*, chap. 4.4, translated in *Pseudo-Dionysius: The Complete Works*, ed. Colm Luibheid and Paul Rorem (London: SPCK, 1987), 74.

14. For a brief summary of Dionysian theory, see Philip Sheldrake, *Spirituality and History: Questions of Interpretation and Method*, 2nd ed. (London: SPCK, 1995/Maryknoll, NY: Orbis Books, 1998), 200–201. Also Georges Duby, *The Age of the Cathedral: Art and Society 980–1420* (Chicago: University of Chicago Press, 1981), 99–100.

15. Pseudo-Dionysius, *The Mystical Theology*, chap. 1.1, in *Pseudo-Dionysius: The Complete Works*, ed. Luibheid and Rorem, 135.

16. Michael Camille, *Gothic Art: Visions and Revelations of the Medieval World* (London: Weidenfeld and Nicolson, 1996), 12.

17. In *De Consecratione*, translated in Panofsky, *Abbot Suger*, 82.

18. William Durandus, quoted in translation in Colleen McDannell and Bernhard Lang, *Heaven, A History* (New Haven: Yale University Press, 1988), 79.

19. Duby, *The Age of the Cathedral*, 95.

20. Aloysius Pieris, "Spirituality and Liberation," *The Month* (April 1983): 120.

21. See Arnold Berleant, *The Aesthetics of Environment* (Philadelphia: Temple University Press, 1992), 62.

22. On the complex nature of interpretation, see Brigitte Bedos-Rezak, "Towards a Cultural Biography of the Gothic Cathedral: Reflections on History and Art History," in *Artistic Integration in Gothic Buildings*, ed. Raguin, Brush, and Draper.

23. Dr. Allan Doig in his deposition to the Court of Arches, cited by Keith Walker, "Jewels in the Dust: Art in Cathedrals," in *Flagships of the Spirit: Cathedrals in Society*, ed. Stephen Platten and Christopher Lewis (London: Darton Longman and Todd, 1998), 116–17.

24. See Roy Spring, *Salisbury Cathedral: A Landmark in England's Heritage* (Salisbury, UK: Cathedral Press, 1991), 71–83.

25. Otto von Simson, *The Gothic Cathedral: Origins of Gothic Architecture and the Medieval Concept of Order* (Princeton: Princeton University Press, 1989).

26. Platten and Lewis, *Flagships of the Spirit*, 123–24, 135–36, 148.

27. Professor Christopher Rowland of Oxford University, in ibid., 30–32.

28. Evidence cited in G. Davie, *Religion in Modern Europe: A Memory Mutates*, 162–67.

29. A. Rouet, *Liturgy and the Arts* (Collegeville, MN: Liturgical Press, 1997), 95.

30. Ibid., 105.

31. Michel de Certeau, "The Weakness of Believing: From the Body to Writing, a Christian Transit," translated in *The Certeau Reader*, ed. G. Ward (Oxford: Blackwell, 2000), 234.

32. Ibid., 226.

33. Ibid., 236.

34. Michel de Certeau, "How Is Christianity Thinkable Today?" in *The Postmodern God*, ed. G. Ward (Oxford: Blackwell, 1997), 151.

BIBLIOGRAPHY

Ackroyd, Peter. *The Life of Thomas More*. London: Random House, 1999.

Aquinas, Thomas. *Sententia Libri Politicorum. Opera Omnia*, VIII. Paris, 1891, Prologue A 69–70.

—————. *De Regimine Principum*, chapter 2. In *Aquinas: Political Writings*, edited by R. W. Dyson. Cambridge: Cambridge University Press, 2002.

Armstrong, R., and I. Brady, eds. *Francis and Clare: The Complete Works*. Classics of Western Spirituality. New York: Paulist Press, 1982.

Ashley, J. Matthew. "The Turn to Spirituality? The Relationship between Theology and Spirituality." *Christian Spirituality Bulletin* 3, no. 2 (Fall 1995): 13–18.

—————. *Interruptions: Mysticism, Politics and Theology in the Work of Johann Baptist Metz*. Notre Dame: University of Notre Dame Press, 1998.

Astell, Ann W., ed. *Divine Representations: Postmodernism and Spirituality*. New York: Paulist Press, 1994.

—————. "Postmodern Christian Spirituality: A *coincidentia oppositorum?*" *Christian Spirituality Bulletin* 4, no. 1 (Summer 1996).

Augé, Marc. *Non-Places: Introduction to an Anthropology of Supermodernity*. London/New York: Verso, 1997.

Augustine. *The City of God* in *A Select Library of the Nicene and Post-Nicene Fathers of the Christian Church*, vol. 2, edited by P. Schaff. Edinburgh: T and T Clark/Grand Rapids, MI: Eerdmans, 1993.

—————. *Confessions and Enchiridion*. Edited by Albert Outler. The Library of Christian Classics. London: SCM Press, 1955.

—————. *Expositions on the Book of Psalms*, Psalm 42, in *A Select Library of the Nicene and Post-Nicene Fathers of the Christian Church*, vol. 8, edited by P. Schaff. Grand Rapids, MI: Eerdmans/Edinburgh: T and T Clark, 1996.

Bachelard, Gaston. *The Poetics of Space*. Boston: Beacon Press, 1994.

Barker, Pat. *Another World*. London: Penguin Books, 1999.

Barnes, Michael, ed. *Spirituality and Ethics. The Way Supplement* 88 (Spring 1997).

Bedos-Rezak, Brigitte. "Form as Social Process." In *Artistic Integration in Gothic Buildings*, edited by Virginia Chieffo Raguin, Kathryn Brush, and Peter Draper, 243–44. Toronto: University of Toronto Press, 1995.

Berleant, Arnold. *The Aesthetics of Environment*. Philadelphia: Temple University Press, 1992.

Boff, Leonardo. "The Need for Political Saints: From a Spirituality of Liberation to the Practice of Liberation." *Cross Currents* 30, no. 4 (Winter 1980/81), 369–84.

―――. *Trinity and Society*. Maryknoll, NY: Orbis Books/Tunbridge Wells: Burns and Oates, 1982.

Bouyer, Louis. *A History of Christian Spirituality*. 3 vols. London: Burns and Oates, 1968.

―――. *An Introduction to Spirituality*. New York: Desclée, 1961.

―――. "Mysticism: An Essay on the History of the Word" in *Understanding Mysticism*, edited by R. Woods, 42–55. London: Athlone Press, 1980.

Brown, Peter. *The Making of Late Antiquity*. Cambridge, MA: Harvard University Press, 1994.

―――. *The Rise of Western Christendom*. Oxford: Blackwell, 1996.

―――. *Society and the Holy in Late Antiquity*. Berkeley: University of California Press, 1989.

Buchanan, Ian. *Michel de Certeau: Cultural Theorist*. London: Sage Publications, 2000.

Bultmann, Rudolph. *Jesus Christ and Mythology*. New York: Scribner, 1958.

Bynum, Caroline Walker. *Jesus as Mother: Studies in the Spirituality of the High Middle Ages*. Berkeley: University of California Press, 1982.

Camille, Michael. *Gothic Art: Visions and Revelations of the Medieval World*. London: Weidenfeld and Nicolson, 1996.

Carr, Anne E. *A Search for Wisdom and Spirit: Thomas Merton's Theology of the Self*. Notre Dame: University of Notre Dame Press, 1988.

―――. *Transforming Grace: Christian Tradition and Women's Experience*. San Francisco: Harper, 1990.

Carrette, Jeremy, and Richard King. *Selling Spirituality: The Silent Takeover of Religion*. London: Routledge, 2004.

Casanova, José. *Public Religion in the Modern World*. Chicago: University of Chicago Press, 1994.

Casey, Edward S. "How to Get from Space to Place in a Fairly Short Stretch of Time: Phenomenological Prolegomena." In *Senses of Place*, edited by Steven Feld and Keith H. Basso, 13–52. Santa Fe: School of American Research Press, 1996.

Clifford, Anne M. "Re-membering the Spiritual Core of Theology: A Response." *Christian Spirituality Bulletin* 3, no. 2 (Fall 1995): 19–21.

Codina, Victor. "Sacraments." In *Systematic Theology: Perspectives from Liberation Theology*, edited by Jon Sobrino and Ignacio Ellacuría, 216–32. London: SCM Press, 1996.

Bibliography

Cohen, Deborah. *Household Gods: The British and Their Possessions*. New Haven: Yale University Press, 2006.

Cortone, Nicola, and Nino Lavermicocca. *Santi di Strada: Le Edicole Religiose della Cittá Vecchia di Bari*. 5 vols. Bari: Edizione BA Graphis, 2001–2003.

Cunningham, David S. "Trinitarian Theology since 1990." *Reviews in Religion and Theology* (1995): 8–16.

Cunningham, Lawrence. *Thomas Merton and the Monastic Vision*. Grand Rapids, MI: Eerdmans, 1999.

Cunningham, Lawrence S., and Keith J. Egan, *Christian Spirituality: Themes from the Tradition*. New York: Paulist Press, 1996.

Davie, G. *Religion in Modern Europe: A Memory Mutates*. Oxford: Oxford University Press, 2000.

Davis, Walter A. *Inwardness and Existence*. Madison: University of Wisconsin Press, 1989.

De Certeau, Michel. "Culture and Spiritual Experience." *Concilium* 19 (1966): 3–31.

———. *Culture in the Plural*. Minneapolis: University of Minnesota Press, 2001.

———. *Heterologies: Discourse on the Other*. Minneapolis: University of Minnesota Press, 1995.

———. "How Is Christianity Thinkable Today?" In *The Postmodern God*, edited by Graham Ward, 142–55. Oxford: Blackwell, 1997.

———. *The Mystic Fable*. Chicago: University of Chicago Press, 1992.

———. " 'Mystique' au XVIIe siècle: Le problème du language 'mystique.' " In *L'Homme Devant Dieu: Mélanges Offerts au Père Henri de Lubac*, vol. 2, 267–91, edited by Michel de Certeau, Paris: Aubier, 1964.

———. *The Practice of Everyday Life*. Berkeley: University of California Press, 1988.

———. "The Weakness of Believing: From the Body to Writing, a Christian Transit." In *The Certeau Reader*, edited by Graham Ward. Oxford: Blackwell, 2000.

De Certeau, Michel, Luce Giard, and Pierre Mayol. *The Practice of Everyday Life*, vol. 2. Minneapolis: University of Minnesota Press, 1998.

De Gruchy, John. *Reconciliation: Restoring Justice*. London: SCM Press, 2002.

De Lubac, Henri. *Exégese Médiévale: Les Quatres Sens de L'écriture*. Paris: Aubier, 1959–63.

Downey, Michael. *Understanding Christian Spirituality*. New York: Paulist Press, 1997.

Downing, Frances-Teresa. *Living the Incarnation: Praying with Francis and Clare of Assisi*. London: Darton Longman and Todd, 1993.

Duby, Georges. *The Age of the Cathedral: Art and Society 980–1420*. Chicago: University of Chicago Press, 1981.

Dupré, Louis, and Don Saliers, eds. *Christian Spirituality III: Post-Reformation and Modern*. New York: Crossroad, 1989.

Dupré, Louis, and J. Wiseman, eds. *Light from Light: An Anthology of Christian Mysticism*. New York: Paulist Press, 2001.

Eckhart, Meister. *Meister Eckhart: The Essential Sermons, Commentaries, Treatises and Defense*, edited by B. McGinn and E. Colledge. Classics of Western Spirituality. New York: Paulist Press, 1985.

———. *Meister Eckhart: Teacher and Preacher*, edited by B. McGinn. Classics of Western Spirituality. New York: Paulist Press, 1986.

Eco, Umberto. *Art and Beauty in the Middle Ages*. New Haven: Yale University Press, 1986.

Egan, Harvey. *What Are They Saying about Mysticism?* New York: Paulist Press, 1982.

Eliade, Mircea. *The Sacred and the Profane: The Nature of Religion*. New York/London: Harcourt Brace Jovanovich, 1987.

Ellul, Jacques. *The Meaning of the City*. Grand Rapids, MI: Eerdmans, 1970.

Endean, Philip. "Theology out of Spirituality: The Approach of Karl Rahner." *Christian Spirituality Bulletin* 3, no. 2 (Fall 1995): 6–8.

Evennett, H. O. *The Spirit of the Counter-Reformation*. Cambridge: Cambridge University Press, 1968.

Faithful Cities: A Call to Celebration, Vision and Justice. London: Church House Publishing, 2006.

Fernández-Armesto, Felipe. "Time and History." In *The Story of Time*, by Kristen Lippincott, with Umberto Eco, E. H. Gombrich, et al., 246–49. London: Merrill Holberton, 1999.

Flanagan, K. *The Enchantment of Sociology: A Study of Theology and Culture*. London: Macmillan/New York: St. Martin's Press, 1999.

Ford, David. *Self and Salvation*. Cambridge: Cambridge University Press, 1999.

Foucault, Michel. *Power/Knowledge: Selected Interviews and Other Writings 1972–77*. London: Pantheon Books, 1980.

Fowl, S., ed. *The Theological Interpretation of Scripture*. Oxford: Blackwell, 1997.

Frugoni, Chiara. *A Distant City: Images of Urban Experience in the Medieval World*. Princeton: Princeton University Press, 1991.

Fry, Timothy, ed. *The Rule of St. Benedict. In Latin and English with Notes*. Collegeville, MN: Liturgical Press, 1981.

Gadamer, Hans-Georg. *Truth and Method*. London: Sheed and Ward, 1988.

Galilea, Segundo. "Liberation as an Encounter with Politics and Contemplation." In *Understanding Mysticism*, edited by R. Woods, 529–40. London: Athlone Press, 1980.

Bibliography

————. "The Spirituality of Liberation." *The Way* (July 1985): 186–94.

Gallagher, Michael P. *Clashing Symbols: An Introduction to Faith and Culture.* London: Darton Longman and Todd, 1999.

Ganss, G., ed. *The Constitutions of the Society of Jesus.* St. Louis: Institute of Jesuit Sources, 1970.

————. *Ignatius of Loyola: Spiritual Exercises and Selected Works.* Classics of Western Spirituality. New York: Paulist Press, 1991.

Garrigou-Lagrange, R. *Christian Perfection and Contemplation.* St. Louis: B. Herder, 1937.

Geertz, C. *The Interpretation of Cultures.* New York: Basic Books, 1973.

Geremek, B. "The Marginal Man." In *The Medieval World,* edited by J. Le Goff, 367–69. London: Collins and Brown, 1990.

Gray, H. "What Kind of Document?" *The Way Supplement* 61 (1988): 21–34.

Gunton, Colin. *The One, the Three and the Many.* Cambridge: Cambridge University Press, 1995.

————. *The Promise of Trinitarian Theology.* Edinburgh: T and T Clark, 1990.

————. "The Trinity in Modern Theology." In *Companion Encyclopedia of Theology,* edited by Peter Byrne and Leslie Houlden, 937–57. London: Routledge, 1995.

Gurevich, A. J. *Categories of Medieval Culture.* London/Boston: Routledge and Kegan Paul, 1985.

Gustafson, James. "The Idea of Christian Ethics." In *Companion Encyclopedia of Theology,* ed. Peter Byrne and Leslie Houlden, 691–715. (London: Routledge, 1995).

Gutiérrez, Gustavo. *On Job: God-Talk and the Suffering of the Innocent.* Maryknoll, NY: Orbis Books, 1998.

————. *We Drink from Our Own Wells,* 2nd ed. Maryknoll, NY: Orbis Books,. 2003.

Hanson, Bradley, ed. *Modern Christian Spirituality: Methodological and Historical Essays.* Atlanta: Scholars Press, 1990.

Hardy, Daniel, and David Ford. *Jubilate: Theology in Praise.* London: Darton Longman and Todd, 1984.

Harton, F. P. *The Elements of the Spiritual Life.* London: SPCK, 1932.

Hauerwas, Stanley. *In Good Company: The Church as Polis.* Notre Dame: University of Notre Dame Press, 1995.

Himes, Michael, and Kenneth Himes. *Fullness of Faith: The Public Significance of Theology.* New York: Paulist Press, 1993.

Hollenbach, David. *The Common Good and Christian Ethics.* Cambridge: Cambridge University Press, 2002.

Isidore of Seville. *Etymologiarum Libri.* Edited by W. Lindsay. Oxford: Clarendon Press, 1911.

Jantzen, Grace. *Julian of Norwich*. London: SPCK, 1987.

————. *Power, Gender and Christian Mysticism*. Cambridge: Cambridge University Press, 1995.

Jencks, Charles. "The Iconic Building Is Here to Stay." *City* 10, no. 1 (April 2006): 3–20.

John, O. "The Tradition of the Oppressed as the Main Topic of Theological Hermeneutics." *Concilium* 200 (1988): 143–55.

John of the Cross. *John of the Cross: Selected Writings*, edited by K. Kavanaugh. Classics of Western Spirituality. New York: Paulist Press, 1987.

Johnson, Elizabeth A. *She Who Is: The Mystery of God in Feminist Theological Discourse*. New York: Crossroad, 1996.

Julian of Norwich. *Julian of Norwich: Showings*. Edited by E. Colledge and J. Walsh. Classics of Western Spirituality. New York: Paulist Press, 1978.

Kardong, Terrence C., ed. *Benedict's Rule: A Translation and Commentary*. Collegeville, MN: Liturgical Press, 1996.

Katz, Stephen, ed. *Mysticism and Religious Traditions*. New York: Oxford University Press, 1983.

Kerr, Fergus. *Theology after Wittgenstein*. London: SPCK, 1997.

LaCugna, Catherine Mowry. *God for Us: The Trinity and Christian Life*. San Francisco: HarperCollins, 1993.

————. "Trinitarian Spirituality." In *New Dictionary of Catholic Spirituality*, ed. Michael Downey, 968–71. Collegeville, MN: Liturgical Press, 1993.

Landry, Charles, and Franco Bianchini. *The Creative City*. London: Demos, 1998.

Lane, Dermot. *The Experience of God*. Dublin: Veritas, 1985.

Lash, Nicholas. *Theology on the Way to Emmaus*. London: SCM Press, 1986.

Leadbeater, Charles. *Civic Spirit: The Big Idea for a New Political Era*. London: Demos, 1997.

Leclercq, Jean. *The Love of Learning and Desire for God*. London: SPCK, 1978.

————. "The Renewal of Theology." In *Renaissance and Renewal in the Twelfth Century*, edited by Robert Benson, Giles Constable, and Carol Lanham, 68–87. Toronto: University of Toronto Press, 1991.

Lefebvre, Henri. *The Production of Space*. Oxford: Blackwell, 1991.

Le Goff, Jacques. "Francis of Assisi between the Renewals and Restraints of Feudal Society." *Concilium: Francis of Assisi Today* 149 (November 1981): 3–10.

————. *Intellectuals in the Middle Ages*. Oxford: Blackwell, 1993.

Lonergan, Bernard. *Method in Theology*. London: Darton Longman and Todd, 1972.

Lonsdale, David. *Eyes to See, Ears to Hear: An Introduction to Ignatian Spirituality*. London: Darton Longman and Todd/Maryknoll, NY: Orbis Books, 2000.

Bibliography

Lossky, Vladimir. *The Mystical Theology of the Eastern Church*. London: SPCK, 1973.

Louth, Andrew. *Discerning the Mystery: An Essay on the Nature of Theology*. Oxford: Oxford University Press, 1983.

———. *The Origins of the Christian Mystical Tradition*. Oxford: Clarendon Press, 1992.

———. *Theology and Spirituality*. Fairacres Publications 55. Oxford: SLG Press, 1978.

Loyola, Ignatius. *The Spiritual Exercises of St. Ignatius*. Edited by Louis Puhl. Chicago: Loyola University Press, 1951.

———. *St. Ignatius Loyola: Personal Writings*. Edited by Philip Endean and Joseph Munitiz. London/New York: Penguin Books, 1996.

Luther, Martin. *Selections from His Writings*. Edited by John Dillenberger. Garden City, NY: Anchor Books, 1961.

Lyotard, Jean-François. *The Postmodern Explained*. Minneapolis: University of Minnesota Press, 1993.

McDannell, Colleen, and Bernhard Lang. *Heaven, A History*. New Haven: Yale University Press, 1988.

McGinn, Bernard. *The Foundations of Mysticism: Origins to the Fifth Century*. New York: Crossroad, 1992.

———. "From Admirable Tabernacle to the House of God: Some Theological Reflections on Medieval Architectural Integration." In *Artistic Integration in Gothic Buildings*, edited by V. C. Raguin, K. Brush, and P. Draper, 41–56. Toronto: University of Toronto Press, 1995.

———. "The Letter and the Spirit: Spirituality as an Academic Discipline." *Christian Spirituality Bulletin* 1, no. 2 (Fall 1993): 1–10.

McGinn, Bernard, John Meyendorff, and Jean Leclercq, eds. *Christian Spirituality I: Origins to the Twelfth Century*. New York: Crossroad, 1986.

McGrath, Alister. *Christian Spirituality*. Oxford: Blackwell, 1999.

McIntosh, Mark. *Discernment and Truth: The Spirituality and Theology of Knowledge*. New York: Crossroad, 2004.

———. "Lover without a Name: Spirituality and Constructive Christology Today." *Christian Spirituality Bulletin* 3, no. 2 (Fall 1995): 9–12.

McManners, John, ed. *The Oxford History of Christianity*. Oxford/New York: Oxford University Press, 1993.

Malpas, J. E. *Place and Experience: A Philosophical Topography*. Cambridge: Cambridge University Press, 1999.

Marion, Jean-Luc. *God without Being*. Chicago: University of Chicago Press, 1995.

Markus, R. A. *Christianity and the Secular*. Notre Dame: University of Notre Dame Press, 2006.

————. *The End of Ancient Christianity.* Cambridge: Cambridge University Press, 1990.

————. *Saeculum: History and Society in the Theology of St. Augustine.* Cambridge: Cambridge University Press, 1970.

Martin, Thomas. *Our Restless Heart: The Augustinian Tradition.* London: Darton Longman and Todd, 2003.

Martinez, Gaspar. *Confronting the Mystery of God: Political, Liberation and Public Theologies.* New York: Continuum, 2001.

Mayernik, D. *Timeless Cities: An Architect's Reflections on Renaissance Italy.* Boulder, CO: Westview Press, 2003.

Meeks, Wayne. "St. Paul of the Cities." In *Religious Interpretations of the City,* edited by Peter S. Hawkins, 15–23. Atlanta: Scholars Press, 1986.

Megyer, Eugene. "Spiritual Theology Today." *The Way* 21, no. 1 (January 1981): 55–67.

Mendieta, Eduardo. "Invisible Cities: A Phenomenology of Globalisation from Below." *City* 5, no. 1 (2001): 1–25.

Merton, Thomas. *The Asian Journal.* London: Sheldon, 1974.

————. *Conjectures of a Guilty Bystander.* New York: Doubleday, 1966.

————. *Contemplation in a World of Action.* New York: Doubleday Image, 1973.

————. *Contemplative Prayer.* London: Darton Longman and Todd, 1973.

————. *Faith and Violence.* Notre Dame: University of Notre Dame Press, 1968.

————. *Ishi Means Man.* Greensboro, NC: Unicorn Press, 1976.

————. "Is the World a Problem?" *Commonweal* 84 (June 3, 1966).

————. *Life and Holiness.* New York: Doubleday, 1964.

————. *The Sign of Jonas.* New York: Harcourt Brace, 1981.

————. *A Vow of Conversation. Journals* 1964–65. Edited by Naomi Burton Stone. New York: Farrar, Straus, 1988.

Meyendorf, John. *Byzantine Theology.* New York: Fordham University Press, 1974.

Milbank, John. *Theology and Social Theory: Beyond Secular Reason.* Oxford: Blackwell, 1990.

Moltmann, Jürgen. *Experiences of God.* Philadelphia: Fortress Press, 1980.

————. *History and the Triune God: Contributions to Trinitarian Theology.* London: SCM Press/New York: Crossroad, 1992.

————. "Teresa of Avila and Martin Luther: The Turn to the Mysticism of the Cross." *Studies in Religion/Sciences Religieuses* 13 (1984): 265–78.

Moore, R. I. *The Formation of a Persecuting Society.* Oxford: Blackwell, 1994.

Morris, Richard. *Churches in the Landscape.* London: J. M. Dent, 1989.

Mugerauer, Robert. *Interpretations on Behalf of Place: Environmental Displacements and Alternative Responses.* Albany: State University of New York Press, 1994.

Mursell, Gordon, ed. *The Story of Christian Spirituality: Two Thousand Years from East to West*. Oxford: Lion Publishing, 2001.

Niebuhr, H. Richard. *Christ and Culture*. New York: Harper and Row, 1975.

Nuth, Joan. *Wisdom's Daughter: The Theology of Julian of Norwich*. New York: Crossroad, 1991.

O'Malley, John. *The First Jesuits*. Cambridge, MA: Harvard University Press, 1993.

O'Meara, John. Introduction to *St. Augustine: City of God*, edited by Henry Bettenson. London: Penguin Books, 1984.

Origen. *Origen: An Exhortation to Martyrdom, Prayer and Selected Works*. Edited by R. Greer. Classics of Western Spirituality. New York: Paulist Press, 1979.

Padovano, Anthony. *The Human Journey: Thomas Merton, Symbol of a Century*. Garden City, NY: Doubleday, 1982.

Pannenberg, Wolfhart. *Christian Spirituality and Sacramental Community*. London: Darton Longman and Todd, 1984.

Panofsky, Erwin. *Abbot Suger on the Abbey Church of St. Denis and Its Art Treasures*. Princeton: Princeton University Press, 1979.

Patrick, Anne E. "Ethics and Spirituality: The Social Justice Connection." *The Way Supplement* 63 (1988): 103–16.

Peake, Laurie. "Smashing Icons." In *Will Alsop's SuperCity*, edited by Laurie Peake, 39–49. Manchester: Urbis, 2005.

Pelikan, Jaroslav. *Christianity and Classical Culture*. New Haven: Yale University Press, 1993.

Platten, Stephen, and Christopher Lewis, eds. *Flagships of the Spirit: Cathedrals in Society*. London: Darton Longman and Todd, 1998.

Pourrat, Pierre. *La Spiritualité Chrétienne*. 4 vols. Paris: Desclée, 1918.

Principe, Walter. "Pluralism in Christian Spirituality." *The Way* (January 1992): 58–60.

————. "Towards Defining Spirituality." *Sciences Religieuses* 12, no. 2 (1983): 127–41.

Pseudo-Dionysius. *Pseudo-Dionysius: The Complete Works*. Edited by Colm Luibheid and Paul Rorem. Classics of Western Spirituality. New York: Paulist Press, 1987.

Raedts, Peter. "The Medieval City as a Holy Place." In *Omnes Circumadstantes: Contributions towards a History of the Role of the People in the Liturgy*, edited by Charles Caspers and Marc Schneiders, 144–54. Kampen: Uitgeversmaatschappij J. H. Kok, 1990.

Rahner, Karl. *The Dynamic Element of the Church*. London: Burns and Oates, 1964.

————. *The Practice of Faith: A Handbook of Contemporary Spirituality*. Edited by K. Lehmann and A. Raffelt. New York: Crossroad, 1984.

————. "Prayer." In *Encyclopedia of Theology*, edited by Karl Rahner. London: Burns and Oates, 1975.

————. *Theological Investigations*, vol. 5. London: Darton Longman and Todd, 1966.

————. *The Trinity*. London: Burns and Oates, 1970.

Raitt, J., ed. *Christian Spirituality II: High Middle Ages and Reformation*. New York: Crossroad, 1987.

Rayment-Pickard, Hugh. *The Myths of Time: From St. Augustine to "American Beauty."* London: Darton Longman and Todd, 2004.

Richard of St. Victor. *De Trinitate*. In *Richard of St. Victor*, edited by Grover Zinn. Classics of Western Spirituality. New York: Paulist Press, 1979.

Richards, Simon. *Le Corbusier and the Concept of the Self*. New Haven: Yale University Press, 2003.

Ricoeur, Paul. *Figuring the Sacred: Religions, Narrative and Imagination*. Minneapolis: Fortress Press, 1995.

————. "Hermeneutics and the Critique of Ideology." In *Hermeneutics and the Human Sciences*, edited by J. B. Thompson, 63–100. Cambridge: Cambridge University Press, 1981.

————. *Interpretation Theory: Discourse and the Surplus of Meaning*. Fort Worth: Texas Christian University Press, 1976.

————. *Time and Narrative*. 3 vols. Chicago: University of Chicago Press, 1984.

Rogers, Ben, ed. *Is Nothing Sacred?* London: Routledge, 2004.

Rogers, Richard. *Cities for a Small Planet*. London: Faber and Faber, 1997.

Rorem, Paul. "The Uplifting Spirituality of Pseudo-Dionysius." In *Christian Spirituality, I: Origins to the Twelfth Century*, edited by Bernard McGinn, John Meyendorff, and Jean Leclercq. New York: Crossroad, 1986.

Rouet, A. *Liturgy and the Arts*. Collegeville, MN: Liturgical Press, 1997.

Ruffing, Janet, ed. *Mysticism and Social Transformation*. Syracuse, NY: Syracuse University Press, 2001.

Ruggieri, G. "Faith and History." In *The Reception of Vatican II*, edited by G. Alberigo, J.-P. Jossua, and J. A. Komonchak, 92–95. Washington, DC: Catholic University of America Press, 1987.

Ruusbroec, John. *John Ruusbroec: The Spiritual Espousals and Other Works*. Edited by J. Wiseman. Classics of Western Spirituality. New York: Paulist Press, 1985.

Saliers, Donald E. "Liturgy and Ethics: Some New Beginnings." In *Introduction to Christian Ethics: A Reader*, edited by Ronald Hamel and Kenneth Himes, 175–86. New York: Paulist Press, 1989.

Sandercock, Leonie. *Cosmopolis II: Mongrel Cities in the 21st Century*. London/New York: Continuum, 2003.

Bibliography

Schneiders, Sandra. "A Hermeneutical Approach to the Study of Christian Spirituality." *Christian Spirituality Bulletin* 2, no. 1 (Spring 1994): 9–14.

————. *The Revelatory Text: Interpreting the New Testament as Sacred Scripture.* Collegeville, MN: Liturgical Press, 1999.

————. "Scripture and Spirituality." In *Christian Spirituality: Origins to the Twelfth Century*, edited by Bernard McGinn, John Meyendorff, and Jean Leclercq, 1–20. New York: Crossroad/London: Routledge, 1986.

————. "Spirituality as an Academic Discipline: Reflections from Experience." *Christian Spirituality Bulletin* 1, no. 2 (Fall 1993): 10–15.

————. "Spirituality in the Academy." *Theological Studies* 50 (1989): 676–97.

————. "The Study of Christian Spirituality: Contours and Dynamics of a Discipline." In *Minding the Spirit: The Study of Christian Spirituality*, edited by Elizabeth A. Dreyer and Mark S. Burrows, 5–24. Baltimore: Johns Hopkins University Press, 2005.

————. "Theology and Spirituality: Strangers, Rivals or Partners?" *Horizons* 13, no. 2 (1986): 253–74.

————. *Written That You May Believe: Encountering Jesus in the Fourth Gospel.* New York: Crossroad, 1999.

Schreiter, Robert J. *The Ministry of Reconciliation: Spirituality and Strategies.* Maryknoll, NY: Orbis Books, 1998.

————. *Reconciliation: Mission and Ministry in a Changing Social Order.* Cambridge, MA: Boston Theological Institute Series, 2000.

Schüssler Fiorenza, Elisabeth. *In Memory of Her: A Feminist Theological Reconstruction of Christian Origins.* New York: Crossroad, 1983.

Schwöbel, Christoph, ed. *Trinitarian Theology Today.* Edinburgh: T and T Clark, 1995.

Scott, J., and P. Simpson-Housley, eds. *Sacred Places and Profane Spaces: Essays in the Geographics of Judaism, Christianity and Islam.* Westport, CT: Greenwood, 1991.

Senn, Frank C., ed. *Protestant Spiritual Traditions.* New York: Paulist Press, 1986.

Sennett, Richard. *The Conscience of the Eye: The Design and Social Life of Cities.* London: Faber and Faber, 1993.

Shannon, William. "Contemplation, Contemplative Prayer." In *The New Dictionary of Catholic Spirituality*, edited by Michael Downey. Collegeville, MN: Liturgical Press, 1993.

Sheldrake, Philip. "Christian Spirituality as a Way of Living Publicly: A Dialectic of the Mystical and the Prophetic." *Spiritus: A Journal of Christian Spirituality* 3, no. 1 (Spring 2003): 19–37.

————. "The Crisis of Postmodernity." *Christian Spirituality Bulletin* 4, no. 1 (Summer 1996).

————. ed. *Ignatian Spirituality in Ecumenical Context, The Way Supplement* 68 (Summer 1990).

————. ed. *The New Westminster Dictionary of Christian Spirituality.* Louisville: Westminster-John Knox Press, 2005.

————. "On Becoming Catholic People: Hopes and Challenges." In *Catholic Learning: Explorations in Receptive Ecumenism*, edited by Paul Murray. Oxford: Oxford University Press, 2008.

————. "Practising Catholic 'Place'—The Eucharist." *Horizons: The Journal of the College Theology Society* 28, no. 2 (Fall 2001): 163–82.

————. *Spaces for the Sacred: Place, Memory and Identity.* Baltimore: Johns Hopkins University Press, 2001.

————. *Spirituality and History: Questions of Interpretation and Method.* London: SPCK, 1995/Maryknoll, NY: Orbis Books, 1998.

————. *Spirituality and Theology: Christian Living and the Doctrine of God.* London: Darton Longman and Todd/Maryknoll, NY: Orbis Books, 1998.

Sölle, Dorothee. *The Silent Cry: Mysticism and Resistance.* Minneapolis: Augsburg Fortress Press, 2001.

————. "To be Amazed, to Let Go, to Resist: Outline for a Mystical Journey Today." In *Mysticism and Social Transformation*, edited by Janet Ruffing, 45–51. Syracuse, NY: Syracuse University Press, 2001.

Spohn, William. *Go and Do Likewise: Jesus and Ethics.* New York: Continuum, 1999.

Spring, Roy. *Salisbury Cathedral: A Landmark in England's Heritage.* Salisbury, UK: Cathedral Press, 1991.

Stewart, Columba. "Asceticism and Spirituality in Late Antiquity: New Vision, Impasse or Hiatus?" *Christian Spirituality Bulletin* 4, no. 1 (Summer 1996): 11–15.

Surin, Jean-Joseph. *Jean-Joseph Surin: Correspondence.* Edited by Michel de Certeau. Paris: Desclée, 1963.

————. *Jean-Joseph Surin: Guide Spirituel pour La Perfection.* Edited by Michel de Certeau. Paris: Desclée, 1963.

Tanquerey, A. A. *The Spiritual Life.* Tournai: Desclée, 1930.

Tickle, Phyllis. *Rediscovering the Sacred: Spirituality in America.* New York: Crossroad, 1995.

Tracy, David. *The Analogical Imagination: Christian Theology and the Culture of Pluralism.* New York: Crossroad, 1991.

————. *Blessed Rage for Order.* New York: Seabury Press, 1975.

————. *On Naming the Present: God, Hermeneutics and Church.* Maryknoll, NY: Orbis Books, 1994.

————. "Recent Catholic Spirituality: Unity amid Diversity." In *Christian Spirituality: Post-Reformation and Modern*, edited by Louis Dupré and Don Saliers, 152–53, New York: Crossroad, 1989.

Turner, Denys. *The Darkness of God: Negativity in Christian Mysticism.* Cambridge: Cambridge University Press, 1995.

Underhill, Evelyn. *Mysticism: The Nature and Development of Spiritual Consciousness.* 1911. Oxford: Oneworld Publications, 1993.

Van Ness, Peter. "Spirituality and Secularity." *The Way Supplement* 73 (1992): 68–79.

Vayne, Paul, ed. *A History of Private Life*, vol. 1: *From Pagan Rome to Byzantium.* Cambridge, MA: Harvard University Press, 1996.

Veale, J. "How the Jesuit Constitutions Work." *The Way Supplement* 61 (1988): 3–20.

Von Balthasar, Hans Urs. *The Glory of the Lord.* Multiple volumes. San Francisco: Ignatius Press/Edinburgh: T and T Clark, 1982–92.

Von Simson, Otto. *The Gothic Cathedral: Origins of Gothic Architecture and the Medieval Concept of Order.* Princeton: Princeton University Press, 1989.

Waaijman, Kees. *Spirituality.* Leuven: Peeters, 2002.

Walsh, James, ed. *The Cloud of Unknowing.* Classics of Western Spirituality. New York: Paulist Press, 1981.

Ward, Graham. *Theology and Contemporary Critical Theory.* New York: St. Martin's Press, 2000.

Weaver, Mary Jo. "Conjectures of a Disenchanted Reader." *Horizons* 30, no. 2 (2003): 285–96.

Williams, Rowan. *On Christian Theology.* Oxford: Blackwell, 2000.

————. *Teresa of Avila.* London: Geoffrey Chapman, 1991.

————. "Trinity and Revelation." *Modern Theology* (1986): 197–212.

————. "The Via Negativa and the Foundations of Theology: An Introduction to the Thought of V. N. Lossky." In *New Studies in Theology, 1*, edited by Stephen Sykes and Derek Holmes. London: SPCK, 1980.

————. *The Wound of Knowledge: Christian Spirituality from the New Testament to St. John of the Cross.* rev. ed. London: Darton Longman and Todd/Boston: Cowley Publications, 1990.

Wilson, C. *The Gothic Cathedral.* London: Thames and Hudson, 1990.

Zizioulas, John. *Being as Communion.* Crestwood, NY: St. Vladimir's Seminary Press, 1985.

INDEX